WEST VIRGINIA

OFF THE BEATEN PATH ®

OFF THE BEATEN PATH® SERIES

NINTH EDITION

WEST VIRGINIA

OFF THE BEATEN PATH®

DISCOVER YOUR FUN

SU CLAUSON-WICKER

FOREWORD BY
SENATOR JAY ROCKEFELLER

Globe
Pequot
Essex, Connecticut

All the information in this guidebook is subject to change. We recommend that you call ahead to obtain current information before traveling.

Globe Pequot

An imprint of Globe Pequot, the trade division of
The Rowman & Littlefield Publishing Group, Inc.
4501 Forbes Blvd., Ste. 200
Lanham, MD 20706
www.rowman.com

Distributed by NATIONAL BOOK NETWORK

British Library Cataloguing in Publication Information available

Library of Congress Cataloging-in-Publication Data: This title is a serial and is covered under LCCN 2002208441.

∞™ The paper used in this publication meets the minimum requirements of American National Standard for Information Sciences—Permanence of Paper for Printed Library Materials, ANSI/NISO Z39.48-1992.

Contents

About the Author vii

Acknowledgments viii

Foreword ix

Introduction xi

Eastern Panhandle **1**

    The Shenandoah Valley 1

    Crossroads. 13

    Springs and Spas. 19

Potomac Highlands. **27**

    The Allegheny Foothills. 29

    Seneca Rocks 37

    The High Valley. 42

    The Western Slope. 45

    Mountain Wilderness 48

Mountain Lakes. **60**

    Summersville Area 64

    Stonewall Country 71

    The Mountain Park 83

New River/Greenbrier Valley Region. **88**

    The Greenbrier and Bluestone Valleys 88

    New River Gorge 108

    Southern Coalfields 115

Metro Valley. **128**

    The Capital Region. 133

    The Tri-State Area 140

Mid-Ohio Valley **154**

    The Western Frontier 157

    Bluegrass Heartland 168

Northern Panhandle **172**

Mountaineer Country **186**

    The Northern Heartland 194

    Morgantown 204

Index 209

About the Author

Su Clauson-Wicker is a Virginian who has spent almost a month of Sundays in West Virginia each year since 1989. She is a regional travel writer and author of *Scenic Driving West Virginia* (Globe Pequot) as well as the *Inn-to-Inn Walking Guide for Virginia and West Virginia*. Her diverse career includes a decade as editor of *Virginia Tech Magazine* and positions in journalism, educational television, medical public relations, and child welfare. She can be found gathering wild edibles, writing occasional features for the *Roanoke Times*, and volunteering at a recycled clothing shop in Blacksburg, Virginia.

Acknowledgments

I'd like to express my indebtedness to the first authors of *West Virginia Off the Beaten Path*, Stephen and Stacy Soltis, whose lively prose and vivacious spirits blazed an exhilarating path to follow in our mutual mining of the hidden and not-so-hidden treasures of the Mountain State. Thank you for the standards; thanks for the zest.

I'd also like to thank scores of friends and colleagues throughout West Virginia for their insight, knowledge, kindness, encouragement, and hospitality. I am especially indebted to: Sissie Summers of West Virginia State Parks, Olivia Litman of Wheeling Convention & Visitors Bureau, Valerie Pritt and Rachael Stebbins of Greenbrier Convention and Visitors Bureau, Kari Thompson of Stonewall Group, Marie Blackwell of Mercer County Convention and Visitors Bureau, Mark Lewis of Parkersburg Convention & Visitors Bureau, Heather Antolini of Country Road Cabins, Mike Smith of Droop Mountain State Park, Steve Jones of North Bend State Park, Bonnie Watts of Cabwaylingo State Forest, the Perry family of Heritage Farm Museum & Village, Mike Foster of Lost River State Park, Steve Jones of North Bend State Park, Doug Wiant of Holly River State Park, and former senator Larry Rowe of Malden, who showed up with the key for the locked gate to the Booker T. Washington Homeplace just as I was preparing to scale the fence. I owe mountains of gratitude to my friend Estill Putney, whose enthusiastic companionship, expert driving, and generous spirit helped propel this book to the finish line. I am also indebted to editor Greta Schmitz at Globe Pequot Press, who has excellent judgment and knows how to get things done efficiently. And thanks to my husband, Bruce Wicker for his great interest, patience, and assistance in identifying the good stories to tell. A heartfelt thanks to all.

Foreword

There is a definite magic, a sense of wonder and adventure and tradition, about traveling the hidden back roads of America. It is a soothing tonic for the daily stresses and distractions of our high-energy lifestyles. We seek relief and escape along these quiet country roads, while always seeking out an adventure around the next bend.

My home state of West Virginia has history and heritage almost guaranteed to provide travelers with the ultimate off-the-beaten-path experience. Our rugged mountains, wild rivers, lush valleys, and warm, welcoming people are a prescription for "getting away from it all." With fewer than 1.8 million people living in towns and communities spread across more than 24,000 square miles, the Mountain State has seemingly limitless places to explore and enjoy.

In the pages that follow, you'll be introduced to scores of overlooked sights, sounds, tastes, and personalities that collectively offer a glimpse into the West Virginia experience. You'll travel from the hauntingly beautiful hollows of the southern coalfields to the aristocratic colonial pathways of the Eastern Panhandle. You'll experience the powerful natural magnificence of the New River Gorge and the simple, easy charms of quiet country inns. You'll hike the backcountry of the pristine Cranberry Wilderness and stroll beneath the gaslight lamps of Victorian Wheeling.

My guess is that you will come away as struck by West Virginia's wondrous beauty and relaxing pace of life as I did some thirty years ago, when I first came to the state as a VISTA worker.

Naturally, West Virginia has changed a lot in that time. Modern interstate highways, a growing tourism industry, and new economic development attract millions of visitors to our state each year. While we may not be "undiscovered" any longer, there are more hidden natural and cultural gems woven into the Appalachians than you could get to in endless weekends.

I hope you will use *West Virginia Off the Beaten Path* to lead you to some of the truly rare American riches found within these borders. It will be time well spent and a travel experience far removed from everyday life, restful and soothing and thick with history, hospitality, natural beauty, and adventure.

—Senator Jay Rockefeller

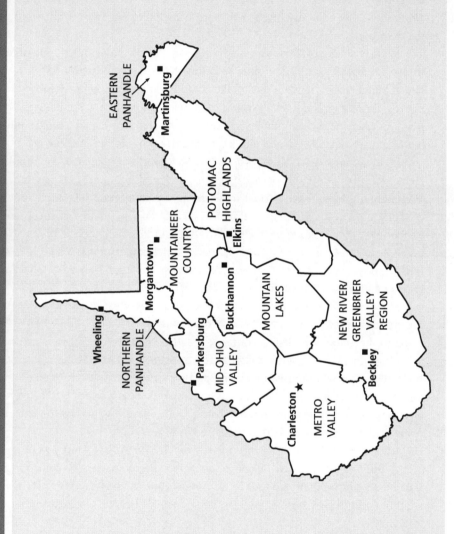

WEST VIRGINIA

EASTERN PANHANDLE
Martinsburg

POTOMAC HIGHLANDS

MOUNTAINEER COUNTRY
Morgantown

Elkins

Buckhannon

MOUNTAIN LAKES

NEW RIVER/ GREENBRIER VALLEY REGION

Wheeling

NORTHERN PANHANDLE

Parkersburg

MID-OHIO VALLEY

Beckley

Charleston

METRO VALLEY

Introduction

While the populace of some parts of the country wax poetic about the notion of "a sense of place," West Virginians, by comparison, seem to take theirs for granted. West Virginians may chafe to get back to the Mountain State should they take a job in the flatlands, but they are never ones to inflict their "West Virginia-ness" on others. Unenlightened outsiders may argue that West Virginians have to adopt this stance; after all, there isn't much to romanticize in this impenetrable land of "hillbillies, moonshiners, and bloodletting coal miners."

West Virginians know perfectly well—as do most visitors who actually get off the interstate—that the tiresome stereotypes are bunk. West Virginians are about the most friendly and most helpful people you'll find. They live in a state that can claim one of the lowest crime rates in the nation and the lowest cost of living. Their state is not only beautiful, but in many spots it's awe-inspiringly gorgeous.

In fact, West Virginia may have the most intense sense of place to be found anywhere in the US. Wedged between the bustling megalopolis of the eastern seaboard and the industrial corridors of the Midwest, West Virginia—thanks to a rugged terrain—has remained lightly populated and overwhelmingly pastoral in character. Yes, it's more rustic than its neighbors, but it's also greener, more relaxed, and refreshingly more informal. It's also more festive, with more festivals, celebrations, and fairs per capita than any other state in the nation.

The late CBS television correspondent Charles Kuralt once said he could have spent all his time in West Virginia—there are that many interesting stories here. This book is an attempt to get travelers to those stories—to the little town that still burns Old Man Winter in the Swiss tradition, to the bejeweled Hare Krishna temple and the "haunted" state prison, to road bowling at the Irish Spring Festival, to base jumping at New River Bridge Day.

West Virginia is a small state with distinctive divisions: some historical, some geographical, some cultural, and some social. The Eastern Panhandle, which reaches east to within an hour's drive of the nation's capital—and is also closer to five other state capitals than its own—is more aligned with the urban lifestyle of northern Virginia than it is with other parts of West Virginia. On the other hand, residents of the industrialized Northern Panhandle consider themselves northerners, while those in southern and central West Virginia are decidedly southern. In the Ohio Valley, many sound and think like Midwesterners.

West Virginia Off the Beaten Path begins in the Eastern Panhandle. From here, we make a clockwise swirl around the state. Sometimes you have to backtrack to see everything, but it's well worth the effort.

A word of explanation is needed here about the dining and lodging pricing key used in this book. Prices in these mountains can seem ridiculously inexpensive to an urbanite. In West Virginia, you can still find respectable hotel rooms for $75 a night, bed-and-breakfast stays for $99, and entrees for $8. Sure, you'll find higher prices in some of the cities and most of the Eastern Panhandle, but in general costs are a little lower than elsewhere.

Our pricing range reflects this. This guide will give you an indication of what you can expect to pay for the average main entree: under $10 is considered budget; $10–$16.99 is inexpensive; $17–$28 is moderate, and more than $28 is expensive.

When it comes to lodging (for a standard double, excluding room tax), anything under $60 is considered budget; $60–$85 is inexpensive; $86–$119 is moderate; $120–$195 is expensive, and anything over $195 is very expensive.

West Virginia at a Glance

Nickname: the Mountain State

Admitted to the Union in 1863 after breaking from Virginia in 1861

Capital: Charleston

Principal cities: Charleston, Huntington, Wheeling, Parkersburg, Morgantown

Population: 1.8 million

Land area: 24,181 square miles

Climate: Average statewide daily minimum temperature: January, 28°F; average daily maximum temperature July, 85°F. Winters can be severe in the Potomac Highlands and Allegheny Plateau, but summers here are free of the humidity that occasionally oppresses the Eastern Panhandle and the Ohio Valley

Major newspapers: *Charleston Gazette*, *Huntington Herald Dispatch*, *Wheeling Intelligencer*, *Parkersburg News & Sentinel*, *Morgantown Dominion Post*

Motto: Mountaineers Are Always Free

State bird: cardinal

State fish: brook trout

State flower: rhododendron

State tree: sugar maple

Famous natives: novelist Pearl S. Buck; Confederate general Thomas "Stonewall" Jackson; actor Don Knotts; pilot Chuck Yeager; diplomat Cyrus Vance; Nobel Prize winner John Forbes Nash Jr.

State Division of Tourism: (800) CALL-WVA; wvtourism.com

The Eastern Panhandle, shaped somewhat like the head of a perched eagle, is West Virginia's easternmost region, and as such bears close association with neighboring Maryland and Virginia and even suburban Washington, DC.

The three-county region is defined by its historic sites, springs and spas, and the Potomac River, which provides the northern border for the area. The far-western portion of the Panhandle (Morgan County) is mountainous and relatively isolated, while the central and eastern sections (Berkeley and Jefferson Counties) roll alongside the tail-end humps and foothills of the Blue Ridge Mountains and are dotted with numerous small towns and a wealth of historical and cultural attractions.

Despite the fact that it's the state's most widely visited region, the Eastern Panhandle still offers an exhaustive array of hidden and unsung treasures. For first-time visitors to West Virginia, this is a good primer trip and a logical starting point if you're coming from the east.

Eastern Panhandle

The Eastern Panhandle, shaped somewhat like the head of a perched eagle, is West Virginia's easternmost region and, as such, bears close association with neighboring Maryland and Virginia and even suburban Washington, DC.

The three-county region is defined by its historic sites, springs and spas, and the Potomac River, which provides the northern border for the area. The far-western portion of the Panhandle (Morgan County) is mountainous and relatively isolated, while the central and eastern sections (Berkeley and Jefferson Counties) roll alongside the tail-end humps and foothills of the Blue Ridge Mountains and are pocketed with numerous small towns and a wealth of historical and cultural attractions.

Despite the fact that it's the state's most widely visited region, the Eastern Panhandle still offers an exhaustive array of hidden and unsung treasures. For first-time visitors to West Virginia, this is a good primer trip and a logical starting point if you're coming from the east.

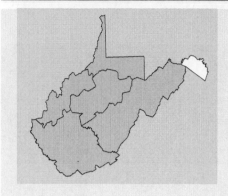

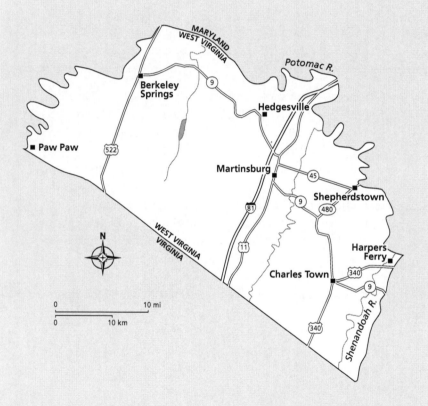

The Shenandoah Valley

The fabled Shenandoah Valley, imprinted on the American psyche through song, stage, and screen, is more synonymous with neighboring Virginia than West Virginia. There's no doubt about it, though, this historic and fertile valley rolls north into the Mountain State along with its namesake river, claiming all of Jefferson County and part of Berkeley County. Also known as the Valley of Virginia, the Shenandoah is one of several geographic entities that make up the Great Valley, a massive, erosion-carved trench stretching from south-central Pennsylvania to northeastern Tennessee. The Great Valley was a major southern migration route for Pennsylvania's Scots-Irish and German settlers, brave and industrious pioneers who lived close to the land, tapping its rich soil for crops and dense hardwood forests for shelter, furniture, and farm implements.

West Virginia's swath of the Shenandoah (an Indigenous term meaning "Daughter of the Skies") is an important agricultural region and a mecca for artisans, writers, cottage-industry entrepreneurs, retirees, and weekend retreaters from nearby urban areas.

This is a land deeply proud of its colonial history and colorful folklife, evidenced by such huge fetes as the Mountain Heritage Arts and Crafts Festival, held each fall outside Harpers Ferry. The laid-back valley is conducive to relaxation, whether it is a lazy day of floating on the Shenandoah River or

BEST ANNUAL EVENTS IN THE EASTERN PANHANDLE

International Water Tasting Festival
Berkeley Springs; last weekend in
February
(304) 258-9147 or (800) 447-8797
berkeleyspringswatertasting.com

**Mountain Heritage Arts
and Crafts Festival**
Charles Town; late September
(304) 725-2055 mhacfestival.org

**Contemporary American
Theater Festival**
Shepherdstown; last three weeks of July
681-240-2283 catf.org

Apple Butter Festival
Berkeley Springs; early October
(304) 258-3738
berkeleysprings.com

**Mountain State Apple
Harvest Festival**
Martinsburg; mid-October
(304) 264-8801
msahf.com

Christmas in Shepherdstown
last weekend in November, first weekend
in December
(304) 876-2786
shepherdstown.info/events

unwinding at the Charles Town Races, where Thoroughbred horses have been going neck and neck since 1786.

Above all, this is a land of immense natural beauty. It was on the way back from a trip to Jefferson County that the late John Denver teamed with songwriter Bill Danoff to pen the words to "Country Roads," an international recording hit that begins with the classic line "Almost heaven, West Virginia." These men knew the Mountain State.

At 247 feet above sea level, **Harpers Ferry** is the lowest point in the Mountain State. It's also West Virginia's easternmost city, wedged in the foot-hills of the Blue Ridge Mountains between Maryland and Virginia.

Harpers Ferry's 300 or so residents live less than an hour's drive from the suburbs of Washington, DC, a blessing or a curse depending on to whom you talk. With urbanization slowly creeping westward, it seems fitting that this post-card village at the confluence of the Shenandoah and Potomac Rivers is the headquarters of the ***Appalachian Trail Conservancy*** (ATC), a nonprofit con-servation group dedicated since 1925 to maintaining and preserving the natural character of the 2,193-mile Appalachian National Scenic Trail. The celebrated foot trail, running from Springer Mountain, Georgia, to Mount Katahdin, Maine, was blazed by the ATC along the crests of the Appalachian Mountains in the 1930s, with help from several federal and state agencies and the Civilian Conservation Corps, the Depression-era organization responsible for developing many of our national parks.

eastern panhandle trivia

The town of Harpers Ferry con-sistently attracts the greatest number of visitors of any West Virginia attraction each year.

Today about two-thirds of the Ameri-can population lives within 500 miles of this strip of mountain wildness. Harpers Ferry is situated near the halfway mark on the trail, and as such it is a natural gather-ing and refueling point for backpack-toting hikers. Much of the ATC's work is centered on ensuring that there is plenty of green buffer land for the tens of thousands of hikers who take to some part of the trail each year, a mission that's backed by a major lobbying presence in the nation's capital. If you've ever stepped foot on the Appalachian Trail, or even just thought about it, make sure to pay homage at its headquarters in the cottagelike structure located on Washington Street. Inside you'll find interesting displays explaining the history and dynamics of the trail; a host of books, maps, posters, shirts, hats, and other hiking accessories; and a hikers' lounge with a huge relief map of the entire trail on one wall. The headquarters, on 799 Washington St., is open 9 a.m. to 5 p.m. daily. Call (304) 535-6331 for more information.

BEST ATTRACTIONS IN THE EASTERN PANHANDLE

Bell Boyd House
Martinsburg
(304) 267-4713
bchs.org

Berkeley Springs State Park
Berkeley Springs
(304) 258-2711
wvstateparks.com/park/
berkeley-springs-state-park

Charles Town Race Track
Charles Town
(800) 795-7001
hollywoodcasinocharlestown.com

Harpers Ferry National Historical Park
Harpers Ferry
(304) 535-6029
nps.gov/hafe

John Brown Wax Museum
Harpers Ferry
(304) 535-6342
johnbrownwaxmuseum.com

O'Hurley's General Store
Shepherdstown
(304) 876-6907
ohurleys.com

From ATC headquarters, you're maybe a five-minute walk to the center of the restored village, virtually all of which is contained in the *Harpers Ferry National Historical Park.* This is the single largest tourist draw in West Virginia. Although not exactly off the beaten path, a stroll through the National Park Service area is strongly advised for American history buffs, for it was here in 1859 that abolitionist John Brown raided the federal armory and arsenal in an attempt to seize guns and munitions needed for his planned slave rebellion. The raiders were ultimately apprehended by US Marines under the command of a young Robert E. Lee; nevertheless, the action was an important catalyst in the growing division over slavery—an issue that ultimately split open the nation with the advent of the Civil War. Here too are sites of special interest in African-American history. Storer College held the 1906 meeting of the Niagara Movement that led to the founding of the NAACP.

A good place to begin touring the town (named after an early settler who operated a ferry service) is at the park service's information center on Shoreline Drive. Rangers answer questions and distribute orientation maps that lead to such sites as the Harpers Ferry Armory fire-engine house, which is at the corner of High and Shenandoah Streets near the main-line tracks of the Baltimore & Ohio Railroad, and which served as the abolitionists' fort. Across the street the *John Brown Museum* chronicles Brown's raid, capture, trial, and hanging in neighboring Charles Town. Up yet another hill, this one overlooking the Shenandoah, stands *St. Peter's Catholic Church,* a gorgeous stone chapel built in 1830 and used continuously until a dwindling congregation prompted its closing as a parish church in 1994. It's still open for visitors as well as for Sunday-morning Mass. A few steep steps away stands the famous *Jefferson Rock,* a granite outcropping with a stunning, three-state view of the Blue Ridge Mountains and the merging rivers. Thomas Jefferson, who helped survey the area as a young man, sat upon the rock and wrote "the scene is worth a voyage across the Atlantic." The National Park Service facilities are open daily year-round (except Christmas and Thanksgiving) from 8 a.m. to 5 p.m. There are parking and walk-in fees, payable at the Cavalier Heights Visitor Center on US 340. A free shuttle bus service transports visitors to the park area. For more information, call (304) 535-6029.

Whether you're meandering through Harpers Ferry's peaceful hills or crowded streets and alleyways, it's impossible to escape the presence of the Shenandoah and Potomac Rivers. The Potomac, while on its 400-mile journey to the Chesapeake Bay from its source spring in Tucker County, West Virginia (see next chapter on the Potomac Highlands), takes on a wild and scenic demeanor as it flows through Harpers Ferry, churning up whitewater as it glides over limestone ridges and rocks. The same can be said of the Shenandoah, the northward-flowing river that ends its 150-mile path from Rockingham County, Virginia, with a gentle whitewater display that attracts anglers and rafters in droves.

Fishing, tubing, canoeing, kayaking, and rafting trips can be organized on both rivers through *River Riders,* located about 2 miles south of Harpers Ferry on Alstadts Hill Road. A best bet for an intermediate-level whitewater experience is to canoe the Shenandoah Staircase, a 6-mile outing with several sets of Class I to III rapids (VI is the most advanced) and a few long stretches of flat water for fishing. The float ends with a dramatic entrance into the Potomac Water Gap at Harpers Ferry. Most float trips, whether by raft, kayak, canoe, stand-up paddleboard, inner tube, or ducky, embark daily from mid-May through October 31. Outfitting fees are moderate; phone reservations should be made by credit card. Call (800) 326-7238 or see riverriders.com for more information on theme weekends with special rates. River Riders also offers zipline canopy tours with lovely views of Harpers Ferry. For an experience, do the evening tour by the light of the moon; visit harpersferryzipline.com for details.

West Virginia contains a treasure trove of offbeat museums, and one of the most unusual is *Harpers Ferry Toy Train Museum,* located 2 miles west of town on Bakerton Road just off US 340. Be prepared for a nostalgic trip back to childhood as you browse through the museum's large assortment of antique Lionel standard-gauge and O-gauge trains and accessories, most of them predating 1939. This was the personal collection of the late Robert E.

Wallich, who in 1970 decided to share his 60-year avocation with the public. The first Harpers Ferry Toy Train Museum was located in downtown Harpers Ferry and housed in a vintage Western Maryland Railroad baggage car. A few years later Wallich constructed an outdoor miniature railroad on his property in the outlying hills and eventually moved the museum to the same site. Wallich's son and grandson now run the museum as well as Joy Line Miniature Railroad, a train ride that's driven by a Cagney steam locomotive and appears to attract as many adults as kids. The museum is open Apr through Oct on Sat, Sun, and major holidays from 9 a.m. to 5 p.m. A small admission fee is charged. Special appointments for parties can be made any time of year. Call (304) 535-2521.

A *Harpers Ferry Ghost Tour* led by storyteller Rick Garland is a must-do if you're spending any amount of time in Harpers Ferry and want the lowdown on its past. You'll gain a darker perspective on this quaint town as you wander the streets behind Garland or sit spellbound in his Civil War parlor on High St. Start at the front patio of St. Peter's Church, then follow him into history. Garland's tales and explanations give his listeners new insight into the town at the time of John Brown and the Civil War. Ghost tours and history tours are available daily except Sundays and Wednesdays year-round. Tours are by reservation; call (304) 725-8019 or (732) 801-0381.

As you leave Harpers Ferry en route to Charles Town on US 340, about a 5-mile trip, the landscape begins to open up, revealing rolling pastures and low, sloping mountains that form the outline of the Shenandoah Valley. *Charles Town,* the seat of Jefferson County, sits in the heart of the West Virginia portion of the valley. The city was incorporated in 1787 and named in honor of George Washington's youngest brother, Charles, a major landowner in the Eastern Panhandle. Charles Washington donated 80 acres to the burgeoning village and was charged with laying out its original streets—George, Samuel, Lawrence, Mildred, and Charles—dutifully named after Washington family members. Not surprisingly, Charles Town's main thoroughfare is Washington Street. The city's current population of just over 5,400 is projected to increase as it acclimates to its newfound status as an exurb of metro Washington, DC.

While in town buy a postcard and have it mailed from the *Charles Town Post Office,* 101 W. Washington St. This is where the Honorary William L. Wilson, Charles Town native and US postmaster general, started the nation's first rural free delivery, or RFD, in 1896. On this site also stood the town jail where John Brown was imprisoned while awaiting his treason trial. The post office is open Mon through Fri from 8:30 a.m. to 5 p.m., Sat 9 a.m. to 12:30 p.m. Call (304) 725-2421.

To dig more into the turbulent history of Brown and Charles Town, stop by the *Jefferson County Museum* on the corner of Washington and Samuel

Streets. Among the hundreds of fascinating curios here are old black-and-white photographs depicting the county's agrarian roots, surveying maps, equipment used by George Washington, and the wagon used to transport John Brown to his execution. The museum is open 11 a.m. to 4 p.m. Tues through Sat, Apr through Nov. Admission is $4 for adults. Call (304) 725-8628 or see jeffcomuseumwv.org for more information.

Strolling among the eclectic blend of businesses in downtown Charles Town, patrons can treat themselves to a facial at Sokel, enjoy a Mexican treat at Ortega's, check out the hobby and yarn shops, then settle into a corner at Fuzzy Dog Books & Music for some serious browsing. Fuzzy Dog opened at 201 E. Washington Street in 2019 after two years of online-only sales of vintage books and records. Now it's expanded to several rooms and hosts regular literary and musical events. It doesn't hurt that the book and music shop has a wealth of comfy chairs and is located steps from Sibling Coffee Roasters.

Although the Eastern Panhandle is one of the most densely populated regions of West Virginia, it still retains a strong rural character underscored by thousands of acres of cattle farms, productive croplands, and apple and peach orchards. The pastoral legacy of the Virginia gentleman farmer lives on in such places as **Hillbrook Inn,** a stunning English-style country manor house/hotel. Five miles southwest of Charles Town, off Summit Point Road (Route 13), Hillbrook sits amid 17 acres of gardens, lawns, woods, and ponds. Bullskin Run (in Virginia and West Virginia, large brooks and streams are known as "runs") dissects the property, enhancing its quiet elegance.

Inside the inn, guests might be greeted with the aroma of roasted pheasant from the kitchen or the sound of an oak-wood fire crackling in the tavern. A colorful mix of antiques and contemporary art fills the private rooms, giving the place an aristocratic aura that begs comparison to the manor homes of England's Cotswolds. Hillbrook's 6 guest rooms and 4 cottages all have private baths, sitting areas, queen-size beds, and air-conditioning. Two rooms have fireplaces. Lodging rates are equally aristocratic, but they typically include a 4-course meal with wine and a country breakfast. If you plan to come just for lunch or a simpler 3-course dinner, it's a good idea to make reservations well in advance. A constituency of affluent—and loyal—Washingtonians apparently has already discovered this hidden gem. Hillbrook is open year-round, except Christmas. Check-in is after 3 p.m. and checkout is noon. Call (304) 725-4223 or (800) 304-4223.

Hillbrook's land, and some 2,200 acres surrounding it, once belonged to the Bullskin, or **Rock Hall Tract,** the first real estate owned by George Washington. The young man and future president actually surveyed the region in 1750 and took part of his salary to purchase Rock Hall Tract from a Captain

Burned Bridges

West Virginians faced conflicting loyalties during the Civil War; neighbor fought neighbor and sons faced off against fathers. In the Eastern Panhandle town of Shepherdstown, this was especially true.

If you look off the Rumsey Bridge on US 340 near Shepherdstown's Bavarian Inn, you can spot the piers of several bridges wiped out by flooding in the 20th century. But you won't see any remains of the first bridge on the spot, a covered bridge burned by Confederate troops in June 1861.

One of the young Confederate soldiers, Henry Kyd Douglas, lived on Ferry Hill Plantation (now C&O Canal Park headquarters), the pillared house directly opposite on the Maryland side of the river. In his memoir, *I Rode with Stonewall,* Douglas described his turmoil as he gazed over at his home, knowing his father was an owner of the property he was destroying. "I knew I was severing all connection between me and my family and understood the sensation of one who, sitting aloft the limb of a tree, cuts it off between him and the trunk," he wrote.

Douglas later became the youngest member of General Thomas "Stonewall" Jackson's staff and rose to colonel. When his father died soon after the war ended, Douglas inherited Ferry Hill. He accepted the inheritance but chose never to live there again.

Rutherford, an early settler. A state historical marker, located in front of South Jefferson Elementary School on Summit Point Road, signals the site of Washington's first farm.

Within earshot of the tiny hamlet of Summit Point, **Summit Point Motorsports Park** unfolds 3 racing courses featuring a total of 6 miles of technical challenges and high-performance driver training circuits. From early March to early December, the Sports Car Club of America (SCCA)–sanctioned track hosts a variety of professional and amateur auto, motorcycle, and go-kart races. Each May, for example, the Jefferson 500 Vintage Sports Car Race rolls back the clock a bit with a pair of 500-kilometer races—one for cars built before 1965 and another for 1965–1980 models. More for fun than competition, a vintage race might begin with an airplane sweeping down and leading the cars off the starting grid. You don't need a vintage car to take to the curvy track of Summit Point. The raceway sponsors a series of high-performance driving schools in your own car on occasional Fridays for wannabe Earnhardts—no pit crew required. Driving at high speeds on the 2-mile, 10-turn raceway is a thrill. If a seat in the grandstand isn't excitement enough, try revving up with a bowl of the track's famous "100 mph" chili and a cold beer. Paved parking, electric hookups, and shower facilities are available at the trackside paddock.

Admission to spectator events is moderate. Call (304) 725-8444 or see summitpoint-raceway.com for event and driving-school information.

Before heading north on Route 1 to Shepherdstown, duck down to the nearby *Harewood* estate, located on Route 51 between Middleway and Charles Town. The Georgian mansion was built in 1770 by Samuel Washington, the next-oldest brother of George Washington and the first in the family to move to the Eastern Panhandle. Like all Washingtons, Samuel was active in public affairs. He was appointed to serve as both county lieutenant and justice of the peace. He died in 1781, and his unmarked grave lies in a family plot on the property. In 1794 Harewood hosted the wedding of James Madison and Dolley Payne Todd, whose sister, Lucy Payne Washington, was the mistress of the estate. The home has been continuously occupied and to this day is owned by a direct descendant. Unfortunately, Harewood is not open to the public, but its exterior and grounds can be viewed from the road.

Claymont Court, just off Route 51, remains the only one of Jefferson County's Washington homes open to the public. In fact, it's possible to spend the night in this 1820 mansion built by George Washington's grandnephew, Bushrod Washington. Claymont is a year-round retreat center run by followers of G. I. Gurdjieff. This estate, on the National Register of Historic Places, includes the magnificent main house, formal gardens, and massive brick stables, which have been adapted as a seminar center. Under the crystal chandeliers of what was always regarded as the grandest of the Washington homes, groups gather to learn more about dance, mindfulness, healing, spirituality, and sometimes scrapbooking. For information about upcoming events at Claymont Court, call (304) 725-4437 or visit claymontseminars.com.

Shepherdstown lies up near the northern tip of Jefferson County, perched beautifully—and sometimes precariously—on the banks of the Potomac River. (The entire northern Potomac Basin is susceptible to dramatic flooding, and for folks living along the river roads, heavy spring rains can turn their homes into islands.)

Laid out by Thomas Shepherd in 1734, Shepherdstown is the oldest burgh in West Virginia, and its painstakingly preserved 18th-century homes and shops have rightfully been deemed a registered district on the National Register of Historic Places. Look for Dickinson & Wait Craft Gallery. Outdoors lovers will want to stop at Kelly's White Fly Shoppe and Pedal & Paddle.

History seeps out of every nook and cranny here. When General Washington called for more support for the siege of Boston in 1775, Shepherdstown paid heed. The famous Bee Line March of southern volunteers to Massachusetts began at Morgan's Spring, now part of **Morgan's Grove Park,** 1 mile south of town on Route 480. Shepherdstown went on to supply more troops to the Revolutionary War than any city its size in the colonies. At one point Washington even considered making the humble town the nation's new capital city.

During the Civil War, Shepherdstown was a strategic river crossing into Maryland. Immediately after 1862's tragic battle of Antietam (just 5 miles away), in which more than 22,000 Americans were casualties of a single day's fighting, Shepherdstown became one massive hospital. Perhaps because of its empathetic nature, the town was spared major damage during the war.

This is equally fortunate for modern-day residents and tourists, who are blessed with one of the most charming townscapes in West Virginia. Over the years Shepherdstown's quiet appeal has lured scores of artisans, writers, merchants, musicians, and scholars—folks who've helped stamp a distinctive impression on the place. Today about 2,000 full-time residents and some 4,100 Shepherd University students call the town home. One friend commented that Shepherdstown has become "West Virginia's answer to Woodstock, NY, the village," a mixture of Norman Rockwellian idyll and bohemian funkiness.

The lifeblood of Shepherdstown has always been **Town Run.** The spring-fed brook runs through the town's alleyways, backyards, and parks and is used as an auxiliary water supply. During the village's infancy, Town Run powered **Thomas Shepherd's gristmill** (midblock of Mill Street), the area's first industry. (Interestingly, the gristmill, now a private home, still contains its 40-foot-diameter, cast-iron waterwheel, one of the largest of its kind in the world.)

At the **Blue Moon Cafe,** corner of Princess and High Streets, Town Run brook flows directly through the restaurant on its way downhill to the river. The waterway is covered to keep out pollutants, but the deli is open to hearty eaters, many coming from the nearby campus of Shepherd University. For a delicious meal, you can't go wrong with a roasted chicken sandwich—a plump, smoked chicken breast covered in roasted corn, avocado, chipotle sauce, and sweet red peppers. Top it off with one of the delicious desserts. In warmer weather, take advantage of the outdoor, streamside seating. Prices are reasonable. The cafe is open Mon through Thurs from 11 a.m. to 5 p.m. and Fri through Sun from noon to 8 p.m. Phone (304) 876-1920 or see bluemoon shepherdstown.com.

Some 20 years before Robert Fulton's *Clermont* steamed up the Hudson River, Shepherdstown resident James Rumsey built and successfully demonstrated a working steamboat on the Potomac. A replica of that boat is located across the street from the Blue Moon Cafe at the **Rumsey Steamboat Museum** (located in the backyard of the Entler Hotel and Shepherdstown Museum). Inside the boathouse/museum you'll also find displays and sketches outlining Rumsey's fascinating life and inventions. In the 1780s George Washington appointed the budding engineer and inventor to manage the development of a navigation company on the Potomac. Washington hoped the company would be a key asset in opening up the West through an elaborate canal system. Rumsey, however, was enchanted with the notion of mastering the river's strong currents by way of a steam-driven piston that created a water-jet propulsion system. On December 3, 1787, Rumsey and a crew of eight Shepherdstown ladies boarded a small test boat appropriately named the *Rumseian Experiment* and chugged up the Potomac at a formidable 3 knots. With Washington's encouragement, Rumsey took the knowledge of his technological breakthrough and went to London to secure financial aid to build a larger and commercially viable ship. Unfortunately, Rumsey died on the eve of completing the new improved steamboat, and the project was soon aborted. These and other tales await visitors to the museum.

If you're lucky enough to be in Shepherdstown in August, the Rumseian Society (the group that runs the museum), under the guidance of Captain Jay Hurley, occasionally takes the steamship replica out onto the river for live demonstrations. The museum, with its colorful outdoor mural depicting the Shepherdstown riverbank as seen through Rumsey's eyes, is open from Apr through Oct, Saturdays from 12 to 4 p.m. Captain Hurley says individual and group tours also can be arranged in advance any time of year. Call (304) 876-6907 for more information and demonstration schedules. Donations of $4 per adult are suggested. Hurley, incidentally, is the proprietor of *O'Hurley's General Store,* a popular stop on most day-trip circuits through Shepherdstown. Stop by on Thursday night for a harmonic blend of dulcimer, harp, and clarinet music. This is the place to find your steam engines, crockery, dinner bells, and much more. While down near the water, be sure to visit the *James Rumsey Monument* at the end of Mill Street. The tall Ionic column supports a granite globe of the world, a reference to the international reach of Rumsey's invention.

The post-and-beam chalets and stone manor of the four-diamond *Bavarian Inn* promise true German fare, and you won't be disappointed. Located just across US 340 from Shepherd University in Shepherdstown, this establishment envelops you in the warm, winey scent of Bavarian food as soon as you enter the dining room. In the ambience of dark, rich hardwood paneling, you can choose among popular German staples such as red cabbage, potato dumplings, and *jaegerschnitzel* (veal smothered in mushrooms and wine sauce). The chef here uses good white wine—not vinegar—in the rich meat dishes, and you'll notice the subtle difference.

The Bavarian Inn is open daily from 7 a.m. to 9 p.m. For more information call (304) 876-2551 or visit bavarianinnwv.com.

Before leaving town, you'll want to stroll through the bucolic grounds of **Shepherd University** (shepherd.edu), founded in 1872 as one of the state's first liberal arts institutions. It was in the building that is now the campus's McMurran Hall, at the corner of Duke and German Streets, that thousands of wounded soldiers were treated in the aftermath of Antietam. The school is widely recognized for its progressive programs in the natural and social sciences and in the arts and humanities. For the past several years, the college has played host to the **Contemporary American Theater Festival**, a showcase of new works by some of the country's most important playwrights. Performances are staged by the state's only **Actors' Equity theater**, a talent pool drawn from Shepherdstown and across the country. Past productions have included such ambitious and poignant works as *Black* by Joyce Carol Oates and *Dream House* by Darrah Cloud. The nearly monthlong thespian festival is typically held during July and also includes staged readings, improvisational comedy, and concerts. For more information about the Contemporary American Theater Festival, call (800) 999-2283, or visit catf.org.

Shepherd University anchors the town's arts scene with its Performing Arts Series, an annual lineup that might host a blues master one month and the Appalachian Heritage Festival the next. During this September fete, energize on the vibes of an old-time string band competition and join in the community square dance. In October, the **American Conservation Film Festival** brings incredible stories and awareness of important ecological issues to the area in films from around the globe. The festival was born in 2003 at the U.S. Fish & Wildlife Service's National Conservation Training Center in Shepherdstown.

Crossroads

Crossroads is the name we've given to the region that sits in the heart of the Eastern Panhandle and contains the historic railroad town of Martinsburg and all of Berkeley County west of US 11, sometimes still referred to as the Valley Pike. In the early 18th century, the region became home to the first settlers in what is now West Virginia and later evolved into a bustling center of wagon, coach, and rail travel to the West. The Valley Pike, now paralleled by I-81, once served as the major north–south artery linking Pennsylvania's Cumberland Valley to the Valley of Virginia.

The legacy of the earliest settlers lives on in Berkeley County's more than 2,000 National Register historic sites, the highest concentration in the state. Crossroads' fruit orchards, cattle ranches, and truck farms, meanwhile, continue to find steady markets in the growing urban corridors of the East, and in recent years they have become the focus of open-space preservation efforts. The gigantic *Mountain State Apple Harvest Festival,* held the third weekend in October in Martinsburg, salutes one of the region's most successful agribusinesses.

With a population of 17,500—and growing—Martinsburg has long been the Eastern Panhandle's principal city, an

eastern panhandle trivia

During the Civil War, the Union army occupied Martinsburg for 32 months.

industrial, agricultural, and transportation center that is just beginning to tap its tourism attributes. Because of its strategic importance as the western gateway to the neighboring Shenandoah Valley, Martinsburg was in the thick of the Civil War, once serving as a command center for Confederate general Thomas "Stonewall" Jackson, a native West Virginian. Though badly bruised during the war, the city remarkably preserved many of its glorious 18th- and 19th-century buildings.

One such structure is *Tuscarora Church,* 2335 Tuscarora Pike, about 2 miles west of downtown. Built from native limestone in 1740 by Scots-Irish Presbyterians, the country church was refurbished in 1803 and is still going strong. In election years the church serves as a polling place. Here's one bit of evidence that even the farthest eastern reaches of West Virginia were once the "Wild West": On the back walls of the church are the two original gun racks worshippers used to hang their pistols during services. The state's second oldest Presbyterian church holds Sunday service at 10 a.m. Call (304) 263-4579.

Another Martinsburg historical gem is the *General Adam Stephen House,* 309 E. John St., a native limestone home built around 1778 by the town's founder. Construction was prolonged by the Revolutionary War, in which General Stephen served as soldier and surgeon. Like most western Virginia gentlemen, Stephen was more intent on creating a home with a natural aesthetic than a grandiose design. He was also as wily as Br'er Rabbit, building his simple, four-room home over a natural underground tunnel system so that the family could escape American Indians or British raiders. The tunnel leads into a man-made underground room with an arched stone ceiling and exits into the cavern below. House tours include the tunnel system, which is a blessing on steamy summer afternoons.

Next to the home on the same property is the *Triple Brick Building,* built in 1874 by Phillip Showers, who at the time owned the Stephen House. The 3-story building supposedly got its name because it contained 3 apartment

West Virginia Firsts

The nation's first rural free mail delivery was started in Charles Town on October 6, 1896.

West Virginia was the first state to have a sales tax, effective July 1, 1921.

Bailey Brown, the first Union soldier killed on the battlefield in the Civil War, died on May 22, 1861, at Fetterman in Taylor County, West Virginia.

The first public spa was opened at Berkeley Springs in 1756.

Mrs. Minnie Buckingham Harper became the first African-American woman to become a member of a state or federal legislative body in the US when she was appointed to the West Virginia House of Delegates in 1928.

Parkersburg citizens founded the first free public school for African-American children south of the Mason-Dixon Line in January 1862.

During the Civil War, Martin Robinson Delany of Charles Town became the first African American to receive a regular army commission. He became a major in the Union Army.

units used by workers rebuilding Martinsburg's Civil War–torn railroad yards. It's now used as a local history museum, complete with quilts, period clothes, Civil War memorabilia, and musical instruments. Both the General Adam Stephen House and the Triple Brick Building are open from 2 to 5 p.m. Sat and Sun, May through Oct. Special viewing appointments can be made by calling (304) 267-4434. No admission is charged.

Three blocks to the north (200 block of E. Martin Street) and across the tracks of the Baltimore & Ohio Railroad stands the **Roundhouse,** one of the finest examples of 19th-century industrial railroad architecture. Abandoned years ago and recently renovated, the unmistakably round building was the nerve center of passenger and freight activity along the B&O route connecting Martinsburg to Baltimore in 1842. Most of the rail yard was destroyed by Jackson's troops during the Civil War, but the Roundhouse was rebuilt in 1866, and 11 years later it was the scene of a major rail-worker strike. The Roundhouse is finishing renovations and is open for Saturday tours April through October as well as craft shows, historical events, and celebrations. For information call the office at (304) 260-4141.

In the rolling hills east of the railroad tracks is the **Old Green Hill Cemetery** on Burke Road. It's patterned on the Parisian mold with an impressive display of stone-carved art. The expansive views of Martinsburg and its environs from atop the cemetery's hills are spectacular. Among those buried here are President Lincoln's bodyguard, Ward Hill Lamon; writer-artist David Hunter Strother (aka Porte Crayon) of *Harper's Weekly* fame; at least 30 unknown Confederate soldiers; and the parents of Belle Boyd. The grounds are open dawn to dusk.

Belle Boyd, you might remember, was a Confederate spy working in cahoots with Stonewall Jackson. She was arrested and imprisoned twice but both times released for lack of evidence. After the war the Martinsburg native married one of her Union captors, went on to become a stage actress in New York and London, and later lectured and wrote a book about her spying exploits. Boyd's father, Benjamin Reed Boyd, built a 22-room Greek Revival mansion in the center of the city, and in more recent years the Berkeley County Historical Society has restored the **Belle Boyd House,** 126 E. Race St., turning a portion of it into a Civil War museum and historical archive. The house contains original family heirlooms, journal entries, and wartime artifacts, as well as a room dedicated to President Abraham Lincoln and his local connection: his former law partner and self-appointed bodyguard, Ward Hill Lamon. Hours are 9 a.m. to 5 p.m., daily. For more information, call (304) 267-4713.

eastern panhandle trivia

Nineteenth-century Bunker Hill Mill, located near Martinsburg, is the only mill in the state featuring dual waterwheels.

Children (and inner children of older folks) delight in the weekend shows at **Wonderment Puppet Theatre**. In a whimsical Victorian house on King Street, art teacher Joe Santoro crafts puppets, sets, and props, presenting six original shows annually as well as specially scripted parties. Visitors are invited to explore rooms filled with puppet curiosities after the show. Shows start at 1 p.m. on Saturdays and Sundays. (304-260-9382; 304-258-4074 or Wonderment Puppet Theater at Facebook.com)

As you wend your way back to I-81, detour to 330 Winchester Ave. and stop in at **WSG Gallery.** Jody Wright's whimsical paintings are displayed with husband Carl Wright's stone sculptures and sleek sculptural furniture. If you see a sculpture you love but can't afford, consider leasing it. Carl has reasonable rental terms for his works, many of which are on display in sculpture gardens across the nation. Call for an appointment (304) 263-2391, or see wsggallery.com.

If you're a chocolate lover, **DeFluri's Fine Chocolates** is a must-see. The Casabona family has won awards for the truffles and other chocolates they create at their family factory at 130 N. Queen St. A corporate favorite, Dr. DeFluri's specially packaged 72% Behavior Modification Tablets helps folks get the cooperation they deserve through "doses" of cacao dark chocolate. For more information, call (304) 264-3698 or visit defluris.com.

From Martinsburg jump on the interstate or the slower but more scenic US 11 and head 8 miles south to Bunker Hill, a village known for its apple orchards and antiques shops. Two miles west of town, on Old Mill Road (Route 26), is the rustic cabin home of West Virginia's first white settler, Colonel Morgan Morgan, a Delaware native who moved his family to this lonely western outpost in the 1730s. *Morgan Cabin,* now a living-history museum of the Berkeley County Historical Society, was made from local hardwoods and stone in 1734, much of which remains in the restored version that is listed on the National Register of Historic Places. Save for a 20th-century farmhouse across the road, little seems to have changed since the 1730s in this rural corner of Berkeley County. Standing in front of the cabin, one can almost imagine a clandestine American Indian gathering taking place beyond the hills a few hundred yards to the south. One of the most violent clashes at Morgan Cabin took place during the Revolutionary War when one of Colonel Morgan's grandsons, an American soldier, was captured by Tories and executed in front of his family. The pioneering Morgans nevertheless went on to become one of the Eastern Panhandle's most prominent families. Neighboring Morgan County and Morgantown, in northern West Virginia, were named after them. Morgan Cabin is open 2 to 4 p.m. Sun, June through Oct. Special tours can be arranged year-round by calling (304) 229-8707.

Heading back into Bunker Hill, you'll pass *Christ Church* on the left. Built in 1740 and frequented by the Morgan family, it is believed to be West Virginia's first house of worship, predating Tuscarora Church by a few months. The brick Greek Revival church has been restored three times. Behind the church is the cemetery where Colonel Morgan and his wife are buried. *Bunker Hill Antiques Associates,* a local landmark, is directly next door at the corner of US 11 and Old Mill Road. The 19th-century mill-turned-emporium houses more than 50 furniture, jewelry, glass, book, and art dealers. It's open Thurs through Mon from 10 a.m. to 5 p.m. For more information, call (304) 229-0709 or see bunkerhillantiques.com.

From Bunker Hill, head back to the I-81 ramp at Inwood, but instead of getting on the freeway, continue west along George Washington Heritage Trail Byway, via Route 51. For about 5 miles, you'll roll past country stores and green pastures dotted with rust-colored barns before arriving in tiny *Gerrardstown.* Once this sleepy, historic district town wasn't so sleepy. Not long after it was laid out in 1784, Gerrardstown became a booming supply center for wagon trains headed west—that is until the westward railroad chose Martinsburg instead. Many of the village's original buildings from the 18th century remain along the byway—Cool Spring Farm, Gerrard House, Prospect Hill, and Marshy Dell.

Scan a map of West Virginia and you're bound to find dozens of towns with intriguing names—places like Burnt House, Toll Gate, Hurricane, Mud, Crum, and Nancy Run. In this region, there's a *Shanghai,* about 10 miles northwest of Gerrardstown. The name probably came from a local furniture manufacturer, according to Don Wood, director of the Berkeley County Historical Society. Another theory, he suggests, is that several citizens of the village were locked up in jail during a crucial election so they couldn't vote and thus were "Shanghaied."

To reach Shanghai, take Route 51 west to Mills Gap and hang a right on Route 45. Continue 3 miles to Glengary, where you'll take the first right onto the kind of country road John Denver immortalized. In 5 miles, you'll see Shanghai—a few houses, a store, and a post office. The sense of being in backcountry is the main attraction, a feeling that increases as you head over Sleepy Creek Mountain.

The peace of Back Creek Valley surrounding Shanghai is marinating at *Lazy-A Campground.* Tucked along a private section of Back Creek, the camp offers tent and RV camping plus rustic cabins with electricity. You can fish, play basketball or pitch horseshoes, but on summer evenings some folks like to plunk their chairs into the creek and zone out to the sound of water spilling over the small dam. For reservations, call (240) 538-3555 or visit lazyacamping.com.

Hedgesville, about 10 miles north of Shanghai on Apple Pie Ridge (next to Potato Hill), has a strong agricultural past. To celebrate this disappearing way of life, farmer L. Norman Dillon left Berkeley County money to start a farm museum. The *L. Norman Dillon Farm Museum* preserves some of the tools and practices of the trade, including apple graders, horse harnesses, milking machines, and hand plows. A quick look around the grounds reveals larger pieces of machinery, including sawmills, tractors, huskers, and harrows. All of this gear is put into action during the museum's fall shows. On those occasions, sulfurous smoke and the ringing of metal on metal summon crowds to the blacksmith shop, where a smithy hammers cherry-red scraps of steel into hooks, knives, and latches. Eventually the farmstead will include a farmhouse, authentic West Virginia barn, and milking parlor. The museum, at the intersection of Route 9 and Ridge Road across from Hedgesville High School, is open free of charge on Sunday afternoon April 1 to October 31. Call (304) 582-5707 or 263-0731 for more information.

Once you've admired the orchards from Apple Pie Ridge, turn west. The landscape takes a definite turn for the vertical as you head into the Springs and Valley Region, toward Berkeley Springs.

Springs and Spas

There's always been a certain mystique, a certain magical attraction, to the western edge of the Eastern Panhandle. Maybe it has to do with the legends left behind by the Tuscarora and Shawnee, who, along with other warring Appalachian tribes, regularly visited the region's "healing waters" in peace. Maybe it stems from the colonial tradition set by George Washington and Thomas Jefferson of "taking to the baths," the plentiful warm springs that cleansed, soothed, and revitalized the body.

Whatever it is, this land of springs and spas is evolving into one of the East's leading health resorts, art and antiques centers, and outdoor recreation areas. Morgan County encompasses 231 square miles of mountains and springfed forest. The northern and western borders are formed by the winding Potomac River, and its rugged spine is shaped by the uplift of the Shenandoah Mountains. The scenic beauty of the landscape and the diversity of residents, from urban transplants to seventh-generation farmers, make for an unforgettable blend of sights and attractions.

Berkeley Springs, the area's largest town, bills itself as "the country's first spa." It's not a hollow claim. Shortly after George Washington's family and friends drew up a "plat" of 134 lots, named the streets, and incorporated the town of Bath, the community emerged as a haven for seekers of respite from a young and troubled nation. President George and First Lady Martha were such regular visitors during the presidency that historians dubbed Berkeley Springs the first "summer White House." Today massage therapists outnumber lawyers three to one in the little town. Visitors may soak in the mineral springs and sample more than 20 different bodywork treatments in 6 full-service spas.

The focal point of the town has always been the warm mineral springs found on Washington Street at what is now *Berkeley Springs State Park,* a 7-acre spring and bathhouse compound. The outdoor springs flow from the base of Warm Springs Ridge at a rate of 1,500 gallons a minute, surfacing at a constant 74°F. The park's Lord Fairfax public tap is a gathering point for locals and tourists who come to fill their jugs with the sweet-tasting mineral water. But the real stars are the bathhouses, the 1815 *Roman Bath House* and its private, heated bathing chambers, and the modern Main Bathhouse with its sauna, baths, and massage therapists—female therapists for the women on one side and males for the men on the other. The historic 2-story bathhouse is the oldest public building in Morgan County. On the second floor is the free *Museum of the Berkeley Springs,* which chronicles the development of the town and its springs through old photographs, sketches, exhibits, and water-bottling memorabilia. There's an 800-lb local crystal, a light-up model of springs geology and

West Virginia Country Music Hall of Fame

Although he never had a chart-topping song, Jim McCoy, who died at 87 in 2016, has managed to make a lifelong career of the country music business. The Berkeley Springs native recorded for a major Nashville label, put Patsy Cline on the airwaves, and played guitar for Cline on tour. McCoy started his own country nightclub and record company just outside of Berkeley Springs. Named in honor of his friend Ernest Tubb, the "Texas Troubadour," the restaurant and lounge is still going and still decorated with photos and memorabilia of stars McCoy knew personally. What's more, Great American Country television network recently named the Troubadour Lounge the top honky-tonk in West Virginia. It's also been called "best dive bar."

The Troubadour acts as a shrine to both Cline and Tubb. Life-size cutouts of the two greet guests as they enter McCoy's country music ranch—a park and amphitheater out back serve up music and barbecue for big Saturday night crowds. Cline—then her name was Virginia Hensley—was just 14 when she was asked him for a chance to sing with his Melody Playboys band on a live radio show in Winchester. "Boy, can she sing," he used to tell listeners.

McCoy and the band toured with Cline when her career took off. They were close. In fact, he had to call her mother and tell her Patsy had been killed in the 1963 plane crash. For years, Charlie Dick, Patsy's husband, would come up from Nashville for the Labor Day celebration McCoy put on in memory of Cline, Tubb, and Johnny Triplett, who played steel guitar with McCoy and Cline. As part of the event, Jim would induct new members into his West Virginia Country Music Hall of Fame—a gallery of plaques and photos that takes up a whole room of the Troubadour. Cline, Tubb, US Senator Robert Byrd, Little Jimmie Dickens, Kathy Mattea, Bluefield singer Mel Street, and others share space on the wall.

The Troubadour offers live shows every Saturday night. The restaurant, lounge, and museum are open Wed through Sat, 5 to 9 p.m.; 3 a.m. on weekends. For more information on the Troubadour visit troubadourlounge on Facebook.com or call (304) 258-9381.

an exhibit of antique bathing wear that brings laughs. The Main Bath House is on the opposite side of the park. The park's baths are open from 10 a.m. to 6 p.m. daily, until 9 p.m. Fridays, Apr through Oct. Water treatments are relatively inexpensive and popular, so it's best to reserve a private bath at least two weeks in advance. The museum is open weekends 10 a.m. to 3 p.m. Feb to mid-Nov, daily in summer, and the park swimming pool serves the public daily throughout summer. Top off your day with some toe-tapping at the park's free summer concerts Saturday nights. The park's number is (304) 258-2711 and the website is wvstateparks.com/park/Berkeley-springs-state-park.

Next door to the springs, the stately **Country Inn & Spa,** One Market St., triples as a hotel, spa, and restaurant. The inn's signature white-columned facade is draped with the flags of the contiguous states and the District of Columbia. Comfortable rooms, many with brass beds, are available in the main house (more like a mansion), while an adjoining modern brick addition houses more contemporary-style digs. No matter where you bunk, you're but a few steps to the spa, where a certified staff will lead you through a choice of whirlpool baths, deep-muscle massages, European-style facials, manicures, and pedicures. The Country Inn is open year-round. Lodging, spa, and dining rates range from moderate to expensive. Call (304) 258-2210; thecountryinnwv.com.

There was a time when small-town America had real movie houses— theaters that were destinations in themselves, not just places where films were screened. Berkeley Springs has such a venue in the **Star Theatre** on Washington Street. The vintage 1930s movie house features a vintage ticket booth, popcorn from a 1940s hot-oil popping machine, and overstuffed love seats in the back. The late Jeanne Mozier and her husband Jack Soronen restored the old theater (formerly a car dealership) with modern sound and air conditioning in 1979 and brought more than 1,500 movies to town. Its current owners, Paul and Trey Johanson, show feature films, family matinees, indies, and classics for classically low prices as well as free Tuesday "movies we all love." Live music shows mix things up on the last Fridays of the month. For information or to reserve a love seat, call (304) 258-1404.

The **Fairfax Coffee House** at 23 Fairfax St., across from the park, has become a sort of art center, neighborhood tavern, and respected eatery. A concert or poetry reading is likely to be going on almost every weekend in May through October and every other Saturday night the rest of the year. Newgrass, bluegrass, Celtic, swing, rockabilly, jazz—it's an eclectic mix. Work by regional artists adorns the walls, changing every few weeks. Serving breakfast, lunch, and light dinners, this *Cheers*-style pub also offers a wide selection of specialty coffee and tea drinks, as well as fine beers and wines. To check on events there, call (304) 258-8019 or visit fairfaxcoffeehouse.com.

Berkeley Springs is a veritable gold mine for antiques and craft collectors, with nearly a dozen shops, studios, and consignment centers located within the central business district. In fact, *American Style* magazine voted Berkeley Springs one of the top seven small-town art destinations in America for its galleries, concerts, theater, and artists' community. These and other outlying boutiques offer two studio tours that let you see firsthand how local artisans create jewelry, pottery, stained glass, and furniture. The tours, offered Memorial Day weekend and in late October, are headquartered at the **Ice House Gallery,** home of the Morgan Arts Council. The Ice House Gallery is a destination in itself for one-of-a-kind crafts, quilts, pottery, and art. For more information, see macicehouse.org or call (800) 447-8797.

Shops that line the streets include the ***Fleur de Lis Cheese Shop***, ***Himalayan Handicrafts***, ***Heath Studio Gallery***, and ***Inspired Chaos Gifts***. ***BlackCat Music Shop & Studio*** on Independence Street carries new, used, and vintage instruments, gives lessons, and hosts weekly jam sessions. Patrons can be recorded or learn sound technology skills in BlackCat's studio. Its Black-Cat School of Rock helps students of all ages apply their skills performing live on stage at real rock venues and local area shows. The shop is usually open seven days a week, (304) 258-4440; blackcatmusicshop.com.

Tucked away in a historic home (and an adjoining building that used to be a mechanic's garage), ***Maria's Garden and Inn,*** 201 Independence St, now operates as a full 9-room bed-and-breakfast run by Curtis Perry. Perry's parents made their mark in Berkeley Springs by running a popular pizza restaurant in the 1970s before becoming a full-service Italian restaurant..

Staying here can be a somewhat spiritual experience—one that extends beyond the food. The rooms are decorated with replicas and paintings of apparitions of the Virgin Mary from around the world. Embedded in the restaurant's stone-wall entranceway, for example, is a reproduction of the Miraculous Cloth of Our Lady of Guadalupe portrait, which has hung in the Basilica in Mexico City for more than 450 years. A small upstairs chapel is dedicated to the Virgin and makes for a pleasant meditation area or wedding site. The garden too is peopled with Virgin statuary. Maria's has several guest rooms done up in a country-chic decor. A first-floor suite comes with a second bedroom and kitchenette. Room rates start at $99 for a single and $195 for the suite, breakfast included. The inn is open year-round, but be sure to make advance reservations for the busy spring and fall months. A two-night minimum is required on weekends. For more information, call (304) 258-2021; mariasgarden.com.

On your way out of Berkeley Springs on Route 9 west, you'll glimpse the stone Berkeley Castle jutting from Warm Springs Ridge. The castle was built in 1885 by Colonel Samuel Suit for his young bride. The road winds up to the 1,000-foot summit of ***Prospect Peak.*** A scenic overlook affords a four-state view of the Cacapon and Potomac River Valleys. The vista was described by *National Geographic* magazine as one of America's "outstanding beauty spots."

A few miles south of town, the ridge turns into Cacapon Mountain and a second state park nestles on 6,000 acres of mountain wilderness. ***Cacapon State Park*** is a full resort with activities open to both day visitors and guests staying at the park's cabins and lodge. There is no entry fee to the park. It's the perfect place to turn your kids loose in nature. The park's stream-fed lake features a sandy beach, lifeguards and a flotilla of paddle and rowboats. The lake's swimming area is free to park guests; there are modest fees for day use. Fishing is free, and no license is required for those under 15 years old. The dam on the east side of the well-stocked lake is often dotted with anglers in pursuit of trout and bass.

Over 20 miles of marked hiking and bridle trails along the mountain range from easy to challenging and boast stunning views and odd rock formations. Other park activities range from an 18-hole golf course, clay tennis courts, and skeet shooting to a children's play area near the lake. Guided horseback rides are offered weekends Apr to Oct as well as Wed through Fri in the summer. For additional information, call Cacapon Resort State Park (304) 258-1022

A fitting final detour in the Eastern Panhandle is to trek west over Great Cacapon Mountain to the little town of **Paw Paw,** the region's westernmost point. Like so many towns in the Eastern Panhandle, Paw Paw lies along the Potomac River and was once a vital rail center. It's named for a tree with a banana-like fruit common to this area. Most of the current 550 residents are direct descendants of the town's original settlers—folks who tamed the river

In Praise of Pawpaws

The last official days of summer in mid-September are the best time for making a pilgrimage down to the pawpaw patch. In Paw Paw, West Virginia, you may have to get down to the riverside a few days early to beat out the raccoons for a taste of this incredibly sweet wild fruit known here as the West Virginia banana.

If you've never sampled a pawpaw (*Asimina triloba*), you should. It tastes like its tropical cousins, the banana and mango, served up in a custard-like pulp popping with vitamins A and C. It has no shelf life, but North America's largest native fruit is credited with being a lifesaver for American Indians and frontiersmen traveling the river valleys of the Southeast and Midwest in the fall.

The pawpaw made the news in 1992 when a Purdue University researcher reported he had isolated a powerful anticancer drug as well as a natural pesticide from the pawpaw tree. Those substances are found primarily in the twigs and smaller branches.

West Virginia native Neal Peterson has been pushing pawpaws for more than three decades. Peterson, known to many as the Johnny Appleseed of the pawpaw, owns the nation's largest mail-order pawpaw nursery, Peterson Pawpaws (petersonpawpaws.com), in Harpers Ferry.

Peterson founded the PawPaw Foundation and eventually joined forces with Kentucky State University to genetically perfect a shippable fruit with fewer seeds. Today at least a dozen universities are running regional trials on a cluster of pawpaw varieties.

and harvested timber from the surrounding virgin forests. There's not a lot of tourism here, save for outstanding river fishing and exploring the ***Paw Paw Tunnel,*** a 0.5-mile mountain tunnel carved by engineers in the mid-1800s during the construction of the Chesapeake & Ohio Canal connecting Washington, DC, to Cumberland, Maryland. Although named after the West Virginia village, the tunnel is actually across the river in Maryland. It's open year-round to hikers and bikers.

Paw Paw is home to the Mountain State's only clothing-optional resort. At the ***Avalon nudist camp,*** it's normal to see naked folks riding golf carts, swimming, playing tennis, dancing, batting around a volleyball, even attending camp church services. There's also an occasional nude prom for adults—and you thought all the fun was dressing up! Actually no one here has to be unclothed, except in the pools, sauna, and spa. "We let people get undressed at their own pace," said former owner Phyllis Gaffney. "We tell people the sooner they try it, the more comfortable they'll be. It's a step toward being more authentic, we think."

But for all the freedom that prevails, some traditional values remain. The resort has canceled memberships and asked men to leave for making harassing comments to women. (No women have menaced men yet, they said.) Avalon is a membership club, but visitors are welcome. Guests are especially welcome at the annual summer ***Avalon Fest*** three-day music festival, when a concert ticket buys admission to all camp recreational facilities. Call (304) 947-5600, or check avalon-resort.com.

The West Virginia Department of Transportation designated the 137-mile ***George Washington Heritage Trail*** as a West Virginia Scenic Byway in February 1998. The trail presents an excellent opportunity to visit some of the more important historic sites and points of interest in the three counties of the Eastern Panhandle. The trail makes a 112-mile loop through the counties, with a 25-mile branch off to the town of Paw Paw. The trail was established to commemorate the life and legacy of our first president and his connection to the Eastern Panhandle. The well-marked trail may be covered in about four hours—but why? It is better to linger along the way and make a day of it. Visitors are never far from gas, food, and lodging at any point on the trail. For a map and more information, call the Martinsburg–Berkeley County Convention and Visitors Bureau at (304) 264-8801 or (800) 498-2386 or visit travelwv.com.

Places to Stay in the Eastern Panhandle

BERKELEY SPRINGS

Cacapon Resort State Park
US 522 (south of Berkeley Springs)
(304) 258-1022
wvstateparks.com/park/cacapon-resort-state-park
Moderate

Highlawn Inn
Market Street
(304) 258-5700
highlawninn.com
Moderate to expensive

CHARLES TOWN

The Carriage Inn Bed and Breakfast
417 E. Washington St.
(855) 516-1090
carriageinn.com
Expensive to very expensive

The Inn at Charles Town
Charles Town Races
US 304
(800) 795-7001
ctownraces.com
Expensive to very expensive

HARPERS FERRY

Angler's Inn
846 Washington St.
(304) 535-1239
theanglersinn.com
Moderate to expensive

Harpers Ferry Campground & Cabins
408 Alstadts Hill Rd
(304) 535-2663
riverriders.com
Inexpensive

Town's Inn
176 and 170 High St.
(304) 932-0677
thetownsinn.com
Moderate

HEDGESVILLE

Woods Resort
Mountain Lake Rd.
(304) 754-7222
(800) 248-2222
thewoodsresort.com
Moderate to expensive

MARTINSBURG

Hilton Garden Inn
65 Priority Dr
(304) 263-0101
Moderate

SHEPHERDSTOWN

Bavarian Inn and Lodge
Route 480 (adjacent to the Potomac River Bridge)
(304) 876-2551
bavarianinnwv.com
Moderate to very expensive

Thomas Shepherd Inn
Duke Street
(888) 889-8925
(304) 876-3715
thomasshepherdinn.com
Expensive to very expensive

FOR MORE INFORMATION

Jefferson County Convention and Visitors Bureau
(304) 535-1813 or (866) 435-5698
discoveritallwv.com

Martinsburg/Berkeley County Convention and Visitors Bureau
(304) 264-8801 or (800) 498-2386
travelwv.com

Berkeley Springs Convention & Visitors Bureau
(800) 447-8797
berkeleysprings.com

Places to Eat in the Eastern Panhandle

BERKELEY SPRINGS

Fairfax Coffee House
23 Fairfax St.
(304) 500-2710
fairfaxcoffeehouse.com
Moderate

Lot 12 Public House
(weekends only)
117 Warren St.
(304) 258-6264
lot12.com
Moderate to expensive

The Naked Olive Lounge
87 N Washington St
(304) 500-2668
Moderate

HARPERS FERRY

The Anvil Restaurant
1270 Washington St.
(304) 535-2582
anvilrestaurant.com
Moderate to expensive

Canal House Cafe
1226 W. Washington St.
(304) 535–8551
canalhousecafe.com
Expensive

MARTINSBURG

Finn Thai Restaurant
748 Foxcroft Ave
(304) 262-2200
Finnthai.com
Moderate

La Trattoria
148 Lutz Ave.
(304) 262-6925
Inexpensive to moderate

SHEPHERDSTOWN

Bavarian Inn and Lodge
Route 480 (adjacent to
Potomac River Bridge)
(304) 876-2551
bavarianinnwv.com
Inexpensive to expensive

Potomac Highlands

West Virginia's grand Potomac Highlands region is the state's premier natural area, with a stunning landscape of rugged mountains, pristine rivers, secluded canyons, unusual ecosystems, and seemingly endless forests.

Sparsely populated and largely unspoiled, the Highlands stretch from north to south along the dramatic uplift of the Allegheny Mountains and Plateau, encompassing the counties of Hampshire, Mineral, Hardy, Grant, Tucker, Randolph, Pendleton, and Pocahontas. Despite the imposing terrain, the mountain roads here, if a little narrow, are well maintained and safe (assuming that you watch your speed) and perfect for relaxed and scenic touring.

Before venturing off the beaten path, be sure to check your fuel tank, because gas stations aren't nearly as plentiful here as they are in the Eastern Panhandle and other portions of the state. When in the backcountry, especially at dusk, keep a watchful eye out for deer and bear on the road.

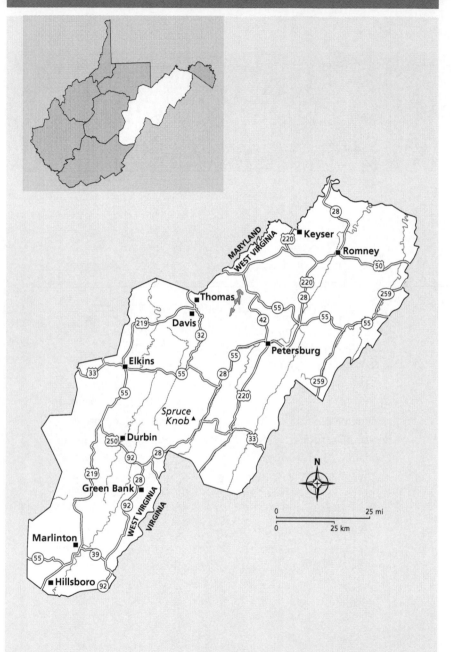

The Allegheny Foothills

The Allegheny Foothills region is located directly west of the Eastern Panhandle. It contains Hampshire, Mineral, Grant, and Hardy Counties, among the prettiest jurisdictions in West Virginia. Although decidedly mountainous, the landscape here is still gentler than other parts of the Potomac Highlands.

A good place to begin a tour of the Allegheny Foothills is in the Hampshire County community of Romney, the oldest incorporated city in West Virginia (1762). From Paw Paw, in the Eastern Panhandle, allow about a 40-minute drive down the winding Cacapon and North River Valleys on Route 29 and then 15 more minutes west on US 50. On your way you may want to make a small detour in North River Valley, home to one of West Virginia's most unusual natural phenomena—*Ice Mountain.* As the state marker proclaims, this peak acts as "nature's icebox." Ice remains into early summer up on Ice Mountain, in crevices that exhale cold air all year. Formed from rock debris tumbling from the mountain's 200-foot cliffs, known as Raven Rocks, the holes and crevices collect ice 50 feet deep in places. The ice usually remains into July, expelling cold air from about 60 pockets.

BEST ANNUAL EVENTS IN THE POTOMAC HIGHLANDS

Fasnacht
Helvetia; Saturday before
Ash Wednesday
(304) 924-5455
helvetiawv.com

Ramps & Rails Festival
Elkins; late April
(304) 636-2717 or 2780

Potomac Eagle Scenic Railroad
Romney; May through October
(304) 424-0736
potomaceagle.com

Wild Edibles Festival
Watoga State Park
Hillsboro; early May
(304) 799-4087
wvstateparks.com/parks/
watoga-state-park

Canaan Mountain Bike Festival
Davis; late June
(304) 894-2662
CanaanMTBFestival @ Facebook.com

Augusta Heritage Festival
Elkins; late July to early August
(304) 637-1209
augustaartsandculture.org

**Autumn Harvest and
Roadkill Cook-off**
Marlinton; last weekend in September
(800) 336-7009 or (304) 799-2509
pccocwv.com

Mountain State Forest Festival
Elkins; late September through
early October
(304) 636-1824
forestfestival.com or elkinswv.com

Because of this strange effect, Ice Mountain's rock talus is dotted with plants associated with subarctic regions or high elevations, such as twinflower, dwarf dogwood, and bristly rose. The preserve, protected by The Nature Conservancy, is open to visitors through guided tours Apr through Nov, by appointment. To minimize impact upon the fragile environment, groups are limited to 15. There is no charge. To schedule a tour, call volunteer guide Steve Bailes at (304) 496-7359.

At the base of Ice Mountain is the small village of North River Mills, which contains the remains of 3 mills. Each year the community holds North River Mills–Ice Mountain Day on a Saturday in May. The event features homemade ice cream, homegrown music, and tours of Ice Mountain.

Romney (historichampshire.org), the county seat, is said to have changed hands 56 times during the Civil War. On September 26, 1867, local citizens erected what they claim is the first Confederate memorial in the US. In the years immediately after the Civil War, federal law forbade monuments explicitly honoring the Confederate States of America, although memorials to the deceased soldiers were acceptable. But the Hampshire ladies purchased a white Italian marble statue bearing the inscription "The Daughters of Old Hampshire erect this tribute of affection to her heroic Sons, who fell in defense of Southern Rights." The last two words probably made the monument illegal, so "Southern Rights" was added through a small opening in the packaging before the statue was shipped from Baltimore. It still stands in Indian Mound Cemetery, which did indeed start out as a burial ground for the so-called Hopewell people in AD 500 to 1000. The fact that two West Virginia governors are buried here (John Jacob and John Cornwell, 4th and 15th governors, respectively) attests to the area's involvement in West Virginia's political life.

Romney is also home to the graceful Hampshire County Courthouse and the **Taggart Hall Civil War History Museum.** Taggart Hall's main claim to fame is an exhibit on the construction and use of the nearby Fort Mill Ridge Civil War battle trenches. The trenches were dug between 1861 and 1862 and lined with chestnut logs by the Confederate artillery, but they were also used in 1863 by Yankees. They are considered the best-preserved Civil War battle trenches and can be seen 3 miles southwest of Romney adjacent to the **Fort Mill Ridge Wildlife Management Area** (US 50/Route 28). Call (304) 463-4040 for information.

Romney's graceful Colonial and Federal-style architecture, with homes and commercial buildings dating from the mid-1700s, stands in stark contrast to the rugged surrounding terrain of mountains and rocky pastures. If you'd like to mix history with pleasure, go east on US 50, then south on Route 259 to visit **Capon Springs and Farm.** This National Historic Register resort of 3-story, porch-lined buildings tucked away in the mountains got its start as a healing spring spa with a state-built bathhouse. In fact, the name "capon" is derived from a Native American word meaning "healing," an indication that folks have been seeking wellness in these waters for many moons.

You can still stop in at the **Hygeia Bath House** for a soak, a massage, some reflexology work, and then a round of golf, if you like. Or you can book a room in one of the gracious old cottages and stay awhile. The fee of $95 to $160 per day includes 3 family-style "all-you-can-eat," home-grown meals, and use of the tennis courts, fishing pond, games, and inclusion in evening programs. In the tradition of an old family resort, these include dances, concerts, campfires, movies, and bingo. The resort also offers special wellness and golf instruction programs.

The springs were believed to carry such healing power that half an acre sold for $900 in gold in the late 18th century. After West Virginia seceded from Virginia, the new state had to compensate Virginia for the loss of the springs. Although no one overtly makes claims of healings today, guests do extol the relaxing effect of the resort and the springs. For a modest fee, you can reserve a tub or even a private pool, or dip outside in the refreshing spring-fed pools on the grounds.

Capon Springs is located off Route 55 southeast of Romney. Warning: This is an off-the-beaten-path resort and you travel 3 miles over a graded dirt road. It is open from the second week of May until November. The spa is open daily. Check for availability by calling the main office at (304) 874-3695 or the spa at (304) 874-3004; caponsprings.net.

After a night or two in the West Virginia woods, you're bound to feel like a frontiersman or frontierswoman. To get a feel for the real McCoy, head north on Route 28 to **Fort Ashby,** the only French and Indian War fort still standing in West Virginia. This 18th-century relic of frontier life gives visitors an all-too-real look at how vulnerable settlers were to American Indian attack. In fact, the fort is named for Colonel John Ashby, who barely escaped a raid here during the French and Indian War.

The large log structure was erected in 1755 on the order of George Washington as one of a chain of 69 forts built to defend the Virginia frontier. Made from hand-hewn logs, it includes a massive chimney that is 14 feet wide and 4 feet thick. Much of the original interior woodwork and wrought iron, including the hinges on the doors, is still intact. After the French and Indian War, Fort Ashby was turned into a schoolhouse. It was restored and opened to the public on July 4, 1939.

The fort, owned by the Daughters of the American Revolution, is located on Route 46, just inside the town limits of Fort Ashby. Visitors must call ahead to arrange tours. Admission is free, but donations are accepted and appreciated. Call (301) 697-9292 or visit www.fortashby.org for more information.

About 12 miles southwest of Fort Ashby on Route 46 sits the quiet riverside town of **Keyser.** Built along a hillside that slopes down to the Potomac River (which is very turbulent here), the Victorian-tinged town makes for a good stopping-off point for tired and hungry travelers. A great spot to unwind is the lovely **Candlewyck Inn,** 65 S. Mineral St., which is perched in the middle of Keyser a few blocks up the river. With its inviting Victorian facade and comfortable modern rooms, the Candlewyck offers a bit of luxury amid the rugged surroundings of the North Branch Valley. The dining room, which is open Wed through Sat from 12 to 8 p.m. and Sundays 12 to 6 p.m., tempts travelers with hearty charbroiled steaks and fresh Maryland seafood delicacies, such as Chesapeake Bay crab cakes and oysters. Call (304) 788-6594 for reservations. Colorful antiques and curio shops along Mineral and Main Streets are just a short stroll away.

The area west of Keyser, along the banks of the North Branch of the Potomac River, was once one of intense surface coal mining, or in the uglier vernacular, "strip-mining." Although mining has kept the region somewhat economically viable, it has laid a heavy hand on its ecosystem. During heavy rains and river flooding, the abandoned coal mines fill with water and then ultimately release a toxic acidic runoff into the fragile Potomac, killing fish in its wake.

During the early 1970s visionaries from the US Army Corps of Engineers decided to construct a special lake to control flooding and environmental degradation. The result is **Jennings Randolph Lake,** a 1,000-acre impoundment

BEST ATTRACTIONS IN THE POTOMAC HIGHLANDS

Lost River State Park
Mathias
(304) 897-5372
wvstateparks.com/park/
lost-river-state-park

Beverly Heritage Center
Beverly
(304) 637-7424
beverlyheritagecenter.org

Canaan Valley Resort State Park
Davis
(304) 866-4121 or (800) 622-4121
canaanresort.com

Elk River Touring Center
Slatyfork
(304) 572-3771
ertc.com

Green Bank Observatory
Green Bank
(304) 456-2150
greenbankobservatory.org

Snowshoe Mountain Resort
Snowshoe
(304) 572-1000 or (877) 441-4FUN
snowshoemtn.com

on the Potomac River bordering Maryland and West Virginia. It's located about 26 miles west of Keyser on Route 46. The lake acts as a receptacle for acid runoff and stabilizes the water downstream by periodically releasing pure water from the dam. The result is cleaner water in the lake and the river. The project has become so successful that brown trout, all but depleted during the 1970s, are now spawning in the tailwaters below the dam, and the river is gaining a reputation as a superior trout stream. A pair of bald eagles have been spotted nesting along its clear waters.

Aside from the environmental good stewardship, the lake has become a major recreational mecca for boaters, anglers, and campers. An interesting geological feature found near the lake's visitor center is *Waffle Rock,* a sandstone structure with a geometric pattern resembling that of a waffle, the result of nearly 300 million years of folding, fracturing, and weathering. The lake facilities are open year-round. For more information call (304) 355-2346 or (304) 788-5732.

South of the lake, on the eastern slope of Saddle Mountain in Mineral County, sits a small, unassuming cabin that was the birthplace of Nancy Hanks, mother of Abraham Lincoln. The spare wooden structure was built in the late 1700s from native hardwoods the Hanks family cleared to farm the hollow. The cabin and surrounding hardscrabble pastures and woodlands are now part of the *Nancy Hanks Memorial,* a state park facility open to the public year-round from dawn to dusk. It is yet another reminder that seeds of greatness are often sown in the most humble of places. There is no admission charge for the area, but getting there can be tricky. From US 50, your best bet is to head south on Maysville Road toward the small farming community of Antioch. About 3 miles beyond Antioch, look for a brown state historic site sign on the right-hand side of the road. Head west about 2 miles to the cabin.

If you're still feeling adventurous, continue on Maysville Road about 10 miles and turn west onto Greenland Gap Road. This short but spectacular 4-mile stretch of road is home to the *Greenland Gap Nature Preserve,* part of The Nature Conservancy's effort to save unspoiled wilderness. In season you'll see spectacular rhododendron blooms, and any time of the year you can catch glimpses of the mountain gap's huge limestone walls, pristine creeks and waterfalls, and perhaps a bobcat or a black bear and her cub. Hundreds of turkey vultures and ravens glide in the gap's warm updrafts in the summer. In the warm months park your car alongside the creek and go for a wade in these gin-clear waters. Chances are you can spend an hour up on the gap and not see or hear another soul pass by. Two trails, one on each side of the gap, provide challenging, rocky climbs for the physically fit. The gap was also the site of an April 1863 battle between a small band of federal troops and Confederate general William Jones's cavalry. The feds holed up in a church, but surrendered when Jones's men set it ablaze. The Mineral County preserve is open year-round from dawn to dusk, and there is no admission charge.

In neighboring Hardy County, down in the bucolic South Branch Valley, be sure to stop by **Old Fields Church,** one of the oldest intact houses of worship in the state. It's located just off US 220, about 3 miles north of Moorefield. The church was built in 1812 and was known at that time as the Fort Pleasant Meeting House. The small redbrick and tin-roof building was used by both Methodists and Presbyterians for more than a century. It also was reported to be the first schoolhouse in West Virginia. A few years ago the church was marked for the wrecker's ball before a local preservation group stepped in and

Bhavana Society—Farther Off the Beaten Path

The *Bhavana Society* in Hampshire County is the practice of simplicity squared. As interest in voluntary simplicity rises, retreats to the Bhavana Society monastery and retreat center are increasing. But a stint at the Theravada Buddhist community isn't for everyone. If you can't see yourself rising at 5 a.m., skipping supper, bunking in spartan cabins, abstaining from electronic communications, and sitting in silence, then you can pass by the US 50 exit for High View. But for some, it's a chance to unwind, rejuvenate, and become more mindful. This can translate into being at peace with what you have, they say. Chances are, what you have is a lot more than what you will have at your Bhavana retreat.

In a typical day, you wake at 5 a.m. for a silent meditation with the monks. After a round of Buddhist chants, you have a silent breakfast, do assigned chores, and clean up around your bunk in the same-sex dorm or *kuti* (single-person hut without electricity or plumbing). At lunch, over which the monastics chant, "not for fun, not for pleasure, not for fattening, but only for the nourishment of this body and keeping it healthy, helping with the holy life," you enjoy your last meal of the day—again, in silence. It seems antisocial, but the quiet allows you to reflect upon your food and the real reason you are eating.

The monastery and retreat center was established more than 25 years ago by Bhante Henepola Gunaratana, a Sri Lankan monk since 1947. A former chaplain at American University, He set out to create a place for monks and nuns to practice the South Asian strain of Buddhism and to offer retreats in this practice for anyone.

The Bhavana Society (304-856-3241; bhavanasociety.org) accepts guests through-out the year for personal or organized retreats at its 97 Meditation Trail campus. The stay includes lodging, 2 daily vegetarian meals, Buddhist teachings, and medita-tions in the Meditation Hall. There is no charge, but donations of $35–$75 a day are recommended.

The Wild Allegheny Trail

The *Allegheny Trail* winds the length of West Virginia along almost 330 miles of backbone ridges, hollows, and high bogs, through some of the Mountain State's wildest, prettiest territory. It purposely avoids civilization, so you can walk for hours without seeing a road. It doesn't lend itself to convenient shuttle points for the day hiker.

Greedy for a hearty helping of natural beauty one September Saturday, my husband and I embarked on a 15-mile segment of the Allegheny—a lot of footwork for 3-mile-a-day walkers. As soon as we entered the eastern Pocahontas County forest, we stumbled upon signs of nature—the skeleton of a 5-foot snake coiled in our path, a blueberry patch raked by giant paws, and the steaming waste of a large animal whose scat indicated it had eaten a mammal for breakfast. "Is this a warning?" I asked.

We saw dozens of specimens of bear scat over the next 11 hours, but no bear. Charleston resident Mike Maxwell, our hiking companion in the last hours of the day, had recently encountered a large cub falling out of a tree. "It squalled when it fell," he said. "That can put the goose bumps on you. Then it looked at me and ran the other way."

We were glad he was with us. Although we saw abundant signs of wildlife, the woods seemed unnaturally quiet. We had the sensation of being like the strangers who bumbled into a country store and brought all conversation to a halt. Everything ceased breathing while the woodland waited for us to pass.

As the forest road dwindled to a single-track path, then to a random passage marked only by occasional gold blazes on the oaks and hickories, we ascended Thorny Creek Mountain into Seneca State Park. The Allegheny Trail passes through four state parks as well as four state forests and the Monongahela and Jefferson National Forests. It stretches uninterrupted from the Mason-Dixon Line at Bruceton Mills to just south of exit 1 off I-64 (Jerry's Run). There the trail disappears like an underground stream, to resurface near Laurel Branch in Monroe County and join the Appalachian Trail atop Peters Mountain. The right-of-way for the 20-mile missing link is still being negotiated.

Hiking the entire length of the Allegheny takes a month. Although we spent only 11 hours on the trail, we weren't spared the plodding weariness of through-hikers. As we ascended to what had to be the summits of Little, Thomas, and Thorny Creek Mountains, we watched the crests flatten out to reveal new heights above us. After six or seven hours on the trail, we stopped thinking, stopped observing, and just stepped, stepped, stepped.

We walked hard all morning, our pulses thudding in our throats, and when we sat down for lunch, we realized we'd gone only 4.3 miles. Allegheny Trail miles feel twice as long as road miles.

When we reached the last mountain, the scrubby, wind-beaten vegetation seemed a mirror for our stoicism. Like the rest of the forest, which was preparing to go dormant until spring, we were ready to lie still for a long, long time.

began renovations. It's now owned by the Duffey Memorial United Methodist Church. Occasional services and social gatherings are still held here. Call (304) 538-6560 for more information.

Hardy County is a mecca for high-quality crafts. Wardensville features regional work in a retrofitted feed store known as **Lost River Trading Post**. **Wardensville Garden Market** is also a great place to stop for farm-fresh, organic produce and award-winning bakery goodies. The thriving nonprofit was created to build skills, confidence, and market savvy in the Appalachian youth who grow the vegetables and hone their culinary skills in the production kitchen.

Visiting this area is also a feast for the eyes. The scenic panorama that unfolds as you cross the Alleghenies into West Virginia's widest valley is worth a dozen Instagrams. West Virginia's only natural lake is hidden here, at the U.S. Forest Service's **Trout Pond Recreation Area**. The "lake" is truly a pond most of the year, but it's manmade sister lake, Rockcliff is a summer hangout for swimmers, boaters, and anglers.

When it comes to water quality, scenery, and isolation, few parts of the country can claim as many ideal canoeing waters as the Mountain State. **Eagle's Nest Outfitters** is ideally situated near more than 80 miles of virtually untouched rivers. Here, in the shadows of some of the highest peaks in northern West Virginia, anglers, campers, and canoeists from all over the US come for clinics, rentals, and outings. Hundreds of trophy-size small- and largemouth bass, catfish, and trout are landed each year on the productive South Branch. For those in search of exciting whitewater, rafting through the isolated Smoke Hole Canyon provides thrills plus beauty. The Lower Smoke Hole Canyon trip begins with breathtaking views of Cave Mountain and Eagle Rock, giant granite and limestone outcroppings that tower more than 100 feet above the river. Canoeing and fishing trip reservations must be made by phone or by mail three weeks in advance for holidays and weekends. For more details call (304) 257-2393.

Those who want milder waters, majestic views, and big fish should plan a trip through the "Trough." **The Trough** is a 6-mile canyon through which the South Branch of the Potomac surges, leaving scant room on one side for the tracks of the Potomac Eagle Scenic Railroad. A stunning 1,000-foot cliff runs along one side and Mill Creek Ridge rises along the other. The majestic setting is made even more dramatic by the dozen or so American bald eagles that inhabit the area and are regularly sighted from the river.

This is an area of trophy bass and catfish that make your arms ache. But the Trough isn't easy to reach. In fact, it's virtually inaccessible except by canoe, kayak, or train. Passengers board the *Potomac Eagle* at Wappocomo

potomac
highlands
trivia

Roughly half the landmass of the
Potomac Highlands is contained in
the Monongahela National Forest.

Station in Romney. Paddlers generally start at Trough General Store, where they pick up their rentals and shuttles to the Trough's opening near McNeill in the South Branch Wildlife Management Area. The Trough's end is at the Harmison's Public Access Site behind Trough General Store. To set up a rental or shuttle, contact Trough Store at (304) 822-7601 or wvcanoerentals.com.

To the east in Hardy County, the Lost River begins as a stream near the villages of Lost City and Lost River. It passes through Lost River State Park, where Robert E. Lee's dad had a springs retreat, then northeast of the village of Baker the Lost River disappears into an underground at an area called "the Sinks" along Route 259. The river emerges again on the other side of a mountain near Wardensville as the Cacapon River. But whatever the name, it is geologically the same river.

Seneca Rocks

Named after the imposing sandstone spires that tower high above the South Branch Valley, the Seneca Rocks region encompasses Pendleton and parts of Grant and Randolph Counties. The deep gorges, jutting rock formations, wild rivers, and arching mountains (including the highest point in the state—4,861-foot Spruce Knob) make for perhaps the most spectacular natural scenery in all West Virginia.

Born of Mother Earth's violent upheaval 185 million years ago, **Smoke Hole Gorge,** running mostly parallel with US 220 in Grant and Pendleton Counties, is one of the most remote and beautiful areas in the US. Most people don't know that, because it's nearly impossible to get to. But it can be done.

Smoke Hole is where the South Branch of the Potomac River squeezes between North Fork Mountain and Cave Mountain, creating spectacular waterfalls, sluices, and whitewater conditions. These raging waters have formed caves, carved canyons, and shaped the wild landscape in an extraordinary fashion. An ever-present fog through the "hole" makes visitors feel like they're in a bygone era. It's easy to believe the old myths here. Earliest settlers said the "smoke" came from a moonshiner's still. Some claimed it came from American Indian fires. The Nature Conservancy considers Smoke Hole Canyon to be one of the most biologically rich spots in the East.

Smoke Hole is managed by the **Monongahela National Forest** as part of the Spruce Knob–Seneca Rocks National Recreation Area. It's a hunting, fishing, hiking, canoeing, and camping paradise. The easiest access into the gorge is via Route 2, near Upper Tract, a tiny town 18 miles southwest of Petersburg along US 220. Route 2 parallels the river into the canyon for about 8 miles. On the way in you might see a few fisherpeople and perhaps a canoeist or two.

After 8 miles the paved road ends at a junction featuring an old country store and a log church. One fork of the road continues along the river; the other rises to the north of the shoulder of North Fork Mountain and down to Route 28. If you take the "high road," notice the small farms nestled in the hollows and the abandoned log cabins decorating the clearings. Traffic is almost nonexistent, so you might want to stop along the photogenic route for an impromptu picnic.

potomac highlands trivia

The Mountain State Forest Festival, held each October in Elkins, is West Virginia's oldest and one of its largest festivals.

If you decide to spend the night, there are some outstanding places to sleep under the stars. The largest is the **Big Bend Campground,** with 46 sites managed by the US Forest Service. It's open April 1 through October 15. As the name implies, the campground is situated along a huge bend of the South Branch of the Potomac River.

Primitive camping sites are scattered along Smoke Hole Road (Routes 28/11) on North Fork Mountain and throughout the backcountry except at trailheads. For camping and other recreation information within the gorge, call the Forest Service at (304) 257-4488.

Just to the west of the Smoke Hole Gorge, off Route 28, about 10 miles south of Petersburg, lies another fascinating natural area, **Dolly Sods.** This 17,371-acre National Wilderness and Scenic Area is characterized by rugged boulder-strewn plains, windswept spruce trees, cool mountain air, and 50-mile vistas.

Dolly Sods was once a forest of giant red spruces and hemlocks, most claiming diameters in excess of 4 feet. These incredible trees were logged in the 1800s, and the hot fires that burned during the logging destroyed the underlying fertile humus layer. About the same time local farmers burned the plains to create grazing land, or sods. One such group of pioneers that cleared the area was the Dahle family. Over the years Dahle somehow became Dolly, as in the present Dolly Sods.

The Sods' plant life and climate are what make it so unusual. It's actually more akin to the boreal forest of northern Canada than it is to any other part of the US. In the summer azaleas, mountain laurels, rhododendrons, and blueberries thrive despite the infertile soil. Cranberries and insect-eating sundew plants are adjacent to more arid, boulder-strewn, open areas. Northern hardwoods are found in the coves and drainages, and red pines grow in several areas.

Save a little energy and appetite for some **berry picking,** a favorite pastime among visitors and native bears. Blueberries, huckleberries, teaberries, and cranberries blanket the area. Ramps (a very strong wild leek) can be found in moist wooded areas. Take your fare to the shady Dolly Sods picnic area to eat, and enjoy the natural surroundings. The picnic area is on FR 19 just south of the scenic area. Picnic tables, grills, and portable toilets are provided.

Dolly Sods has several hiking trails, all marked only by ax blazes or rock cairns (mounds). Distances are not indicated. When you're ready to pull off your hiking boots, you can bed down overnight in the area's only campground, Red Creek. It has 12 campsites (3 walk-in and 9 suitable for trailers). Portable toilets and a water well are provided.

A visit to Dolly Sods, rated one of the top 10 backpacking trails in the nation by Trails.com, is well worth your time, but you should observe a few cautions. Because it sits directly atop the Allegheny Plateau, at elevations ranging from 2,600 to 4,000 feet, weather can change suddenly. Storms can be severe and life-threatening, and dense fog can confuse even the most experienced outdoorsperson. The area is noted for its fierce westerly winds (note the one-sided red spruce trees), snow in the fall, winter, and spring, and low temperatures during any month of the year. Also be watchful of venomous snakes. And if that's not enough, be on the lookout for old mortar shells.

potomac highlands trivia

Pendleton County claims more than 250 noncommercial caves, most of which are located on private land.

Yes, mortar shells. The area was used for military exercises during World War II, and some live shells remain. If you come to a shell, don't touch it! For more information about Dolly Sods, call the US Forest Service at (304) 636-1800, (304) 257-4488, or (304) 567-2827.

Straight down the highway (literally) from Dolly Sods are the fabled **Seneca Rocks.** Named for one of the American Indian tribes that passed through the area, these sandstone rock formations rise more than 900 feet above the North Fork Valley and Route 28 and US 33. This is one of the most popular rock-climbing areas in the East, and on any given weekend—or weekday, for that matter—you'll see cars with license plates from as far away as Vermont, Florida, and Illinois.

If you're brave (or crazy) enough to scale these narrow spires, look for the words d.b., september 16, 1908, carved into the top of the south peak. No one is quite sure who D.B. was, although one theory claims he may have been D. Bittenger, a civil engineer who surveyed the area for the Forest Service. Whoever he or she was, D.B. beat Paul Brandt, Don Hubbard, and Sam Moore to the top, a trio credited with being the first recorded climbers to master the rocks and reach the summit in 1938.

Since that time thousands of thrill seekers have climbed Seneca Rocks, including members of the US Army's Tenth Mountain Division, who trained here during World War II. For those who yearn to see the view from the top but don't want to risk life and limb in the process, there is another way. A steep and relatively safe 1.3-mile, self-guided interpretive trail ascends the north edge of the rocks to a viewing platform.

If you'd rather keep your feet firmly planted on the ground, there's still plenty to do in the area, starting with a visit to the Seneca Rocks Discovery Center. Inside you'll find exhibits and a video explaining the history and geology of the area. There's also a small indoor rock-climbing wall. In the adjacent picnic area, you can watch the brave climbers cling precariously to the rocks, or you can stroll down to the South Branch for a bit of catch-and-release trout fishing. The **Sites Homestead** is located at the picnic area, within walking distance of the Discovery Center. The first area home built by a European-American settler, the Jacob Sites house was originally constructed as a single-pin log home in 1839. Tours of the home are available on summer Saturdays. Seneca Rocks Discovery Center is open Wed through Sun, Apr through Oct. For more information, call the visitor center at (304) 567-2827 or visit www.fs.usda.gov/recarea/mnf/recarea.

The wild beauty of Seneca Rocks serves as a spectacular backdrop for **Harper's Old Country Store** (harpersoldcountrystore.com), a thriving early 20th-century retailer that shows no signs of slowing down. It's one of the oldest continuously operated businesses in the state, still run by members of the Harper family. The wood-frame store was built in 1902 and originally operated under the name of D. C. Harper and Co. Its interior today is much the same as it was then. Inside you'll find groceries, hardware, clothing, snacks, gifts, and hunting and fishing equipment. While you're stocking up, take a look at the store's original board floor, the antique ceiling, and the original shelving and counters. You can't miss the mounted West Virginia black bear that stands guard over the store's ground floor.

If you're in the mood to eat, step up to the ***Front Porch Restaurant***, located on the second floor of Harper's. It's nothing fancy, just simple, tasty, and well-prepared food in a casual atmosphere. The view isn't bad either. Try a slice of fresh dough pizza, or sample one of the wheat pita pocket sandwiches. They're good enough to lure you down from the rocks.

Harper's Old Country Store is located at the intersection of US 33 and Route 55 in Seneca Rocks. Store hours are 7 a.m. to 8:30 p.m. weekdays and Sat, and 8 a.m. to 8 p.m. Sun. The restaurant is open daily April 15 through October 15 from 11 a.m. to 9 p.m. Call (304) 567-2555 for more information.

Teens getting car claustrophobia? Or maybe you're ready to climb the walls. Seneca Rocks Mountain Guides offer guide service for rock-climbing expeditions as well as two-day climbing fundamentals classes from their base at the junction in Seneca Rocks. Every climber is supervised by a certified instructor. Call (800) 451-5108 or (304) 567-2115 or visit senecarocks mountain guides on Facebook.com.

Now that you're loaded with provisions from Harper's, it's time to explore the state's highest mountain, ***Spruce Knob,*** and take in what's probably the finest vista in West Virginia. From Seneca Rocks, drive 10 miles south on US 33/28 before taking a right on CR 33/4 (look for the sign to Spruce Knob National Recreation Area). After a mile or so, the paved mountain road will give way to gravel for the next 8 miles until you reach the summit of the 4,861-foot mountain. Budget a half hour to get up the mountain (if you make it quicker than that, you're probably driving too fast), and keep your eyes posted for wildlife that will frequently dart onto the road. This isn't a place where you want to apply the brakes quickly; skidding on gravel on a narrow mountain road without guardrails isn't exactly conducive to relaxation.

potomac highlands trivia

Spruce Knob, the tallest mountain in West Virginia (over 4,800 feet), marks the geographic center of the Potomac Highlands region.

Once you reach the summit of this gorgeous mountain, you'll be glad you made the trip. Near the top of the mountain, the gravel returns to blacktop and winds around to a parking lot. An easy 0.5-mile foot trail takes you along the summit ridge, which is sprinkled with massive limestone and granite boulders; windblown, one-sided red spruce trees; and dense pockets of blueberry, huckleberry, and mountain ash. The trail ends at a two-story observation deck that affords views of more than 75 miles in any direction, including an eastern vista extending all the way to Virginia's Shenandoah Valley.

Chances are, a stiff wind will be blowing from the west; it always is. Fog and storms arise quickly, even in summer, and the weather can turn from sunny to icy in minutes. So strong and so constant is the wind that the western branches of exposed red spruce never develop, and the one-armed trees point eastward as reliably as a compass points north.

Like the Dolly Sods Wilderness Area, the Spruce Knob region was once farmed by hearty Scots-Irish and German settlers, and traces of the pastures they forged by clearing timber can still be seen more than 100 years later. If you plan to camp out, the US Forest Service maintains the 43-site Spruce Knob Campground about 3 miles down from the summit, next to Spruce Knob Lake, a 25-acre pond that provides some good trout fishing. A 1-mile boardwalk circles the lake. Backcountry camping also is allowed throughout Spruce Knob, and the same types of precautions you would take on Dolly Sods should be applied here. The recreation area is open year-round, except during snowy and icy periods, when the roads can be life-threatening. For more information stop by the Seneca Rocks Visitor Center, or call (304) 567-2827.

The High Valley

The High Valley region is the area in and around Tucker County's Canaan Valley, pronounced "keh-NANE" by locals. It's the highest valley in the East and one of the most peculiar, geologically and geographically speaking, in the US.

Canaan Valley is a place of quiet beauty where the deer will eat out of your hand—though allowing them to do so is illegal, unhealthy for the deer, and forbidden under any circumstances. The oranges, reds, and yellows of Octobers here are incomparable, and the lush springs, mild summers, and deep winter snows make the mountain vistas breathtaking. The 3,200-foot-high, 14-mile-long valley is located in Tucker County, near the Maryland border, and is bisected by Route 32.

Portions of Canaan have been designated a National Wildlife Refuge because of the unusual Canadian forest plant life and the 8,400 acres of fragile upcountry wetlands—the largest wetland area in the central and southern Appalachians. Here more than 580 plant and 290 animal species thrive. For more information on the refuge, call (304) 866-3858 or visit fws.gov/canaanvalley.

The high Allegheny Mountains that rim the valley seem to act as magnets for snow. In fact, Canaan receives 150 to 200 inches of the white stuff each year. Late-spring snows aren't uncommon. As you might guess, the valley has become one of the best ski areas in the Mid-Atlantic, boasting two downhill ski resorts, ***Canaan Valley Resort State Park*** (800-622-4121) and ***Timberline Mountain*** (304-403-2074), and the ***White Grass*** cross-country ski resort

To Canaan's Land, I'm On My Way

You can get a feeling for eternity sitting on the slope behind Canaan Valley Resort's lodge watching the light fade over miles of high marsh and forest. Life appears to go on forever in some form in nature's endless cycle. Could any small, petty thinking exist against sweeping perspectives like this?

You hear a distant "Who, who for you?" A barred owl? A little later, a woodcock circles with a high "chee." A doe saunters within feet, pausing to gracefully rub the top of her head with her back hoof.

Canaan Valley is a place of quiet loveliness where summers are mild and the winter snows deep (an average of 175 inches annually). Frosts have been recorded every month of the year, and cool night air slides down the mountains, leaving a dreamy fog over the valley most mornings between May and November.

Underneath its apparent tranquility, Canaan Valley is still in recovery mode. In the earlier part of the 20th century, this country was logged out of its spruce and hemlock forests. Even earlier, when Lord Fairfax's surveyors reached Canaan in 1746, there was hardly room to walk for the growth sprouting from the fertile, 8-foot duff layer of decomposing vegetation. Surveyor Thomas Lewis wrote, "Ye laurels and spruce grow so thick one cannot have the least prospect of seeing light except they look upwards."

But a century and a half later, fires kindled by logging detritus swept over the land, burning the deep, peaty soil that had taken thousands of years to develop. Through some rash will for survival, the vegetation we see today has managed to migrate back into this cool, humid climate. Many of these plants—including red spruce, balsam fir, high-bush cranberry, swamp saxifrage, and Jacob's ladder—are considered boreal species, two vegetation zones below tundra. They persist in portions of Canaan Valley now designated a National Natural Landmark.

For more information about lodging and nature programs at Canaan Valley Resort State Park, call (304) 866-4121.

(304-866-4114). With a drop of 1,000 vertical feet, these resorts give you some of the longest ski runs in the East—up to 2 miles. The terrain and weather are conducive to Nordic skiing, and lessons are offered on the forest trails of Canaan and White Grass.

When the weather warms up, hiking, golfing, mountain biking, and fishing take center stage. Hikers take to the Blackwater/Canaan Trail, an 8-mile mountain path connecting Blackwater Falls State Park to Canaan Valley State Park. In early March, trout fishing revs up on the tea-colored Blackwater River and stays hot through the summer months. For those who'd rather swing a club than a fly rod, the 18-hole championship golf course at Canaan Valley State Park (800-622-4121) offers a great summertime escape. Canaan recently added sporting clays to its mix of paintball, Eurobungy, hiking, and mountain biking.

At the northern edge of Canaan Valley sits the eclectic little town of Davis. Looking a bit like Juneau in the legislative off-season, Davis is the highest incorporated town (elevation 3,200 feet) east of the Mississippi. Here you'll find a number of unusual attractions, such as 4 very different outdoor stores, including a secondhand gear exchange. Another popular stop is *West Virginia Highlands Artisans Group* (wvhighlands.net), a collection of local craftspeople producing contemporary and traditional crafts. Browse here and you're likely to meet the maker of the watercolor, necklace, or lamp you might be examining.

Leaf Peepers' Special

When the autumn leaf watch is just beginning in the lower elevations, Pocahontas County's 4,800-foot ridgetops blaze orange, gold, and crimson. The Greenbrier, Elk River, and Deer Creek valleys, more than 2,000 feet below, reach their peak display of red maple, yellow beech, and rusty oaks two to three weeks later in mid-October. Starting just after summer officially ends, the Potomac Highlands color show slides a little farther down the mountains each day.

And when the mountaintops are bare, it's easier to spot the last hawks and eagles on their southern migration.

One great way to enjoy the colorful vistas—especially if you have children in tow—is from the open passenger cars of Cass Scenic Railroad. The restored village of Cass remains relatively unchanged since it began life as a company town for the West Virginia Pulp & Paper Company around 1900. For 58 years, residents awoke to the mill whistle and lived to the rhythm of the comings and goings of the rowdy wood hicks from their logging camps up on Cheat Mountain.

Luckily for leaf peepers, the mixture of spruce and hardwoods has grown back; now the restored Shay locomotive pulls retrofitted logging cars full of passengers up the 11 percent grade to Whittaker Station and Bald Knob. With thick black smoke gushing from the stack, huff-huffing and clanking like a kitchen band, the Shay transports you back in time as it pulls you up the mountain.

Even at full speed, the steam locomotive reaches only about 4 miles per hour uphill and 6 miles per hour down, so there's plenty of time to admire the scenery and look for deer, turkey, and bear along the tracks.

The view from Whittaker (1.5-hour round trip) is lovely; above the spruce forest from Bald Knob (5-hour round trip), it's stunning. But take a jacket for the chilling wind whipping around the observation tower at 4,842 feet.

The Division of Forestry will provide weekly leaf-color reports late September through the end of October on its Facebook page, facebook.com/wvforestry, or by telephone, (800) 982-3386.

Across the street from the gallery is **Bright Morning Inn,** a bed-and-breakfast that was once a boardinghouse for itinerant lumberjacks. Proprietors Robert and Linda Darfus took over the restored wood-frame building in July 1999. The B&B includes 7 bedrooms and 1 suite, all with private baths. Right next door you can find even roomier accommodations at **Doc's Guest House,** a 3-bedroom Victorian home. Breakfast is provided to all guests. Reservations are suggested for lunch and dinner, which typically feature local fish, meats, and produce prepared in a "country gourmet" fashion. The inn is open year-round. Rates range from $110 to $169 for double occupancy. Call (304) 259-5119 or visit brightmorninginn.com.

The Western Slope

The Western Slope of the Allegheny Mountains shows its face in Randolph County, where the hills tend to come down on top of one another, adding to the mythical spirit of the place. The remoteness of the land seems only to intensify the friendliness of the people who live here.

From Davis, follow US 219 south through the Monongahela National Forest to Elkins, the Randolph County seat. This is the home of the **Augusta Heritage Center** (augustaartsandculture.org), a haven for traditional Appalachian music, crafts, dancing, and folklore.

The world-renowned musical performance and craft-learning center was founded in 1973 on the secluded, tree-lined campus of Davis and Elkins College. Its guiding mission is to keep alive the spirit of West Virginia's mountain culture by sharing it with natives and visitors alike. It's been a huge success. Each July and August hundreds of students of all ages from across North America descend on Elkins to take part in Augusta's intimate workshops taught by master artists and musicians. Courses range from fiddle and banjo instruction to log-house building, Celtic stone carving, and African-American storytelling.

Late July also ushers in the **Augusta Festival** (augustaartsandculture.org) in Elkins City Park, a weekend celebration of free concerts, juried craft fairs, children's art and music exhibitions, dancing, food, and storytelling. The Fiddler's Reunion and Old-Time Week in October is a homecoming of sorts for mountain musicians from throughout the US and from as far away as Nova Scotia, Ireland, and Scotland. Most Wednesday evenings you can enjoy old-time jam sessions from 7 to 10 p.m. at Davis and Elkins College's Hermanson Center, from October to May, and at Elkins City Park June to September. For more information on courses and programs provided by the Augusta Heritage Center, call (304) 637-1209.

West Virginia battles played an important and largely ignored role in the Civil War. On July 11, 1861, in one of the first major engagements of the war, Union regiments under General George McClellan attacked and defeated Confederate troops defending a strategic mountain pass on the Staunton-Parkersburg Turnpike. This Union victory gave federal forces control over much of what is now West Virginia, eventually leading to its creation as a new state. Today you can find bullet marks and soldiers' names scratched in rocks atop Rich Mountain. But the best place to start a Mountain State Civil War tour is at the **Beverly Heritage Center,** a museum and visitor center 6 miles south of Elkins. The facility combines 4 historic buildings to tell the stories of the Battle of Rich Mountain, the Civil War in West Virginia, and daily life in 19th-century Beverly. Summer hours are 10 a.m. to 6 p.m. Thurs through Sat, and 11 a.m. to 5 p.m. Sun through Wed. The rest of the year, hours are 11 a.m. to 5 p.m. Thurs through Mon. More information is available at beverlyheritagecenter .org or by calling (304) 637-7424.

If your travels haven't yet taken you to Europe, you can at least get a glimpse of what one European country must be like with a visit to the Randolph County community of **Helvetia.** This hidden village, tucked into the folds of the Alleghenies about an hour south of Elkins off US 250, was settled by feisty German and Swiss immigrants in 1869 and today has all the flavor of a true Alpine community. It was the first town district in the state to be placed on the National Register of Historic Places.

Helvetia claims about 60 year-round inhabitants, considerably fewer than the 1,200 or so who populated the village and surrounding hills and hollows around the turn of the 20th century during the area's logging boom. As you stroll the tidy streets, don't be surprised to hear a few residents chatting in their ancestors' High German tongue.

It is the native cuisine, however, that keeps many outsiders returning to Helvetia on a regular basis. Find the sign that says *Grüß Gott, tritt ein, Bring Glück herein* ("Praise God, step in, bring luck within"), and you've found *The* **Hütte Restaurant**, known for its locally grown food prepared in Swiss style. It's the hub of activity in Helvetia. Most of the staff are descendants of Helvetia's original settlers. Menu items include *pfeffernüsse,* a ginger cookie; Stout Country Soup, a thick vegetable beef soup; and a locally made cheese. All of this and more is served at *Bernerplatte,* the Swiss version of Sunday brunch. Other menu items include sauerbraten, bratwurst, homemade sausage, homemade breads, pineapple, and pickled beets. The Hütte is open daily from noon to 7 p.m. Call (304) 924-6435.

If you arrive on a weekday and want to stay over for the brunch, ask about a room at **The Beekeeper Inn** (304-924-6435), a bed-and-breakfast. It's a cozy,

3-room affair complete with private baths, a common room overstuffed with books, and a large deck shaded by huge pine trees. Rooms are also available over the country store.

After a sumptuous repast or a long afternoon nap, take a walk around this fairy-tale village. Don't miss the flag-bedecked bridge leading to the pottery shop; the Cheese Haus, formerly a working cheese shop; the circa 1880 church; and the town museum housed in an original settler's cabin—10 historic buildings in all. For tours of the museum, call (304) 924-6435. The latter is filled with interesting artifacts, including the original Swiss flag the settlers brought with them from the old country.

Helvetia is no theme park. It's an active community with deep pride in its roots. As such, it celebrates its heritage with several endearing customs and festivals. Hundreds come from far and wide to attend such events as Swiss Independence Day in August, the Helvetia Fair in September, and Fasnacht, a Mardi Gras–like fete in February that celebrates the coming of spring. Fasnacht participants hang Old Man Winter in effigy and don costumes to "scare away" winter. If visitors arrive without proper costumes, they're encouraged to rummage through local attics to find something fitting to wear. The celebration is usually held the Saturday before Ash Wednesday and is kicked off with a community-wide Swiss feast and an Appalachian music show. Helvetia also hosts a ramps (the pungent wild leeks so prized in the mountains) dinner in April, a Swiss fair in September, and Helvetia Day in mid-October.

Nearby, deep in the heart of the hardwood forest, along a fork of the Buckhannon River, lies the small town of **Pickens.** Founded in the 1890s, Pickens doesn't have a lot going on these days. The town's post office has to be one of the smallest in the nation, only slightly larger than outdoor storage sheds commonly seen in the yards of suburban homes. The town has the distinction of being the wettest place in West Virginia. It receives more annual precipitation than most any place in the eastern US—an annual 66 inches—much of it in snowfall. The snows received by Pickens are comparable to the lake-effect snows experienced by Buffalo, New York. The high mountains, cool weather, and wet conditions have conspired to produce an abundance of sugar maple trees in the area—such as one would expect to find only in Vermont.

With such a wealth of maple trees, the production of maple syrup is a booming concern—and the reason for Pickens's annual **Maple Syrup Festival**. Each year on the third full weekend in March, people come down from the hills and hollows to socialize, feast on pancakes and maple syrup, listen to good mountain music, and sell a few crafts made during the long, cold mountain winter.

The festival features a pancake feed on Saturday and Sunday, a 5K run, a muzzle-loading competition, and woodchopping and carving demonstrations. Free musical entertainment is found at the town pavilion and in the Opera House. Visit the sugarhouse and watch the syrup-making process firsthand. Artisans are at work—the most interesting of which may be the chain-saw sculptor, who in a short period of time makes a piece of art from a chunk of wood using only his chain saw.

Tradition says that American Indians discovered the sweetness of the sugar maple when a hatchet was thrown into a maple trunk. A taste of the oozing sap was found to be sweet. Figuring a way to concentrate that sweetness, they would gather the sap, place it in a trough, and drop heated rocks into it to cause evaporation. There is about a 50-to-1 ratio in the process: 50 gallons of sap, when processed, will produce 1 gallon of syrup, and evaporation is still at the heart of syrup production today.

Early settlers in the region used maple trees as their primary source of sugar, as imported white sugar was very expensive. They would boil the syrup down to dry brown chunks. Only in the mid-1800s, when white sugar produced in the Caribbean brought down the price, was maple sugar displaced.

The sap is gathered over a six- to eight-week period from February to mid-March and must be processed right away. A succession of freezing nights and temperatures reaching the mid-30s to mid-40s in the day starts the sap coming up into the tree. Gathering involves drilling a hole about 2.5 inches into the tree trunk and driving a tap, which is nothing more than a spout, into the hole. Either a bucket is dangled from the tap for sap collection or plastic tubing is attached. The tubing connects many trees and drains into large collection tanks. Each tree may have up to three or four taps. For more information call the Pickens Improvement and Historical Society at (304) 924-5096 or visit pickenswv.com.

Mountain Wilderness

The Mountain Wilderness region consists of Pocahontas County and parts of Randolph County. As its name implies, this is one of the most mountainous parts of West Virginia, and it contains the largest swath of the Potomac Highlands.

Any place that's called a "most beautiful spot" by someone as noteworthy as American inventor Thomas Edison must be special. The New Jersey–born inventor was referring to West Virginia's *Cheat Mountain Club,* an 1899 lodge along the banks of the Shavers Fork River and high atop the namesake mountain that contains nine of the state's 10 tallest peaks. Edison, Henry Ford, and Harvey Firestone journeyed to this mountain in a Model T to enjoy the region's hunting and rustic charm. The club is now open only to large groups that rent the entire facility, but people still make pilgrimages from urban areas to see mountainsides tricked out in ice crystals or fiery foliage and to hunt, ski, snowshoe, or hike.

The shriek of a train whistle in the village of Durbin below Cheat Mountain is no fantasy. Durbin maintains its tradition as a key railroad stop, but now ***Durbin & Greenbrier Valley Railroad*** excursion trains carry passengers into pristine mountain valleys where no wood saws whine.

The Cheat Mountain Salamander, the Tygart Flyer, the Mountain Explorer dinner train, and the Durbin Rocket haul passengers up mountains and through hidden valleys accessible only by foot or by rail. The Salamander, Flyer, and Explorer operate out of Elkins, while the Durbin Rocket departs from the center of its namesake town. Trips run from May 15 through Halloween and range from a 2-hour jaunt to an 8-hour, 88-mile expedition. If the children get restless, the friendly engineer may invite them to ride up front with him and take turns helping to operate the controls. Or they can look out for bears; black bear sightings are a regular feature on several runs.

If you've ever wanted to be a hobo or experience wilderness miles from the nearest railroad, rail camping may be in your future. You can board the train with your tent only and disembark at one of several remote campsites near the tracks, or you may rent the railway's ***Castaway Caboose*** for an overnight at the end of the line. Campers are dropped off in the afternoon and don't hear another sound of civilization until the approaching train whistles almost 24 hours later. Caboose accommodations include refrigerator, linens, modern shower, and bathroom, for $330 the first night, $260 the second night. For train rides and overnights, call (877) MTN-RAIL or visit mountainrailwv.com.

A few miles east of Durbin at the junction of US 250 and Route 28, look for the historic marker for ***Travelers' Repose.*** The private home standing here was once a stagecoach-stop inn favored by Confederate general Stonewall Jackson for its fresh venison and trout. The original building survived being in the line of fire during the Civil War's Battle of Greenbrier River in October 1861, only to burn down after the war. The front of the house is original to the 1866 rebuilding. Confederate trenches are located about 3 miles up the small side road, CR 3, behind the house.

Tourists with an interest in the scientific must find time to visit an impressive and somewhat eerie facility in eastern Pocahontas County, about 30 minutes south of Durbin in the town of Green Bank. Established in 1956, the ***Green Bank Observatory*** was built to provide state-of-the-art radio astronomy communications equipment for exploring the universe. The sprawling campus looks like something from the set of the 1997 film *Contact.*

In radio astronomy, celestial objects are studied by examining their emission of radio-magnetic radiation. It is a fairly recent science, with its earliest roots dating only from the 1930s. It was then that a researcher for Bell Laboratories, Karl G. Jansky, discovered extraterrestrial radio waves coming from a source near the center of the Milky Way galaxy.

Grote Reber, an astronomer and radio engineer, is largely responsible for developing radio astronomy. Prompted by Jansky's discovery, Reber built the world's first radio telescope in 1937. He did it right in his backyard in Wheaton, Illinois. Thirty-one feet in diameter, this bowl-shaped telescope must have presented an unusual specimen of lawn art. It certainly must have provoked some strange looks and speculation by his neighbors. Why did he choose a 31-foot diameter? His building project was limited by the length of the boards he could obtain at the local hardware store. Reber's invention served as the world's only radio telescope until after World War II. His telescope is now on display by the entrance to the Green Bank observatory.

Set back deep in **Deer Creek Valley**, the observatory is ideally situated because the remoteness of the area and the surrounding mountains protect the sensitive receivers used on the telescopes against any human-made radio interference.

As you approach the installation on Route 28, you'll see several giant satellite dishes dotting the quiet valley, a startling sight against the lush landscape. The observatory houses a 140-foot radio telescope used to discover new molecules in the spaces between the stars. "Molecules," explains one of the tour guides, "reveal the birth sites of stars." This huge telescope is linked electronically around the world with other similar devices, helping create some of the sharpest images possible in radio astronomy.

The **Green Bank Telescope** (GBT or Great Big Telescope, as locals call it), is the largest fully steerable radio telescope on the planet. This huge iron ear, which resembles a satellite dish, is the size of one and a half football fields and is 30 stories tall. Weighing 16.7 million tons, GBT took 249 ironworkers nine years to build. The telescope turns and tilts as it gathers information from outer space—radio wave data about the births of galaxies and the composition of interstellar dust. GBT sits at the center of a National Radio Quiet Zone, a restricted area off-limits to cell-phone towers, set up by the Federal Communications Commission to protect the purity of signals from outer space from competing cell-phone or radio signals. Because it is a radio-frequency quiet zone, you can't use your cell phone or even your digital camera here. In fact, National Radio Astronomy Observatory (NRAO) interference technicians have tracked down distracting "noises" to a neighbor's faulty heating pad 10 miles away. Push an electronic button and they'll have you in their sights within a few minutes.

In October 2002 the National Radio Astronomy Observatory opened a $6.1 million education and visitor center, featuring hands-on displays that explain the instruments and discoveries of radio astronomy. Full-time science educators answer questions and guide visitors through a real-world research environment as they try out the role of astronomer. Through a connection to the GBT, visitors can eavesdrop on scientists receiving data via the real telescope. Visitors can explore the effects of signal interference from radio stations, manipulate a laser beam, and learn how NRAO scientists became interested in astronomy, all in the science center. The observatory became an independent entity in 2016, although it is still used by national and international astronomers.

Tours are offered for a fee at the visitor center daily from 9 a.m. to 6 p.m. Memorial Day through Labor Day. The rest of the year, the facility is open Thurs through Mon from 10 a.m. to 6 p.m. with tours at 11 a.m., 1 p.m., and 3 p.m. Planetarium shows are held every Friday at 2 p.m. and special High-Tech Tours leave the science center at 3:30 p.m. on second Thursdays. Star parties for optical views are held on the occasional Saturday night. The observatory has a gift shop and cafe for guests. Call (304) 456-2150 or see gb.nrao.edu for details.

All abooouuarrrddd! No, it's not the Chattanooga Choo Choo, but it may inspire you to sing just the same. For some good old land travel, head up the road to *Cass Scenic Railroad State Park.* Cass Scenic Railroad is a delight any month of the year, but in the fall the locomotive's 11-mile winding journey through the area's breathtaking foliage is really a treat. It's the nation's only authentic and operating museum of lumber railroading.

Tourists board the train in the small railroad town of Cass, on the eastern slope of Cheat Mountain and less than 45 minutes from Green Bank. The village, located on Route 66 at the Greenbrier River, has remained virtually unchanged since the early years of the 1900s, when it was a company lumber town. At that time West Virginia led the nation with more than 3,000 miles of logging railroad line. The renovated, state park–operated line was the same used to haul lumber from the mountaintop to the mill in Cass.

Steam- and coal-powered locomotives haul passengers up an 11 percent grade (a 2 percent grade is considered steep on conventional railroads) using several switchbacks, then wind through open fields to Whitaker Station, where passengers disembark long enough to enjoy lunch or a cup of coffee from a park-run snack bar. Round-trip to Whitaker is 90 minutes. A 4-hour trip is offered to 4,800-foot Bald Knob, the second-highest point in the state. You can also take the 4.5-hour trip to the ghost town of Spruce. If you're going in the fall, be sure to have a warm sweatshirt or coat handy; except for the enclosed Leatherbark Creek car, all cars are unheated.

Before or after the ride, most visitors stop in at the Cass Country Store. It was once the world's largest company store but now exists as a gift shop and restaurant. It's located near the depot, along with a small wildlife museum, a Cass history museum, a Cass historical diorama, and a Main Street full of locally made crafts.

For those who really want a taste of how 19th-century railroaders lived, choose overnight lodging from among several completely furnished state park cabins. These restored cottages sleep six to eight people, include private bathrooms, and come fully equipped with utensils, tableware, towels, dishcloths, and linens. Wood stoves and electric heaters provide heat. Open year-round, the cabins are rented by the day up to a maximum of two weeks. The rates are very reasonable—a six-person cabin goes for roughly $950 per week and $180 a night May 15 through September, and a little higher in the winter ski season. The cottages are only available for one-night stays Sun through Thurs.

Rail excursions are offered from Memorial Day through the end of October. Cottage and train reservations can be made by calling (800) 933-7275 or (304) 456-4300, or visit www.wvstateparks.com/reservations.htm.

Snowshoe Mountain Resort may not seem off the beaten path in winter, when as many as 3,000 visitors hit the slopes, but on its 11,000 acres you'll find trails seldom trod by human feet. Some 120 miles of hiking and mountain biking trails wind through Cheat Mountain's spruce forests, and several of these paths lead to Snowshoe's Sunrise Backcountry Cabin, a lodge so off the beaten path it's not even on the power grid.

Sunrise offers catered meals by lamplight, ghost stories in front of a roaring fire, and a nocturnal silence so profound you can hear the scream of a bobcat 2 miles away. You may reach the cabin by hiking or biking but usually by riding a 4-seat Polaris.

Snowshoe also sets up snowmobile and—of course—snowshoe expeditions, as well as skiing, snowboarding, and snow tubing in season. Split Rocks Pools is a great place to splash around any time of year. With a geyser, slides, and hot tubs, the pool is the place to unwind. The Ballhooter lift, open year-round, offers one of the best vistas of autumn leaves in the Potomac Highlands.

potomac highlands trivia

West Virginia's Snowshoe Mountain has been named the top ski resort in the Mid-Atlantic and Southeast by *Ski Magazine.* The resort boasts 60 downhill runs and usually the best ski conditions south of Vermont.

Summer fun at Snowshoe often begins at its Raven Golf Course, consistently ranked as one of the top three public courses in West Virginia by

Golfweek magazine. Mountain biking clinics for women, men, and children are also extremely popular. But you can choose from activities as leisurely as wildflower walks up to rock climbing and kayaking and paddleboarding adventure tours. The mountaintop adventure center also offers electric bike riding and guided fly-fishing trips topped off by trout cooking class, and bass float trips, sporting clays, caving, and canoeing.

Segs on the mountain—you bet! Guests can learn to ride the resort's popular personal transporters. After a brief off-road training session on the Segway, they're ready for the resort tour on pavement. Then, if they're ready to step it up a bit and have their balance under control, they can do the backcountry Segway tour. Riding a Segway is intuitive; to go forward, lean forward. To go backward, lean gently back. To turn, twist your handlebar. It's a little like a rocking horse or a unicycle at first. Call Snowshoe's Outdoor Adventure Center at (304) 572-5917 for further details, pricing, and date of availability or check Snowshoe's website, snowshoemtn.com.

There's no better—or quicker—way to get off the beaten path in West Virginia than by jumping on a mountain bike (the nonpolluting variety) and heading into the distant backcountry of Pocahontas County. Granted, this is not for everyone, but if you're in decent shape and lean toward the adventurous, give the good folks at the **Elk River Touring Center** a call. This mecca for eastern mountain bikers, located in Slatyfork off US 219 (about 45 minutes from Cass), can outfit you for day, weekend, and weeklong guided fishing, cycling (including inn-to-inn tours), or ski trips through the Potomac Highlands. Elk River rents comfort bikes for trail riding. For overnight treks, you can choose to bunk down in a remote backcountry campground or the cozy bed-and-breakfast at great group rates.

If you're in pretty good shape, request a trip on the famous **Greenbrier River Trail**, at 77 miles one of the nation's longest and most scenic mountain biking trails. It follows the path of the abandoned Greenbrier River railroad line, with a 0.5 percent grade the entire trip. Along the way you'll see some incredible vistas of the river valley and the namesake river, one of the cleanest and clearest in the country. You can also pick at the remnants of old logging villages, including an abandoned (empty) bank vault that marks the ghost town of Watoga. For more information call Elk River at (304) 799-4087 or visit greenbrierrivertrail.com.

Park rangers at **Watoga State Park** (watoga.com) on the eastern side of the Greenbrier River can give you directions to the remains of the Watoga bank, Located southwest of Marlinton, Watoga is the largest state park in West Virginia. Two campgrounds provide more than 90 campsites and 34 rental cabins, some rustic CCC cottages, others modern all-season cabins. Numerous trails lead through the woods and the 400-acre arboretum.

Northeast on the park on Route 39, look for an interesting geological feature. Just before the Knapp's Creek Bridge east of Huntersville, look south. The huge arch of exposed sandstone, known as **Huntersville Arch** or Devil's Backbone, is a dramatic part of Browns Mountain's anticline. The rock was folded under tremendous pressure as the mountains formed.

To call the **Thorny Mountain Fire Tower** a room with a view is an understatement. The Seneca State Forest fire tower is *all* view, 360 degrees, with a couple of cots and chairs thrown in. And steps. You earn the view in this unique lodging accommodation by climbing 69 steps—5 stories. The only bathroom is a pit toilet at the tower's base. But the view makes this inconvenience as petty as mosquitoes buzzing a bear, neither of which you are likely to see up here, by the way.

Up top in the 14-foot x 14-foot quarters, the wind is always blowing, making even August evenings refreshing. Wooded ridges ripple off into the blue distance in every direction. Although **Cass Scenic Railroad** lies within a 30-minute drive, it isn't visible from the tower. Four distant homesteads to the south and an array of twinkling stars overhead supply the only lights you'll see from the tower. A flashlight is a necessity. Also water, potty bucket, food, and sleeping bag or bed linens. What you won't need is a mobile phone; here in the National Radio Quiet Zone around the Green Bank Telescope, cell towers, wireless internet routers, and other devices generating electromagnetic radiation are banned.

But there is quite enough to do within Seneca State Forest's 11,684 acres. Twenty-three miles of biking and biking trails traverse the forest. Visitors can rent canoes, rowboats, and paddleboats at small Seneca Lake, where trout, bass, bluegills, and catfish are ready to take the right bait. Children enjoy catching newts here, and the bird-watching is especially good in the low areas near the lake. For information, call (304) 799-6213 or visit wvstateparks.com/park/seneca-state-forest.

Virginia and North Carolina may have the Blue Ridge Parkway, but West Virginia has the equally spectacular and much-less-traveled **Highland Scenic Highway** (Route 39/55). The 46-mile two-lane highway gives motorists a look at some of the most scenic and unusual countryside in America. The road begins north of Marlinton, off US 219 (about 20 minutes south of Slatyfork), and leads you through the wilds of the Monongahela National Forest to an elevation of more than 4,500 feet, ending in the old logging town of Richwood. This is extremely remote country, and the roads aren't taking you anywhere fast—but that's the point, after all. Unless you're camping, it's a good idea to make advance gas, food, and lodging arrangements in Richwood, Webster Springs, or Marlinton.

There's much more to experience here than what you see from your car. For those who want to camp out, pitch a tent at one of three rustic campgrounds located a short drive from the highway. **Summit Lake Campground** is just 2 miles off Route 39/55, and it's near a beautiful reservoir. The 42-acre lake, cherished by trout and bass fishermen, has a boat ramp and a wheelchair-accessible fishing pier. An easy 1.5-mile footpath with views of the lake begins here, as do several challenging hikes into the national forest. Tea Creek Campground is 1 mile from the parkway portion of the highway, and Day Run Camp is 4 miles away; both are located along the beautiful **Williams River.** Recreational vehicles are allowed, but no hookups are available. Backcountry camping also is available in selected sites along the Williams River.

More than 150 miles of nearby trails lead hikers, backpackers, mountain bikers, horseback riders, and even cross-country skiers through such memorable natural attractions as **Falls of Hills Creek,** a series of cascading waterfalls. This popular 114-acre area contains 3 waterfalls: 25 feet, 45 feet, and 63 feet. The lower falls, at 63 feet, is the second-highest waterfall in West Virginia. A 0.75-mile trail leads visitors to spectacular views of the waterfalls as Hills Creek descends 220 feet. Practically a drive-in waterfall, the first can be reached by a paved, 0.25-mile, wheelchair-accessible path. The rest of the trail is a workout. Observation platforms at each falls give visitors unobstructed views of the cascading water. The complete trip takes about an hour—longer if you pause often to breathe deeply and enjoy the scenery.

Three rivers in the area—the Cherry, Cranberry, and Williams—provide some of the best trout fishing in the nation. The West Virginia Department of Natural Resources stocks these waters year-round with rainbow, brown, and golden trout. Native brook trout are also abundant in these cold and clear waters.

The **Edray Trout Hatchery** at nearby Marlinton is the place to see all species of the Mountain State's trout in one location. Operated by the West Virginia Department of Natural Resources, the hatchery raises brook, brown, rainbow, and golden trout. Ask a hatchery worker to tell you about the process: The male and female fish are milked of their eggs and sperm, which are mixed by humans in a special solution to up the chances of fertilization. Mostly you'll see trout of varying sizes swirling around the nursery tanks. About 3 miles north of Marlinton, turn onto Woodrow Road for about 1 mile. You'll see the sign. It's open daily from 7:30 a.m. to 3:30 p.m. Call (304) 799-6461 for more information.

Back on the Highland Scenic Highway, look for the eastern boundary of the 35,864-acre Cranberry Wilderness, a protected natural area of cranberry bogs, rare orchids, ferns, lilies, and numerous wildflower species. At an elevation of 3,400 feet, the tundra-like bowl holds several bogs that contain a relic population of plants more commonly found in northern Canada. These plants, including the carnivorous sundew, flourish in the cool, acidic setting. Stop in at the *Cranberry Glades Nature Center,* open Thurs through Mon, Apr through Oct, and located at the junction of Route 150 and Route 55.

The bogs lie on the edge of the wilderness area. Locally known as the "glades," the bogs consist of spongy peat (partially decayed plant material) covered by sphagnum moss. A wheelchair-accessible boardwalk leads 0.5 mile through the bogs and the surrounding forest. Look for miniature cranberry bushes. Guided tours of the bogs can be arranged in advance throughout the summer months by contacting the Cranberry Glades Nature Center at (304) 653-4826. The same number will provide you with information on all the above camping and natural areas.

The *Cranberry Mountain Lodge* is an isolated retreat for outdoor enthusiasts in some of West Virginia's highest mountains. The lodge is in a remote location, 6 miles from Hillsboro on John Wimer Road, behind a locked gate. Located at a 4,000-foot elevation on top of Cranberry Mountain, the lodge borders Monongahela National Forest. The deck views are spectacular, exceeding 40 miles. You can hike, bike, or ski right out the front door to a vast trail system through the national forest. The entire 7-bedroom, 4-bath facility is rentable through Airbnb. Nearby attractions include Cranberry Glades Botanical Area and Black Mountain Black Bear Sanctuary. For more information call (304) 242-6070.

Driving the Highland Scenic Highway, or in any part of West Virginia, for that matter, brings you up close to an amazing variety of hardwood trees, still among the state's most lucrative natural resources.

Lumberjacks and literary folk have always lived side by side in West Virginia. In Hillsboro, 8 miles south of Marlinton, travelers and literary enthusiasts can tour the restored home of one of America's greatest novelists, Pearl S. Buck. Buck wrote 85 books, including *The Good Earth,* for which she received the Pulitzer Prize. In 1938 she was awarded a Nobel. Until her death in 1973, she continued to publish and was active in civil rights and women's rights groups. While most of her books deal with China, she wrote several biographical books that showed Buck's emotional ties to the hills of West Virginia.

The *Pearl S. Buck Homestead* was built by Buck's mother's family—the Stultings—who emigrated from Holland in 1847. Buck (her married name) was born here in 1892 as Pearl Comfort Sydenstricker. Her father's birthplace, the

Sydenstricker House, was originally built in neighboring Greenbrier County but was dismantled and reconstructed on the museum grounds to serve as a cultural center.

A tour of the 13-acre homestead, her cars, and the ingenious furnishings her grandfather created gives insight about her life, from missionary child to celebrity author. You can purchase rare autographed first editions by Buck in the gift shop. If you're really interested in Buck, come back on the last Saturday in June for her birthday celebration or the autumn Harvest Moon Festival that Buck loved. The Pearl Buck Birthplace is open Fri though Mon, May through Oct. An admission fee is charged. Call (304) 653-4430 or visit pocahontas countywv.com/p-s-buck-birthplace for information.

Covered bridges hold a fascination for many, especially those old enough to remember the romance of parking with a date in the shelter of an old "kissing bridge." Locust Creek Covered Bridge, built in 1888, rates placement on the National Register of Historic Places. From Hillsboro, drive 2.2 miles south on US 219, then turn onto Locust Creek Road and go 3 miles to the bridge.

Civil War history still figures prominently in this part of West Virginia, especially just down US 219 at *Droop Mountain Battlefield State Park.* If you hear shots on the second weekend in October, it's not your imagination—West Virginia's largest and last significant Civil War battle has been reenacted on its 150th anniversary in 2013 and in subsequent even years (2014, 2016, etc.). It was actually on November 6, 1863, that Union troops under General William Averell pinned in place the Confederates under General John Echols by attacking them on the ridge from the right, left, and rear. While the main federal force bombarded the Confederates, another blue-coated wing circled around to surprise the Confederates' left flank. Following nearly six hours of artillery fire, musketry, and hand-to-hand combat, Averell's infantry forced the Confederate troops into a wedge, and their retreat became a rout. After much bloodshed Echols fled south into Virginia with the remnants of his command. The decisive Union victory ended Confederate efforts to control the new state.

The battle cost 600 men their lives; a few are still buried here. Long after the battles were over, veterans gathered on Droop Mountain to remember the fierce struggle and mourn their dead. They proposed a memorial, which became West Virginia's first state park in 1928. The site of the raging battle is now a peaceful 267-acre park with footpaths, picnic facilities, children's play areas, a lookout tower, and a small museum containing artifacts from the battle. Confederate earthworks are still visible in the forest. For more information call (304) 653-4254 or visit wvstateparks.com/park/droop-mountain-battlefield-state-park.

Places to Stay in the Potomac Highlands

BRANDYWINE

Cowger Guest House
4121 Corner Rd.
(304) 249-5004
Moderate

DAVIS

The Billy Motel
1080 William Street
(304) 851-6125
Thebillymotel.com
moderate

Blackwater Falls State Park
Route 32
(304) 259-5216
wvstateparks.com/park/
blackwater-falls-state-park
Moderate

Canaan Valley Resort State Park and Conference Center
Route 32
(304) 866-4121
(800) 622-4121
canaanresort.com
Moderate to expensive

ELKINS

Graceland Inn and Conference Center
on the campus of Davis and Elkins College
(304) 637-1600
gracelandinn.com
Expensive

FRANKLIN

Loafer's Glory B&B and Camping
3576 Dry Run Road
(304) 358-7034
Loafersglorywv.com
Inexpensive

LOST RIVER

Guest House at Lost River
288 Settlers Valley Way
(304) 897-5707
Guesthouselostriver.com
Expensive

MARLINTON

Jerico Cabins and B&B
Jerico Road
(304) 799-6241
jericobb.com
Inexpensive to moderate

SENECA ROCKS–SMOKE HOLE

North Fork Mountain Inn
235 Canyon View Lane,
Cabins, WV
(304) 257-1108
northforkmtninn.com
Expensive

Places to Eat in the Potomac Highlands

CANAAN VALLEY

Big John's Family Fixin's
Route 32
(304) 866-4418
Budget

DAVIS

Big Belly Deli
438 William Ave
(304) 259-2222
Bigbellydeliwv.com
Inexpensive

Milo's Café
454 Williams Ave
(304) 259-5119
Brightmorninginn.com
Moderate

Sirianni's
William Avenue
(304) 259-5454
Inexpensive

ELKINS

Graceland Inn and Conference Center
100 Campus Dr.
(304) 637-1600
gracelandinn.com
Moderate

MARLINTON

Dirt Bean
217 8th St.
(304) 799-4038
dirtbean.com
Inexpensive

MINGO

Brazen Head Inn
US 219
(304) 339-6917
(866) 339-6917
brazenheadinn.com
Inexpensive

MOOREFIELD

Mullins 1847 Restaurant
104 S Main St.
(304) 530-1847
Mullins1847.com
Moderate

FOR MORE INFORMATION

Grant County Convention & Visitors
Bureau
(304) 257-9266
grantcountycvb.com

Pocahontas County Convention and
Visitors Bureau
(800) 336-7009
pocahontascountywv.com

Hampshire County Convention &
Visitors Bureau
(304) 822-7477
cometohampshire.com

Elkins-Randolph County Convention
and Visitors Bureau
(304) 635-7803
elkinsrandolphwv.com

Hardy County Convention & Visitors
Bureau
(304) 897-8700
visithardywv.com

Tucker County Convention and
Visitors Bureau
(304) 259-5315
canaanvalley.org

SENECA ROCKS

Front Porch Restaurant
Junction of Routes 28, 55,
and 33
(304) 567-2555
Inexpensive

SNOWSHOE

**Snowshoe Mountain
Resort, Old Spruce
Tavern**
Route 66 and US 219
 (304) 572-1020
snowshoemtn.com
Moderate

THOMAS

Farm Up Table
272 East Ave
(304) 924-4944
Farmuptable.com
Moderate

WARDENSVILLE

Kac-Ka-Pon Restaurant
Route 259
(304) 874-3232
kackaponrestaurant.com
Inexpensive

Mountain Lakes

The Mountain Lakes region covers seven counties near the center of the state: Gilmer, Lewis, Upshur, Braxton, Webster, Nicholas, and Clay. It is a gentle place of small towns, tidy farms, country roads, and rolling green woodlands. The region is dotted with communities whose names are as distinctive as the people who have lived there for centuries. Hominy Falls, Tallmansville, Stumptown, and Erbacon line the two-lane roads with little stores, a few houses, and some of the friendliest people to be found anywhere.

The region is a sportsman's paradise. Its landscape is dominated by five major lakes: Summersville Lake (the largest in the state) in Nicholas County, Sutton and Burnsville Lakes in Braxton County, Stonewall Jackson and Stonecoal Lakes in Lewis County, and the small Big Ditch Lake in Webster County. The heart of the Mountain State is also a land of rivers. Here the Elk, the Williams, the Cherry, the Buckhannon, the Cranberry, and the Little Kanawha snake through the fields and forests, providing great fishing and canoeing opportunities. In fact, this is one of the most abundant wildlife regions in West Virginia, with more than 8,400 acres for lake fishing and 60,000 acres of wildlife management area.

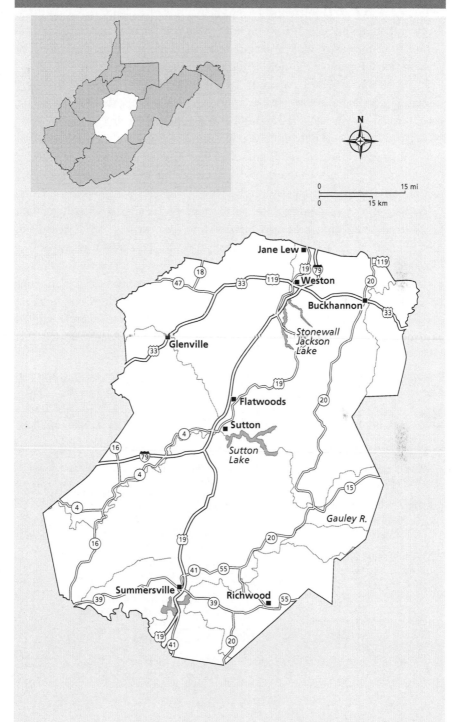

The area's low population density means there is plenty of space to get away and enjoy the natural surroundings. This is a remote land but one that's sprinkled with unusual attractions and festivals. Take your time and enjoy the scenery, for the pace of life here is relaxed and good for the soul.

The Mountain Lakes region is an area studded with sparkling though underutilized lakes and traversed by winding miles of lonely but scenic country roads. In far eastern Nicholas County, about a 90-minute drive from the town of Clay, is **Richwood** (cityofrichwoodwv.com), the gateway to the Mononga-hela National Forest and the Highland Scenic Highway (which we visited in the Potomac Highlands chapter). The former lumber town was the world's first and largest clothespin manufacturer. If those clothespins were still around, they could be put to good use to close sensitive noses each April when Richwood hosts its annual **Feast of the Ramson**—and, yes, that is the correct spell-ing—one of the state's largest ramp festivals, and for sure an event not for the gastronomically challenged. A ramp is a potently flavored wild scallion, a vegetable with staying power. It grows abundantly in rocky West Virginia hills and is often the first green vegetation to sprout on the hillsides in late March and early April. In pioneer times the ramp supposedly saved many a starving soul and helped prevent scurvy. Today the hearty leek-like vegetable is a local

BEST ANNUAL EVENTS IN THE MOUNTAIN LAKES REGION

Irish Spring Festival
Ireland; mid-March
(304) 452-8962

Feast of the Ramson
Richwood; mid-April
(304) 846-6790

West Virginia State Folk Festival
Glenville; mid-June
(304) 462-9644 or (304) 462-8762
wvstatefolkfestival.com

Flatwoods Monster Fest
Flatwoods; early July
(304) 678-7334
Flatwoods Monster Fest @ Facebook
.com

West Virginia's Largest Yard Sale
Buckhannon, Weston, and surroundings;
early August;
(304) 473-1400
visitupshur.org

Potato Festival
Summersville; early September
(866) 716-0448
nicholascountypotatofestival.com

Grape Stomp Wine Festival
Summersville; mid-September
(304) 872-7332
kirkwood-wine.com

WV Glass Gathering
Weston; mid-October
(304) 269-5006
magwv.com

Ramp Up to Spring, West Virginia Style

When the tree frogs are announcing spring along tributaries of Nicholas County's Big Coal River, West Virginians know it's time to look for ramps. Ramps (*Allium tricoccum*) are wild leeks. For at least three centuries, the unfurling of ramps' pungent shoots in Appalachian valleys has signaled the end of winter and the time to eat spring greens.

Here in West Virginia, that time is celebrated with the **Feast of the Ramson**, using the folk name of ramps' relatives in the British Isles. In fact, Richwood claims the title of Ramp Capital of the World. It is true that the National Ramp Association began here 80 years ago and that Richwood's *West Virginia Hillbilly* newspaper once impregnated its newsprint with ramp oil and received a federal reprimand for fouling rural post offices with the odor.

Although early 20th-century schoolchildren who ate ramps may have been sent home from school to purge the stench from their systems, to the early settlers and American Indians, the odor seemed trivial. Ramps were a nutritious change from their winter diet of game, dehydrated vegetables, nuts, and dried meats. The wild leeks are a good source of vitamin C as well as prostaglandin, a fatty acid useful in lowering blood pressure. Studies by Oregon State University biochemistry professor emeritus Phil Whanger, a native West Virginian, have indicated that women who eat ramp leaves increase their resistance to breast tumors.

The late wild-foods evangelist Euell Gibbons considered ramps "the sweetest and best of the wild onions."

At festivals, ramps are served up with beans, corn bread, potatoes, trout, or in gourmet circles, with black beans, sole, or artichokes. Specialty vendors extend ramps' April through May season with offerings of pickled ramps, ramp vinegar, and ramp jelly.

For more information about Richwood's annual April Feast of the Ramson, call (304) 846-6790.

favorite and is often fried with ham and served with beans and potatoes. The Richwood festival, sponsored by the locally based National Ramp Association, is held at the local high school, at 1 Valley Way, where you're seated elbow to elbow with those who come back for more every year. Afterward, don't skimp on either the Alka-Seltzer or the breath mints.

If you overindulge, you can walk off your discomfort on the **Tri-Rivers Trail**. The 16.5-mile course begins in Richwood and follows three rivers—the Cherry, Gauley, and Cranberry—to end at a tunnel.

From Richwood, you're also about equal distance from the attractions of nearby Summersville Lake and the high mountain country of the Cranberry Wilderness area (see "Potomac Highlands").

Summersville Area

At the heart of Nicholas County is the fast-growing town of Summersville—a virtually insignificant town 35 years ago. The expansion of US 19 changed all that. The road is part of a major north–south thruway, with Summersville being near the midway point for Canadian snowbirds headed to Florida.

Labor Day weekend marks the traditional end of summertime activities, but not in Summersville. The *Potato Festival* is held the following weekend, along with the reenactment of the Battle of Carnifex Ferry, and then the Gauley River Fest.

Events at the Potato Festival include a beauty pageant, a potato cook-off, a potato judging and auction, a parade, a classic car show, arts and crafts, and a 5K run. Nearby, the *Carnifex Ferry Battlefield State Park* has Civil War camps set up by reenactors for public viewing on Saturday and Sunday. Throughout Saturday, living-history events take place, while on Sunday morning the reenactors conduct an outdoor church service. The reenacted Battle of Carnifex Ferry takes place on Sunday afternoon in odd-numbered years (2023, 2025, etc.). The weekend warriors demonstrate how on September 10, 1861, Union troops led by Brigadier General William Rosecrans forced the Confederates to abandon the ferry. The Confederate commander, Brigadier General John Floyd, retreated to Lewisburg, giving the Union control of the Kanawha Valley. As a result, the movement for West Virginia statehood proceeded without major resistance. The battle commences, with booming volleys of cannon fire, drifting smoke, and earnest soldiers. Participants come from as far away as Canada and California.

Although the Potato Festival draws quite a number of people to the area, an even larger attraction brings people from all across the US and several foreign countries: the opening of the Gauley season.

The name *Gauley River* strikes fear into hearts of the whitewater timid. The Gauley River is among the most challenging whitewater rivers in the US. Every year, for six consecutive weekends in September and October, during the annual drawdown of the Summersville Dam, people flock to the area to experience the whitewater-rafting thrill of a lifetime. During the drawdown the water is released at a constant rate of 2,800 cubic feet per second. The Gauley is a pounding, swirling, tumbling, fast-and-furious river.

Located in the heart of mountainous West Virginia, the Gauley flows through some of the most remote and gorgeous scenery in the eastern US. It is channeled through a steep canyon that is an average of 500 feet deep. Recommended only for commercial rafting trips and expert kayakers, the river crashes in Class V rapids over and around boulders the size of homes. This high-velocity creek is one of the top 10 whitewater rivers in the world, offering more than 100 major rapids in its course. Riding the Gauley is as pure an adrenaline rush as one could possibly hope for—or want. Just listen to the names of some of the rapids: Heaven Help You, Upper and Lower Mash, and Pure Screaming Hell.

Gauley season starts the Friday after Labor Day. Dam release days are Fri through Mon for five weeks, then Sat and Sun the last weekend. Saturday and Sunday book up fairly quickly with the commercial rafting companies. Friday and Monday find fewer people on the river.

Don't think you will be doing the Upper Gauley your first time out. Rafting companies require a minimum age of 15 or 16, depending upon the company. All recommend that rafters have whitewater experience on either the New River or Lower Gauley. (Brochures make it sound like a requirement, but there is no way to fully enforce such a rule.) The Gauley is a mighty river, however, and it simply wouldn't make sense to attempt it with no whitewater experience.

The Lower Gauley is quite thrilling, with rapids from Class III through Class V, with some easy flat water in between. The Upper Gauley is Class III to Class V+, with back-to-back rapids and almost no flat-water breaks.

For a complete listing of rafting companies in the state, phone (800) CALL-WVA. Call the Summersville Convention and Visitors Bureau at (304) 872-3722 for more information on the Battle of Carnifex Ferry Reenactment and the Potato Festival.

BEST ATTRACTIONS IN THE MOUNTAIN LAKES REGION

Audra State Park
Buckhannon
(304) 457-1162
wvstateparks.com/park/
audra-state-park

Trans-Allegheny Lunatic Asylum
Weston
(304) 269-5070
trans-alleghenylunaticasylum.com

West Virginia University Jackson's Mill and Farmstead
Weston
(304) 269-5100
jacksonsmill.wvu.edu

West Virginia Museum of American Glass
Weston
(304) 269-5006
magwv.com

West Virginia Wildlife Center
French Creek
(304) 924-6211
www.wvdnr.gov/wildlife/wildlifecenter
.shtm

Along with Gauley season comes the ***Gauley River Fest and Races,*** held in the third weekend of September at the Veterans Memorial Park in Summersville. Started in 1983 to celebrate the derailment of a hydroelectric project that would have disrupted the flows on the Gauley River, Gauley Fest has become the largest paddling festival in the world. In addition to plenty of running the raging rapids, music, and food, this is a rowdy paddler's party with howl-at-the-moon fun that sometimes includes late-night mud wrestling and boxing. Several years ago there was a Rock-Paper-Scissors tournament involving 1,000 people. Winners got boats and paddles. The event is sponsored by the American Whitewater Association (304-658-5016; americanwhitewater.org).

A ***lighthouse*** in the Mountain State? Oh, yes. Its creation was a major school project for pre-engineering and welding students from Nicholas County Career and Technical Center, who collaborated with older students at Fayette Institute of Technology to construct a 100-foot lighthouse overlooking Summersville Lake. The lighthouse, actually a leftover tower from a wind turbine project, stands 2,000 feet above the lake at Mount Nebo. Visitors have unparalleled views of Summersville Lake, Gauley Mountain, and Carnifex Ferry Battlefield State Park from its gallery deck. But they must climb 122 spiraling steps to get there. Admission is $7 for adults and $5 for seniors and children under 12. In addition to daily tours April through Oct, sunset and full-moon tours are offered occasionally May through Oct, weather permitting. To check on availability, call (304) 872-5975 or visit summersvillelakeretreat.com. Camping and lodging are available on the site.

Probably the last place most people think of to go scuba diving is West Virginia, but few lakes in the US have the extraordinary water clarity found in 2,800-acre ***Summersville Lake,*** which is actually a dammed section of the Gauley River in central Nicholas County. In some parts of the lake, underwater visibility exceeds 50 feet. ***Sarge's Dive Shop*** (sarges.net) leverages this natural attribute by offering a host of dive charters and snorkel trips along the clifflike shores of the lake. If you're new to scuba diving, owners Mark and Eric Allen offer certified courses, including private instruction, and have plenty of gear for rent. In addition, rescue courses are offered for those who want to take the scuba experience a bit further. Dinner cruises and pontoon boat tours of the lake also are offered from here.

Sarge's is located at Long Point Marina, a mile south of Summersville off US 19. Diving reservations are preferred, but walk-ins are welcome, says Mark. You may also rent kayaks and paddle boards, if you want to stay on top of the water. The shop is open daily 10 a.m. to 5 p.m. mid-Apr through mid-Sept. Call (304) 872-1782 for more information.

Summersville's dining options have been growing as more visitors arrive at West Virginia's largest lake. Three new establishments are especially worth noting: the Vault on Main serves creamy scallops, salmon tacos with strawberry salsa, and other gourmet items in the cloistered atmosphere of an old bank, and Original Flavor Bistro on Broad Street blends Venezuelan and Puerto Rican recipes with local ingredients. Gad Dam Brewery—named for the town of Gad that is now under Summersville Lake and the dam that might have taken its name—has a reputation around the lake for its craft beers, premium coffee, tasty food, live music and family-friendly fun and games.

For some, the right beverage goes hand in glove with a fine meal. If you have any interest in the inside operations of spirited libations, stop by ***Kirkwood Winery*** and its adjoining ***Isaiah Morgan Distillery,*** just off US 19 on Phillips Run Road north of Summersville. The staff are happy to explain the makings of a Kirkwood wine, whether it's a specialty ginseng or garlicky ramp wine or one of their award-winning Fochs, a chardonnay, or a Seyval mead.

A newer operation, the Isaiah Morgan Distillery is housed in the tasting lodge. Forget your impressions of tarnished green copper stills; this West Virginia distillery is a gleaming stainless steel apparatus that converts bubbling corn, rye, or grape mash into 180 proof whiskey. (Of course it's watered down by more than half for market.)

You can purchase any one of Kirkwood's multitude of wines here, as well as the whiskey. Now Southern Moon Whiskey can be purchased on site in this craft distillery. For a good time, visit during the ***Grape Stomp Festival,*** held each year on the third weekend of September. Call (304) 872-7332 or go to kirkwood-wine.com for more information.

After Summersville, you might also want to get off the main drag and do a little sightseeing on county roads as you head up to ***Sutton.*** Take Route 41 to Route 55 to Muddlety, then take the county road through Enoch before catching Route 16 again near Clay. This time go north; then get on I-79 briefly to Sutton. It may sound out of the way (what isn't in this part of the state?), but the drive through the countryside is interesting and serene.

In Sutton get ready to be entertained, for here's another not-to-be-missed opportunity at Main Street's ***Landmark Studio for the Arts,*** housed in a beautiful 19th-century building that has been a Baptist, a Presbyterian, and a Methodist church. (Note the art nouveau stained-glass windows.) The studio's stage hosts the some of the best local thespians and musicians in the state, including occasionally the West Virginia Symphony's string quartet. Recent productions have included *Mamma Mia!*, *Rock of Ages*, and *The Rocky Horror Picture Show*. Call (304) 644-3166 for hours and more information.

The **Flatwoods Monster Museum** gives some eerie zing to Sutton's attractions. It is a part of the **Braxton County Convention & Visitors Bureau** on Main Street. Stir around in West Virginia folklore and you'll find a number of aliens and monster creatures such Mothman, Bigfoot, and the Flatwoods Monster, who made enough of a resurgence in 2020 to be featured in one of Blenko glass company's most popular art glass creations.

The story of the Flatwoods Monster began September 12, 1952, in the village of Flatwoods. Schoolboys playing football saw a fiery object fall from the sky, so they and two adult bystanders hiked up the hill to check it out.

"Something was moving. An overwhelming rotten-egg smell burned their eyes," said Andrew Smith, director of the Braxton County CVB and founder of Flatwoods Monster Museum.

What they saw, they reported to police, was a 10-foot-tall monster hovering above the ground, spewing smoke and gas. Its head was red and spade-shaped with a pointed top. It had glowing eyes, and its body was covered in what looked to be green armor.

"It was emitting a shrieking sound," Smith said.

The group fled. Other than a lingering smell, police could find no evidence of the monster. The Flatwoods Monster legend lives on, though the telling gets embellished. Some think a government conspiracy was involved; others claim a dog died from the noxious gas.

The monster has a surprising Japanese following dating back to 1980s Japanese video games. Japanese people have visited Sutton expressly to see the museum. In fact, the Flatwoods Monster Museum has become an epicenter of all the different interpretations of the monster. What started as one small shelf of Flatwoods Monster paraphernalia in the office has turned into a museum that draws 95 percent of the storefront's visitors, Smith says

Visitors entering the building are greeted by a life-sized Flatwoods Monster costume. The walls are lined with other interpretations of the monster—drawings, figurines, lanterns, stickers, T-shirts, and video games. Another huge Flatwoods Monster stands in the back, fashioned from a green graduation robe, PVC pipes, and a red pizza pan. A bust of the monster peers down from a top shelf, its dark red, bony face resembling the grim reaper.

The monster museum was featured in such programs as America's Got Aliens, Nerdist's Bizarre States, and The Unseen World. The museum is open 9 a.m. to 5 p.m. on weekdays and from 10 a.m. to 4 p.m. on weekends. Admission is free. You can spend your money on monster shirts, stickers, shot glasses, and lanterns. A Flatwoods Monster Festival is held each year around the Sept 12 anniversary of the sighting.

Sutton is haunting with monsters it seems. Two blocks down Main Street from the Flatwoods Monster museum sits West Virginia Bigfoot Museum, housed in the *Mountain Laurel Country Store*. Bigfoot sightings have occurred all over Braxton County with a concentration around Sutton Lake. The local marina claims to rent many boats annually to bigfoot hunters. The free bigfoot museum provides a somewhat scientific look at the legendary creature and displays West Virginia bigfoot track castings and accounts of encounters with the large primate. The shop also carries bigfoot merch as well. An annual Bigfoot Festival is held in late June. The museum is open Wednesday through Friday 10 a.m. to 6 p.m. and Saturdays 10 a.m. to 4 p.m.

While you're in Sutton, you'll have a good opportunity to get wet. *Sutton Lake* has 1,500 surface acres of water recreation, including a newly expanded marina with boat rentals. This is the place to rent canoes, paddleboats, party boats, fishing boats, even a houseboat. The lake is located just off I-79, and anglers come from everywhere to hook into the excellent largemouth, small mouth, and spotted bass. No wonder—Sutton Lake logs about 40 fishing tournaments a year. Even if you don't enjoy fishing, you can take a spin around the lake in a boat, enjoying the beautiful scenery of the *Elk River Wildlife Management Area,* which abuts the lake. The park is open year-round, dawn to dusk. Call (304) 587-7652.

Just north on I-79 is the reputed center of West Virginia. An enterprising businessman decided this was reason enough to establish an outlet-store complex and conference center at *Flatwoods.* Among the array of factory outlets, you'll find Amish bulk food, books, fashion, leather goods, tools, sleepwear, an, craft shops, and an outlet store specializing in Fiestaware, from vibrant colors of dinnerware to accessories and bakeware. It's all made and designed right here in West Virginia. The outlet is open 9 a.m. to 5 p.m. Mon through Sat and noon to 5 p.m. Sun. The phone number is (304) 765-5384.

mountain
lakestrivia

The town of Sutton, located along the banks of the Elk River about 60 miles northeast of Charleston, is considered the geographic center of the state.

But while some are shopping in the Mountain Lakes region, others are fishing. So glorious is this area for fishermen that some say it's where righteous anglers go when they die. You can also grab your fishing rod and splash over to nearby *Burnsville Lake.* Just north on I-79, this lake was formed when the US Army Corps of Engineers dammed the Little Kanawha River. Bass, crappie, muskie, and channel catfish are abundant in these 968 acres of water. Surrounding the reservoir are 12,000 acres known as the ***Burnsville Wildlife Management Area,*** which at the right time of year is home to migrating waterfowl, grouse, quail, turkey, deer, and innumerable bowhunters. Motel accommodations and camping are abundant, including the ***Bulltown Campgrounds,*** which is waterside. Operated by the Corps of Engineers, more than 200 sites are available from the third week in May through Nov. For reservations and information, call (304) 452-8006. Bulltown is named for Captain Bull, chief of the Delaware tribe that once lived in the area.

After you've done all the fishing you can stand (or all your spouse can stand for you to do), there's a lot to see around the lake on foot. Head over to the ***Bulltown Historic Area,*** where the US Army Corps of Engineers moved several log structures to prevent their destruction when the dam was being built. Originally built between 1815 and 1870, the pioneer settlements were disassembled by the corps, moved, then reconstructed right near the campgrounds. Today, during the warm-weather months, living-history demonstrations show how quilting, clothes washing, gardening, cooking, and other household chores were accomplished by 19th-century pioneers of the backcountry. This site was also where the ***Battle of Bulltown*** raged, a 12-hour skirmish between Union and Confederate soldiers fought on October 13, 1863. The Southerners, led by Stonewall Jackson's cousin, Colonel William L. "Mudwall" Jackson, were attempting to capture the Union garrison stationed at Bulltown. They failed, and Union forces held their ground in West Virginia.

Also in Bulltown don't miss the early 19th-century ***Cunningham Farmhouse,*** a dogtrot-style house seized by the Union forces during the war and which bears the bullet holes to prove it. Farther down the trail, which takes you along the ***Weston and Gauley Bridge Turnpike***—used by both North and South to transport supplies—you'll find ***Johnson House,*** built in 1883 by a freedman, and the log ***St. Michael's Church,*** one of the first Catholic churches in the state. It rests on a hill, overlooking the battle site. During the second week of October in odd years (2023, 2025, etc.), reenactors restage the Battle of Bulltown.

An interpretive center shows a six-minute show on the lake and its facilities and houses 19th-century memorabilia and Civil War battle artifacts. Follow the one-mile interpretive trail around the grounds, or better yet, take the 2 p.m. tour of the houses, church, and battlefield. The center is open from mid-May through mid-Sept, 10 a.m. to 6 p.m., but closes two hours earlier from Sept 1 to Oct 30. It's closed Oct 30 to May 1. Call (304) 452-8170 or (304) 853-2370 for more information.

Stonewall Country

Lewis, Gilmer, and Upshur Counties contain the largest towns in the region, most of which are close to I-79. But don't spend all your time on the interstate, because most of the goodies are way off the beaten path. This route will leave your car trunk filled with arts and crafts, your head swimming in history, your stomach filled with good food, and your toes tapping a happy beat.

From Burnsville Lake, veer slightly to the west on Route 5 to **Glenville.** If you're in town on the third weekend in June, follow your ears to the **West Virginia State Folk Festival** (304-462-5000). Fiddles, banjos, mandolins, autoharps, and hammered dulcimers ring through the streets. If you've ever wanted to learn how to mountain dance, the festival is the place to be. There's also storytelling, a quilt show, and a shape note singing workshop as well as a chance to serenade the local nursing home. One of the most unusual sights is the parade of elderly "belles" in hoop skirts. To be selected as a belle—an honored guest of the festival—the lady must admit to being over 70 and portray true "pioneering mountain spirit." The festival opens on the third Thursday of June at the Country Store Museum and ends with a Sunday service at a historic church.

Now head north, either back on I-79 or on US 33, into **Weston,** a community planned by Stonewall Jackson's grandfather. This charming little city with Victorian mansions and gingerbread-bedecked homes is famous locally as the **Christmas Town** because of its spectacular light show during the holidays. Beginning the day after Thanksgiving and lasting through New Year's Day, a quarter of a mile of Main Street is illuminated with blue and white snowflake lights. They used to dance along to a choreographed computer program. A lighted, waving Santa and his reindeer fly overhead, above all the downtown storefronts, which also have been adorned with an incredible array of lights and designs. Angels protect the glass museum on Main Street. Across the street from the courthouse, on Center Avenue, sits a 37-foot blue spruce, glowing brilliantly with hundreds of colored lights. Every year the display gets bigger.

Interesting landmarks abound in Weston, such as the **Trans-Allegheny Lunatic Asylum,** located on Second Street. This imposing structure is actually the world's second largest hand-cut stone building—only the Kremlin is larger. Probably not creepier, though. Although the 200,000-square-foot structure was known as Weston State Hospital for as long as most locals remember, the new owner has taken back its original name of Trans-Allegheny Lunatic Asylum, a name that doesn't sit well with advocates for the mentally ill.

Thousands were committed to the facility over its 130 years in operation, and hundreds have died in these rooms. Open for a variety of history and spooky tours Tuesday through Sunday from Apr 1 through Nov 1, the asylum has become a favorite haunt of ghost hunters who've detected unexplainable voices and sounds, weird vapors, and other seemingly paranormal activity. SyFy's *Ghost Hunters*, Travel Channel's *Ghost Adventures* and *Paranormal Challenge,* and an episode of CMT's *My Big Redneck Wedding* have been recorded here. For the invincible visitor, occasional overnight ghost hunts begin at 9 p.m. and last until 5 a.m.

But for even the daytime guest, this building's history holds fascinating, sometimes chilling stories from the Civil War, the early days of mental-health treatment, and the efforts of determined individuals to better the lives of the mentally ill. The asylum's exhibits reveal horrifying treatments once considered routine: electroshock therapy, lobotomies, cold-water baths, and cagelike cribs that were hung from the ceiling.

The first patient was admitted in 1864, an Ohio woman said to be suffering from "domestic trouble." In those days it was possible for a husband to have a relative committed for afflictions as vague as "female disease" or "novel reading." Too much political or religious fervor also was a symptom that could merit hospitalization. Before psychotropic drugs and electric shock, the only treatment was to stop the behavior. Patients who couldn't be controlled were chained or caged, even children. Stepping into the dim cells today encourages thoughts of earlier miseries that took place there. Wouldn't a ghost tour here be overload? Apparently not—the October tours, enlivened by a cast of almost 100 actors, are extremely popular.

If you're not up for a ghost tour, the asylum offers a number of historical tours, including several on medical history, as well as a 75-minute Civil War tour. This walking tour recounts fascinating stories of local Civil War raids, gold robberies, and soldiers who would become presidents. On the medical side, the asylum's 7 museum rooms feature nurses' logs, superintendents' records, and more than 120 pieces of art made by patients in therapy, as well as other items related to the treatment of the day.

During the summer months, concerts, outdoor drama, fairs, and mud-bog races are held on the grounds. In October things get spookier with amped-up ghost tours every Wednesday through Sunday, culminating in the largest costume ball in West Virginia on October 26.

Tours are held Tues through Sun between noon and 5 p.m. and on Fri and Sat night. Prices range from $12 to $100, with the proceeds going for building restoration. You can obtain more information at trans-alleghenylunaticasylum.com or by calling (304) 269-5070.

Another building of note is Lewis County's only public library. It is housed in the historic *Jonathan-Louis Bennett House,* 148 Court Ave., once home to one of Weston's most prominent families. The 17-room high-Victorian Italianate mansion contains a few pieces of original furniture and other furnishings amid the book stacks. Visitors to the library are allowed into certain sections of the home that offer a glimpse of life during the Victorian era. The entire house can be viewed by special tour arrangements. The Louis Bennett Library is open Mon through Fri from 10 a.m. to 5 p.m. and Sat from 10 a.m. to 2 p.m. Call (304) 269-5151 for more information.

Just off US 33 at *Appalachian Glass & Gifts,* you can find Chip Turner blowing glass dipped from a red-hot kiln. Turner and his father, Matt, honed their skills at nearby Princess House before the glass factory closed. "It's a dying art," says Chip, "and because we want people to appreciate it, we take our portable kiln out to festivals and fairs. We want to keep our heritage alive."

mountain lakestrivia

West Virginia native son and Confederate hero Thomas "Stonewall" Jackson died from wounds inflicted after being accidentally shot by one of his fellow soldiers in a battle near Fredericksburg, Virginia.

Turner twirls and dips the hot gobs of glass until he has a bubble the size of a Red Delicious apple. Though the finished product looks like something to hang on your Christmas tree, they call it a friendship ball. "Folks didn't have much money, so they'd wrap up one of these for birthdays and give it with something homemade, like a pie or an apron. The one who got it would pass it on to somebody else with another homemade gift. It made its way around a community like that," Turner says.

Appalachian Glass offers over 500 traditionally produced crystal pieces in a vast array of colors. From novelty items to elegant stemware and vases, all are handcrafted and mouth-blown in West Virginia. In the same long building, other crafters make quilts to sell. Appalachian Glass & Gifts also features a stained-glass artist, a potter, a woodworker, a candymaker, and other artists demonstrating their crafts at various times. The craft store is open 6 days a week, and Turner is likely to be working in the glass studio in the morning. Their annual Glass Fest is in late April. Call (304) 269-1030 for more details.

Downtown Weston is the home of the *West Virginia Museum of American Glass,* open noon to 4 p.m. every day June 1 through Sept 1, and on Mon, Tues, Thurs, Fri, and Sat the rest of the year. Here you'll see fine representatives of many of the 20th-century glassmaking operations in Ohio, Pennsylvania, and especially West Virginia. Once West Virginia alone boasted more than 500 glass plants. Of the dozens of companies that produced marbles, window glass, tableware, and art, only about a half dozen remain in the whole state. But they left a sparkling legacy. The museum's gems are its Tiffany glass tiles and winners of its paperweight contest. It also boasts the largest collection of glass toilet bowl floats in the nation, and its glass-eye holdings are nothing to sneeze at. The museum also has 561 glass hens, including a few made by the now-defunct Kanawha Glass plant in Dunbar. It recently acquired the collections of the American Marble Museum, including a Roman glass marble dating to AD 100.

The Weston museum has a gift shop where you too can begin a glass collection—items range from $2 to several thousand dollars—or buy books about glass collecting. No admission is charged, but donations are welcome. The museum is on the corner of Main Avenue and Second Street in downtown Weston. For more information, call (304) 269-5006 or visit wvmag.com.

One thing Weston has in abundance is carp. The West Fork River that runs through the center of town is full of the olive-brown bottom feeders. Many a Weston resident has been awakened at night by the sounds of big bull carp "barking" by puffing and blowing bubbles to attract females. Since each female can lay up to 2 million eggs and they have no natural predators, carp can take over a river. They are eaten only by the Chinese, some Europeans, and West Virginians—and for years a carp tournament was held in town. Although the competition has been discontinued, visitors are welcome to fish along the West Fork River as it flows through the town northward from Stonewall Jackson Lake.

If you're in the mood for a picnic, Weston has a delightful ***Farmers' Market*** Saturdays, bursting with fresh local produce, handcrafted furniture, and some very good West Virginia wines. It's on the right just as you come into town on US 33. Also, a few turns off US 33 is an unusual place to help fill up your picnic basket. ***Smoke Camp Crafts*** has homegrown table teas, Appalachian herbs, and almost 50 varieties of jams and jellies made with wild and organically cultivated fruits (you can also pick up a few cleansing lotions at the same time). Traditional and exotic herb blends here run the gamut: the Headache Blend, the Herbal Moth Repellent, the High-Blood-Pressure Blend, the Hot Flash Tea, Menopause Blend Tea, and PMS Capsules. Smoke Camp Crafts is located on Smoke Camp Run Road, about 5 miles northwest of Weston. Call (304) 940-1142 for more information and for directions.

Smoke Camp Crafts is located on Smoke Camp Run Road, about 5 miles northwest of Weston. Call (304) 269-6416 for more information and for directions.

Stonewall Jackson Lake meanders close to the interstate at the Roanoke exit south of Weston. Before the ***Stonewall Jackson Dam*** was built in 1986, there really was a small town called Roanoke here. Now Roanoke lies underwater, and a Roanoke plaza at ***Stonewall Resort State Park*** headquarters

West Virginia's Biggest Liar Takes to the Parks

Bil Lepp has just told 400 adults his hound dog hauled a 168-car CSX train loaded with West Virginia bituminous coal clear from Cowen to Grafton, West Virginia, and he hasn't cracked a grin. In fact, he's earnestly elaborating on the quality of the coal, that it's scrubbed, "so as not to pollute the great state of West Virginia," and not one of the highly educated librarian types in the audience shows any sign of incredulity. No, they're totally with him in the tailwind of that train, howling with delight, tears of laughter streaking down their cheeks.

The spectators hang on as Lepp drops West Virginia–born test pilot Chuck Yeager to the wheel of that engine and fastens himself by the tongue to an ice-steel boxcar "like scandal to Martha Stewart." They don't flinch when he pulls out a 74-function Swiss Army knife ("What, yours doesn't have a sewing machine function?") to save his hide.

They leap to their feet, cheering. This bunch would follow Lepp anywhere. Boyish-looking Lepp shrugs, hands in the pockets of his faded jeans. Should an ordained Methodist minister be getting away with this? Lepp's life is as good as an Appalachian Jack Tale, and he is crafty Jack.

Lepp, who left the pulpit in 2003 to become a full-time storyteller, has won the *West Virginia Liars Contest* at the Vandalia Festival so many times he's no longer allowed to enter; he's the emcee these days. He's also pushed credibility several notches above believable in performances at the Smithsonian Folklife Festival, Timpanogos (Utah) Storytelling Festival, Washington Storytellers Theatre, and many other venues across the nation.

It takes a liar to know one. So Lepp won a gig with the History Channel's *Man vs. History* series traveling around the nation to discover the truth behind the mysteries and legends of American history. In each episode, Lepp investigates, decodes, and debunks iconic figures, like Billy the Kid, Johnny Appleseed, Davy Crockett, Houdini and more. He works to proclaim whether each story is fact, fiction, or somewhere in between.

You can often hear Lepp tell his own outrageous lies in West Virginia's state parks and festivals from June through September. His stories usually take place among West Virginia landmarks, especially in the Mountain Lakes region where he spent his youth, and they almost always involve his dog, his fishing rod, a bear, and a train.

Lepp describes his original yarns as Appalachian stories. "Not traditional stories, maybe—everything I tell I wrote or my brother Paul did. The stories we tell come out of the culture and people of Appalachia, hill people from West Virginia to mid-Ohio."

To see Lepp's schedule, check his website, leppstorytelling.com, or that of West Virginia state parks: www.wvstateparks.com.

commemorates the vanished village. It has been replaced with the 198-room **Stonewall Resort** and its 10 furnished cottages. And 40 campsites offer direct contact with the surrounding natural beauty. On a pretty weekend when the Arnold Palmer signature golf course is in full swing, the place is livelier than bygone Roanoke during harvest season.

Stonewall Jackson Lake's clear waters and 82 miles of shoreline make the state's second-largest lake extremely popular with anyone who likes to boat and fish. Largemouth bass, muskie, crappie, catfish, and bluegills are more likely to take your bait here than at any other West Virginia lake. The bass fishing rates among the best in the nation. The lake's tailwaters are stocked with trout.

Little Sorrel, the resort's 100-passenger excursion boat, provides regular lake tours. Smaller watercraft are available to rent and are the perfect way to enjoy the beautiful lake and surrounding landscape. Call (888) 278-8150.

Among the resort's numerous short trails, the 3.5-mile Hevener's Orchard Trail leads past an overgrown orchard where West Virginia's first patented apple, the Red York, first appeared. The Cairns Trail travels along a line of small stone towers, walls, and rock piles that have become an archaeological curiosity. The mysterious stone structures, called cairns, have been remarkably difficult to place in history. Some believe they might have been constructed by Native Americans, while others note a likeness to the dry stone walls of Ireland.

If you're more of an indoor person, you could conceivably spend your whole vacation in the grand, Adirondack-style Stonewall Resort lodge. When you tire of ogling the lake and mountains, you could swim in the indoor/outdoor pool, mellow out in the hot tub, check out the game room, or try any of two dozen services at Mountain Laurel Spa—from a coconut scrub to an artsy nail polish to the Golfer's Advantage massage. The Time for Two pampers two with massages, facials, manicures, pedicures, and champagne.

Stillwaters restaurant continues the lodge's tradition of pampering with locally sourced favorites such as corn-crusted rainbow trout, cherry-smoked brisket, and farmers' market salad. The upholstered twig furniture is surprisingly comfy, so you can blame it if you have a hard time pushing away from the table.

Of course you should get outside. The 3,800-acre park offers dinner cruises, miles of hiking and biking trails, a wildlife exhibit, a 374-slip marina with boat rentals, and an outstanding golf course. The cart-only golf course reputedly is not for the faint of heart. However, six sets of tees give golfers of various abilities a chance to score.

The golf course, cottages, and resort are operated by Benchmark Hospitality, which also developed the $42 million project within the state park. The park and resort are open year-round. Call (304) 269-7400 or check out stone-wallresort.com for more information.

About 15 miles east of Stonewall Jackson Lake is the community of **Buck-hannon,** named one of the Top 100 Small Towns in America by Random House books. It's a college town with a surprising number of unusual attractions, including a 40-seat underground theater where foreign and independent films are screened each Friday evening at 7:30. Patrons often bring wine to share. The **Lascaux Micro-Theater,** named after a French cave, is located at the rear entrance of 33 E. Main St. (304-473-1818) underneath founder Bryson Von Nostrand's architecture office. Von Nostrand has created a small restaurant and an intimate music venue in the bottom floor of the same Main Street building.

Another nearby attraction is **West Virginia Wesleyan College,** the largest private institution of higher learning in the state. Founded in 1890 by the Methodist Church, West Virginia Wesleyan is a learning community of more than 1,200 students from 30 countries. Take a stroll around the beautiful, century-old, Georgian-style campus near the Buckhannon River and recall your school days. Be sure to duck into the gorgeous **Wesley Chapel,** a classic Greek Revival structure that seats 1,600 worshippers, making it the largest church in the state. The chapel, with its signature white steeple and Casavant organ with 1,500 pipes, holds regular religious services as well as special performing arts events, lectures, and community activities. The adjacent rhododendron garden blooms spectacularly in the late spring and early summer. During the tour you may also notice the modern Rockefeller Athletic Center, named for WVWC's former president Jay Rockefeller, also once the governor of West Virginia and now a US senator. Campus tours are available, and reservations are requested. To make arrangements, call (304) 473-8000.

If you're in Buckhannon in the middle of May, you're in luck—the city's most anticipated event is forthcoming. The **Strawberry Festival** promotes the harvesting of the local crop of berries. This weeklong event includes three days of parades with bands from all over the US, dozens of floats, and even a Strawberry Queen and her court floating down Strawberry Lane. Tons of strawberries are served every imaginable way—and then some. Senior citizens are invited to compete in the "capping" of the strawberries, a contest of speed in removing the hulls. You'll also find the usual festival food fare along with music and scores of craft exhibits, antique cars, and sports competitions. For more information on the citywide festival, call (304) 472-9036 or visit wvstraw-berryfestival.com.

Two miles north of town is an unusual attraction: a tree with a great story. At the spot where Turkey Run Creek enters the Buckhannon River (just off US

119), look for the **Pringle Tree.** This large, hollow sycamore tree is the third-generation descendant of one that provided shelter for two brothers, John and Samuel Pringle, who had deserted from the British army. The brothers ran from Fort Pitt (now Pittsburgh) in 1761 and, on finding the tree in 1764, lived in its cavernous base for more than three years before venturing away from the area for ammunition. When they discovered the war was over, they returned to civilization but soon came back to the area to show others where they had lived in the wild. As legend goes, the party was so impressed by the bounty of the land, they decided to settle the area, making the spot the first permanent settlement west of the Alleghenies in Virginia. The tree is symbolic of the movement into the western frontier.

Pringle Tree Park is open May 1 to November 1 during daylight hours. Facilities include picnic grounds, a playground, bathrooms, a boat launch, and ample fishing spots on the West Fork River. Call (304) 472-1722 or visit visit-buckhannon.org for more information.

The more recent history of this area has been linked with its manufacture of fine glassware. Although most of the glass factories have closed, a Buckhannon artisan is following his heart to continue the craft. **Ron Hinkle Glass** studio and gallery are open for demonstrations of the old art of glassblowing, Mon through Fri, 9 a.m. to 3 p.m. You can visit his gallery between 9 a.m. and 5 p.m. Mon through Fri and 9 a.m. to 2 p.m. Sat. To get there, take Route 20 south from Buckhannon 5 miles to Sago Road and follow the signs.

Yes, it is the same road that leads to nearby Sago mine, where 12 miners died on January 2, 2006. The road, renamed **Coal Miners' Memorial Roadway,** follows the winding Buckhannon River to the now-closed mine. Near the mine and beside the Sago Church, a small park commemorates the miners. A 6-foot **Sago Miners' Memorial** is etched with the photographs of each of the miners who died and bears a quote from the note Sago miner Martin Toler Jr. left for his family: "We'll see you on the other side." A nearby bench is adorned with the photo of the sole Sago mine disaster survivor, Randal McCloy.

Ten miles south of the Sago turnoff on Route 20 is the community of **French Creek** and the **West Virginia State Wildlife Center.** The center has roots in a game farm established on this 329-acre tract during the 1920s. The original facilities were beyond renovation, so an entirely new exhibit area was designed and built beginning in 1984. The woodland enclosures allow the animals to interact with their environment and exhibit more natural behavior.

Many visitors come out especially to see French Creek Freddie, the weather-prognosticating groundhog who appears on television around February 2. Each Groundhog Day, Wildlife Center staff wake the grumpy rodent and bring him out of his winter hibernation hole to allow him to look for his shadow and predict the severity of the remaining six weeks of winter. After making his forecast before an audience of hundreds of groundhog fans, including news media from around the state, Freddie is eager to get back to bed. Visitors to the center can also see elk, bison, mountain lions, timber wolves, white-tailed deer, black bears, coyotes, river otters, and many species of birds, all native or formerly native to the state, in their natural habitat. Although Jack, a 700-pound black bear, died after 21 years at French Creek, he's back now, stuffed for display in the gift shop. Other animals can be seen along a 1.2-mile wheelchair-accessible loop walkway through the habitat lined with interpretive signs to help you learn more about the animals and their impact on West Virginia history.

Enjoy the picnic area, then take a walk to check out the snake exhibit so you know what to be afraid of, and what not to be. The park is open year-round. Hours are 9 a.m. to 5 p.m. April through Oct. and 9 a.m. to 3 p.m. Nov. through March. Admission is $4 for adults, $2 for children under 15, and free Nov through Mar. For information call (304) 924-6211 or visit www.wvdnr.gov/wildlife/wildlifecenter.shtm.

If you're fortunate enough to be in the Mountain Lakes region in mid-March, then by all means head over to the aptly named Lewis County town of *Ireland,* about 10 miles west of Rock Cave. By the second week of March, most West Virginia fields are beginning to green—a rich, dark green, reminiscent of the rolling hills of the Emerald Isle itself. In the town of Ireland, the locals are celebrating their Celtic roots with one of the state's most festive Irish celebrations. The weeklong *Irish Spring Festival,* usually starting around the 15th of the month and always including St. Patrick's Day, is alive with so-called pot o' luck dinners, Mulligan stew cook-offs, Irish gospel choirs, leprechaun contests, Irish jig contests, harp concerts, road bowling, a parade, a kite-flying contest, and many more distinctively Irish pastimes.

The region around Ireland, like most of West Virginia and the southern Appalachians, was settled by Irish and Scottish pioneers, many of whom were ostracized by the British gentry who owned the sprawling plantations of the flatter and infinitely more fertile lowlands of Virginia, the Carolinas, and Georgia. Irelanders claim their community was first settled by an Irishman named Andrew Wilson, a gentleman who in his later years was known affectionately as "Old Ireland." According to local legend, Wilson "lived to see 114 springtimes." When folks from around the countryside learned of this long life, many were convinced that there was something about the quality of life in Ireland—West Virginia—that was conducive to long life. Hence the town grew in numbers and prestige. Today it's home to a little more than 200 souls, but the population more than doubles during the festival. The town also receives a deluge of cards and letters from around the country to be postmarked "Ireland" for St. Patrick's Day. For more information on the festival, contact the Lewis County Convention and Visitors Bureau at (304) 269-7328.

Lodging is somewhat scarce along the back roads of the Mountain Lakes region, so you might want to take a spin over to **Holly River State Park,** located just off Route 20 at Hacker Valley on the northern tip of Webster County. The park is the state's second largest in area; 10 fully equipped cabins of rustic stone or logs are interspersed among the lushly forested hills and along the namesake river. Trout fishing is good here, especially in the spring and fall, when trout raised in the park pond are released in the river. The park also has a visitor center, pool, and game courts. Its **Holly River Restaurant**, open daily in summer and on weekends in the spring and fall, has been named one of West Virginia's unique places to dine several times. The friendly cook will chat with you about menu items and let you know if a local farmer has just delivered sweet corn or blueberries. Featured menu items

Playing in the Road

Brush up on your underhand throw. There's a new old sport catching on in central West Virginia. The West Virginia Irish road-bowling season goes into swing in March with the Irish Spring Festival in—of course—Ireland, West Virginia.

Like their Irish counterparts who started the game 350 years ago, these strong-armed bowlers hurl an iron ball down a 1.2- to 2-mile country-road course. The player or team reaching the finish line in the fewest shots wins. A good shot, not counting the 15-foot running start, is 150 yards. The Mountain State record is 422 yards, but it was downhill—well, it's hard to find a flat place in West Virginia.

Veteran bowlers compete side by side with newcomers and giggling sixth-grade girls at these friendly events. Eleven years ago David Powell saw a televised Irish road-bowling game and brought the sport back to West Virginia, where it has been gaining popularity on back roads.

"We've had record numbers for most of our matches lately," says Powell, who has been coordinating Irish road bowling throughout West Virginia for the past decade.

The West Virginia road-bowling circuit holds nearly 20 events on 14 stretches of road throughout the state. The season opens annually with Lewis County's Irish Spring Festival and ends with the Yankee Skedaddle at nearby Stonewall Resort in November. In between, bowlers keep their arms in shape through competitions at the West Virginia Strawberry Festival, Mountain State Forest Festival, Preston County Buckwheat Festival, Barbour County Fair, and events at West Virginia state parks. For more information, contact the West Virginia Road Bowling Association at (202) 387-1680 or http://www.wvirb.com.

include chocolate peanut butter pie, blackberry cobbler, roast beef, and spiced pork chops. If you're looking for a more primitive experience, Holly River has 88 campsites, all wooded and private with outdoor fireplaces and grills. Don't leave the park without hiking over to the 2 scenic waterfalls, Tecumseh and Tenskwatawa. Call (304) 493-6353, or check the website at wvstateparks.com/park/holly-river-state-park

If you're looking for a little regional entertainment while at Holly River Park, look no further than *Jerry Run Summer Theater,* just 1.5 miles north on Route 20. Saturday nights are devoted to bluegrass in its many shades, from traditional to newgrass, young grass, and gospel. Sometimes you'll hear classic rock and roll too at this rustic theater seating 150. Allegheny Outback Bluegrass, Little Roy & Lizzy, Staats & Shafer, West Virginia Travelers, Blessed Beyond—you hear the talented musicians of the region on this stage.

Shows begin at 7 p.m. on Saturday, and occasionally Friday too. Admission is usually $5 for adults and $3 for children. For information, call (304) 493-6574 or visit online at members.citynet.net/jerryrun.

Four miles north of Weston is *Jackson's Mill Historic Area,* the boy-hood home of Confederate legend General Thomas "Stonewall" Jackson. His grandparents settled the land and built the area's first gristmill along the banks of the West Fork River. Their son Cummins, Thomas's uncle, took possession of the property upon the death of his father and ran the lucrative business, which included two mills, carpenter and blacksmith shops, and a store. While Thomas Jackson had a hard early life, orphaned before age 8, he remembered good times growing up at Jackson's Mill. Now, more than 150 years after Jackson's death, the farmstead visitors see looks much as it did when Jackson roamed its fields in the 1830s. He lived with various aunts and uncles in a cabin similar to the one on the site today.

The state-run farmstead allows visitors to experience such Appalachian farm crafts as gristmilling, weaving, spinning, basket making, candle dipping, woodworking, blacksmithing, paper marbling, and other heritage arts. These activities are set against a historic backdrop that features the original mill as well as a newer, turbine-powered mill that grinds corn and wheat. The historic area includes the Jackson Mill Museum, a functioning gristmill, and the Moun-tain State Heritage Center.

In addition to site-milled flours, the general store sells West Virginia pre-serves and crafts; it's also a sitting spot after you've toured the 523-acre farm. Don't miss the half-hour film on the life of Stonewall Jackson; then feel free to wander among the artifacts, tools, and other items remaining from another era. See the apple-butter kettle, the chicken-watering jug, the varmint trap, and the cheese press, among other authentic curios.

Also of interest on the property are **Blaker Mill** and the **McWhorter Cabin.** The mill, disassembled stone by stone from another part of the county and moved to its new location at Jackson's Mill, is a fully operating gristmill. Today you can see 19th-century technology at work as locally grown grains, actually used in the conference center's kitchen (see later), are ground and even sold to the public.

The 200-year-old, hand-hewn log McWhorter cabin, also relocated here, was the handiwork of Henry McWhorter, a New Yorker who had served in the Revolutionary War before moving south. He and his family lived in the one-room cabin for 37 years. It is located on the original site where the Jackson home once stood. Admission is $4 for adults, $2 for children under 12. Jackson's Mill is open Memorial Day through Labor Day from 10 a.m. to 4 p.m. and on weekends only in Apr, May, Sept, and Oct; closed Mon. For further information and specific times, call (304) 269-5100 or visit jacksonsmill. wvu.edu.

If you're near Jackson's Mill in the summer, stay around for one of the best festivals anywhere in the US. Usually around Labor Day weekend, hundreds of artisans gather here for the **Jackson's Mill Jubilee** exhibit traditional Appalachian handicrafts. Blown and stained glass, pottery, quilts and dolls, handmade lace, and dozens of other items are displayed here.

Crafters aren't the only ones who show up. This is one of the state's premier mountain music showcases. Singers and musicians from around the region put on quite a show with mountain dulcimers, guitars, banjos, and fiddles echoing through the hills deep into the night, along with the stomping of cloggers. History buffs, meanwhile, will enjoy the eerily realistic Civil and Revolutionary War battle reenactments, while others will enjoy workshops in mandolin and banjo playing. Past turkey-calling champions compete in turkey- and owl-calling contests. With all that gawking you'll be doing, you'll need sustenance. Mouthwatering vittles are everywhere, including pork barbecue sandwiches, catfish platters, cobblers, corn bread and beans, pancakes, barbecued chicken, and ice cream made on the spot. Call (304) 997-4141 Mon through Fri, 9 a.m. to 4 p.m., for admission prices and further information. Visit jacksonsmill. wvu .edu.

When you're through enjoying the historic area at Jackson's Mill, it's time to take in the park's more modern amenities. Today it has a beautiful stone **Conference Center** providing year-round activities for those seeking to get away from the office or simply to take a vacation. Originally a youth camp (this was the site of the nation's first state 4-H camp, established in 1921), it now has a contemporary 24-room stone lodge and 14 cottages to house guests. Various private rooms also are scattered around the campus. More than 20 meeting facilities are available for groups as large as 400 or as few as 10.

Rates are very reasonable and in the off-season are offered at a sizeable discount for Sunday through Friday morning stays for groups. For information, call (304) 269-6140.

The Mountain Park

The rugged lifestyle and athletic prowess of the lumberjacks—those responsible for timber harvesting—are brought to life every spring at the **Webster County Woodchopping Festival** in Webster Springs. The backbreaking competition is held in late May, and choppers competing for the Southern World title hail from as far away as Australia and New Zealand. For the past several years, the finals of the competition have been televised on ESPN. For those who haven't been working on upper-body strength all year, there is a turkey calling contest, a 5K race, and a cornhole tournament as well as a truck show and craft fair. For more information on the festival, contact the Webster County Development Authority at (304) 847-7666 or visit woodchoppingfestival.org.

Another Webster County event not to be missed is the annual **Webster County Nature Tour** at Camp Caesar near Cowen the first weekend in May.

Elk Mountain is just one beautiful area covered by the annual Webster County Nature Tour. A favorite activity is the hike up an old railroad grade along Leatherwood Creek for 2.5 miles to Leatherwood Falls. Aqua-green water roars 30 feet over a rock ledge to a pool below. All weekend activity is centered in Camp Caesar's 300 wooded acres. **Camp Caesar** has been open since 1922 and offers 10 rustic cabins. Sleeping arrangements for the weekend are dormitory style, and guests need to bring pillows and sleeping bags.

The cost for the weekend event is under $150 per person. The fee covers accommodations, tours, refreshments, 5 meals served over the 3 days, and entertainment for 2 days. Besides the nature tour, the camp hosts a ramp dinner, concerts, and various summer camps. For more information, call Camp Caesar at (304) 226-3888 or visit Camp Caesar at Facebook.com.

Perhaps more than any other Mountain State county, Webster County lays claim to world-class fishing in numerous crystalline mountain streams and rivers. Truly outstanding trout fishing can be experienced in the Williams River, Cranberry River, and Elk River above Webster Springs. Special regulation areas, such as the fly-fishing-only section on the Dogway Fork of the Cranberry River and the catch-and-release trout fishing areas on the Back Fork of Elk, Cranberry, Williams, and upper Elk Rivers may appeal to the Orvis crowd. If you're seeking the West Virginia golden trout, try the Little Kanawha River, Holly River, Sugar Creek, Fall Run, and Desert Fork. The West Virginia Department of Natural Resources lists the Elk and Little Kanawha Rivers among the

The Golden Apples of Clay County

Anderson Mullins of Clay County was mighty fond of apples, enough so that he traded a larger farm for his brother Bewell's 36 acres of bottomland and hillside orchards on Porters Creek.

A.H., as he was called, experimented with some stock from Stark Brothers Nursery, but he knew the golden apples that won him first prize at the Clay County Fair every year didn't come from any tree he'd planted. In September 1914 Mullins sent samples of the miraculous golden apples to Stark Brothers Nursery in Missouri. Paul Stark knew red apples dominated the market, so he wasn't impressed with the freckled yellow apples—until he took a bite.

"With one in hand, you can't be sure whether you're eating an apple or drinking champagne," Stark later wrote in his catalog. He hopped on a train, traveled over 1,000 miles, then rode a horse an additional 25 miles to a remote farm near the Clay/Kanawha County line. The tree was everything he'd hoped for—vigorous, prolific, and able to produce large golden apples that stayed crisp until spring.

Although no one knows for sure how much he offered the Mullins family—some say $5,000; others say $10,000—when Stark left, the tree was enclosed in a wire cage and Stark Brothers had a deed for the 900-square-foot plot it stood on.

The Golden Delicious, as Stark named it, came about by accident. The result of natural pollination, the apple was literally created by the birds and the bees. Within two years the grafts he took back to Missouri were producing apples, and word of the "great, glowing, glorious apple" spread across the nation.

The great horticulturist Luther Burbank wrote, "After observing the Golden Delicious in my experimental gardens . . . I have no hesitation in stating that it is the greatest apple in all the world."

Although the original Mullins Golden Delicious tree died in the 1950s, a roadside plaque marks the spot where it once sprouted. In 1973 Clay County baked up a 6-foot apple pie and began the annual tradition of a *Golden Delicious Festival*.

To find it, go to downtown Clay on the third weekend of September and follow the scent of baked apples, or call (304) 587-7652 or see claygoldendeliciousfestival.com.

state's best smallmouth bass streams. What aren't listed are the best native trout streams—small, cold tributaries with shaded pools deep in the forest. After a day of wandering along the rivers, it's time to relax in the pool or picnic grounds at *Baker's Island Recreation Area,* in the Elk River right in downtown Webster Springs.

A three-quarter-mile boardwalk called *Lover's Lane* is another Webster Springs attraction. David Gillespie, who was nearly 80 when he finished constructing the walkway, was too young to remember seeing the original boardwalk that snaked along the Back Fork of the Elk River near his home. But the retired university librarian devoted five years and a pile of money to bring that boardwalk back.

The original boardwalk was erected along the steep bank of river in 1875 by retired Confederate army Captain Benjamin Conrad to spare his gristmill customers a slog over the perpetually muddy road. With sweeping views of the river, the boardwalk became a popular venue for strolling and acquired the nickname "Lovers Lane." It was featured on postcards and became the site of wedding ceremonies. Webster Springs enjoyed an era as a mineral springs resort with six hotels catering to guests who sought to boost their health in the town's salt sulfur spring waters. But by the 1940s, the town's era as a spa destination was ending and the saggy boardwalk was torn down.

Gillespie bought land where the original boardwalk was located and worked solo several years before realizing he was in over his head. He had to tear down the first two sections of his work and start over with a crew to secure the 4-foot-wide boardwalk to the steep slope. The walkway includes three rain shelters as well as angler access to the river. Swinging bridges near each end of the boardwalk connect with a trail on the other side of creek, creating a two-mile hiking loop. Visitors are urged to take a relaxing stroll over Lovers Lane and enjoy the local scenery.

mountain lakestrivia

The Elk River, which bisects central West Virginia, is widely regarded as one of the best trout fisheries in the state.

No matter the season, folks around Webster Springs are screaming for, not ice cream, but **_Custard Stand_** custard. The chain started here as a takeout dairy back in 1991, offering zany ice cream flavors such as root beer, apricot, and watermelon, as well as a century-old family recipe for hot dog chili. Folks loved the chili so much that the Cowger family converted a car wash behind their restaurant into a USDA-approved production facility and began selling to groceries, restaurants, and convenience stores in more than 13 states. Custard Stands have sprung up in Flatwoods, Oak Hill and Summersville, West Virginia. The Cowger family still operates the original Custard Stand from 10 a.m. to 10 p.m. daily year-round on Route 20 a short walk from Baker's Island in Webster Springs. To find out more, see custardstand.com or call (304) 847-7774.

Places to Stay in the Mountain Lakes Region

BUCKHANNON

Bicentennial Inn
90 E. Main St.
(304) 472-5000 or
bicentennialinn.com
Moderate

JANE LEW

Sunny Pointe Guest House
374 Linden Lane
(304) 884-7935
Sunnypointewv.com
Expensive

RICHWOOD

Guest House & Cottage of Richwood
76E Walnut St.
(304) 276-9105
Moderate

SUMMERSVILLE

Chalets at the Lake
4357 Summersville Lake Rd.
(304) 741-4459
bchaletsatthelake.com
Inexpensive to moderate

Sleep Inn
701 Professional Park Dr.
(304) 872-4500
choicehotels.com
Moderate

SUTTON

Days Inn by Wyndham
350 Days Dr.
(304) 765-5055
www.wyndhamhotels.com/
days-inn/sutton
Moderate to expensive

WEBSTER SPRINGS

Mineral Springs Motel
1 Spring St.
(304) 847-5305
mineralspringsmotel.net
Inexpensive

FOR MORE INFORMATION

Upshur County Convention and Visitors Bureau
(304) 473-1400
visitupshur.org

Lewis County Convention and Visitors Bureau
(304) 296-7328
stonewallcountry.com

Summersville Convention and Visitors Bureau
(304) 872-3722
summersvillecvb.com

Webster County Economic Development Authority
(304) 847-2145
websterwv.com

Richwood Convention & Visitors Bureau
(304) 846-9218
richwoodchamberofcommerce.org

Places to Eat in the Mountain Lakes Region

BUCKHANNON

CJ Maggie's American Grill
16 E. Main St.
(304) 472-6522
cj-maggies.com
Moderate

88 Restaurant & Lounge
88 E. Main St.
(304) 473-1988
88loungewv.com
Moderate to expensive

Hillbilly Grill
1235 Stonecoal Road
(304) 471-2223
Inexpensive

SUMMERSVILLE

Gad Dam Brewing
922 Broad St
(304) 880-5735
G.D.B at Facebook.com
Moderate

Original Flavor Bistro
860 Broad St
(304) 872-2301
Facebook.com/
originalflavorbistrowv
Moderate

The Vault on Main
800 Main ST
(304) 872-1770
thevaultonmainwv.com

New River/Greenbrier Valley Region

The New River/Greenbrier River region offers the most diversity in land, character, and attractions of any area of the state. These eight counties in southeastern West Virginia make up a land of extremes—stupendous wealth in the millionaires' homes in historic Bramwell and the grinding poverty of played-out mining towns several miles away; the pristine Greenbrier River as well as creeks choked with mining runoff or buried by mountaintop removal operations. It's a region of piercing beauty and glaring neglect, of comely horse farms and crumbling coal camps, of ATVs, waterfalls, and hickory-club golf. That's what makes it such an interesting place to visit. Take your time on the back roads (don't try to do otherwise on the notorious county one-laners); stop at the country stores, diners, and roadside attractions. This is diverse, quirky America at its best.

The Greenbrier and Bluestone Valleys

This scenic stretch in southeastern West Virginia runs roughly from White Sulphur Springs in the north to the Bluestone River Gorge in the south and contains virtually all of Greenbrier and

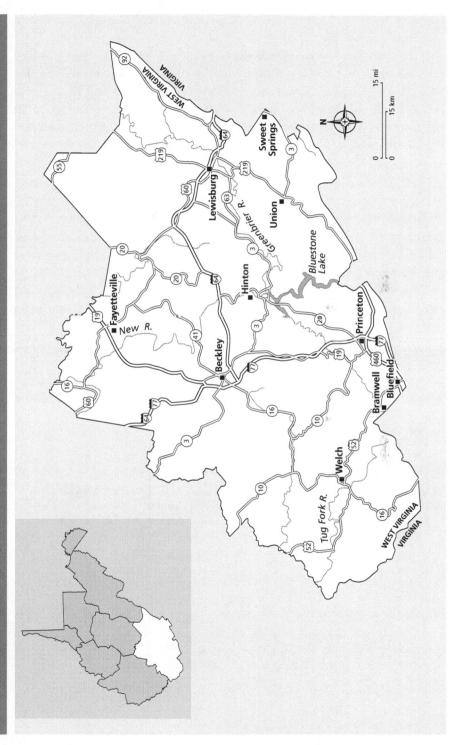

NEW RIVER/GREENBRIER VALLEY REGION

Summers Counties. It's a region of verdant rolling farmland, inviting old inns, and remote getaways.

The luxurious **Greenbrier Resort** (greenbrier.com) is perhaps the most on-the-beaten-path attraction in West Virginia. (You know you're on the beaten path when your past clientele has included Prince Rainier and 26 US presidents.) There are, however, some off-the-beaten-path features here, such as the **Greenbrier Bunker.** This secret hideaway—at least it was until the *Washington Post* blew its cover in 1992—is a 112,000-square-foot maze of barracks and storage areas reserved for congressmen and other government officials in case of a nuclear attack. The two-story underground structure was designed to accommodate 1,500 people at a time. The site was selected because the Greenbrier has always been a popular vacation spot for politicians and other members of Washington officialdom. It is also far from any large population center, yet accessible by interstate, Amtrak, and an airport boasting the Mountain State's longest runway. The outside entrance to the bunker no longer remains a well-kept secret, even though Washington is trying to distance itself from this embarrassing relic of the cold war. The renovated bunker is open for

BEST ANNUAL EVENTS IN THE NEW RIVER/ GREENBRIER VALLEY REGION

Historic Bramwell's Tour of Homes
Bramwell; second Saturday in
May and December
(304) 248-8381 or (800) 221-3206

WV Renaissance Festival
Lewisburg; every weekend in June
(304) 992-6178
wvrenfest.com

**Appalachian String Band
Music Festival**
Clifftop; early August
(304) 438-3005
Facebook.com/stringband

State Fair of West Virginia
Lewisburg/Fairlea
second week of August
(304) 645-1090
statefairofwv.com

Appalachian Makers Market
Beckley; late August
(304) 252-7328
appalachianfestival.net

Taste of Our Towns (TOOT) Fest
second Saturday in October
(304) 645-7917
Carnegiehallwv.org

Hinton Railroad Days
Hinton; mid-October
(304) 466-5420
hintonwva.com/rrdays.html

New River Gorge Bridge Day
Fayetteville; mid-October
(800) 927-0263
officialbridgeday.com

tours several times each week at the cost of $39 for adults, $20 for children over 10. (This tour doesn't accept younger children.) Call (304) 536-7810.

Guests visiting the revered five-star resort for the day or longer have myriad options for filling their time, with new ones coming on line all the time. With the purchase of the Greenbrier by Jim Justice in 2009, the resort has added a casino (for overnight guests only). Like the bunker, it's underground. Take a spin on 320 slot machines, try your luck at 37 table games including blackjack, craps, roulette, baccarat, and three-card poker, or test your skill at the Texas Hold'em poker tables. Or stop by Twelve Oaks and place your wager on the horses at tracks around the country.

The sportsman or -woman will want to head up Kate's Mountain to the Greenbrier Gun Club for sporting clays, skeet, and trap. Pheasant-hunting excursions are also available. The facilities are open to beginners and advanced marksmen alike.

For those more inclined to watch wild creatures, a falconry academy is offered in the ancient art of working with raptors. Now add a roster of other activities, including shooting the whitewater down West Virginia's Gauley or New Rivers, flying along the zipline over Mill Creek, hitting the trails on a mountain bike, swimming in the infinity-edge pool, learning how to make truffles, taking the spa treatment, or playing a round on one of the famed golf courses.

While you're in the interested in the history of golf, why not take a short drive over to the nine-hole course in White Sulphur Springs to see the first US golf course and organized golf club in 1884—***Oakhurst Links.*** Purchased by the Greenbrier in 2012, the Links also boasts having the first known golf tournament in the States, in 1888.

Although the historic course has been closed due to extensive flood damage, golfers here once played on a rough Scottish green, use hickory clubs, and hit gutta-percha balls off tees fashioned from sand and water—the same way it was done more than 130 years ago. Players in knickers and wandering sheep no longer frequent the course, but a small museum in the clubhouse is awaiting renovation. For information, see greenbrier.com/Golf/Oakhurst.aspx.

The village of White Sulphur Springs is unusual in that it has a national trout hatchery on Main Street at the east (Oakhurst Links) end of town. ***White Sulphur Springs National Fish Hatchery*** is one of three primary broodstock stations in the nation for rainbow trout. The small hatchery harvests rainbow trout eggs from adult fish and ships about 10 million eggs per year to 20 state, federal, and tribal hatcheries in 13 states. It also raises freshwater mussels to shore up endangered species and replace those lost in toxic spills.

The hatchery began raising freshwater mussels, also known as freshwater clams, from the Ohio River in 1995 after a toxic spill near Marietta, Ohio, killed a million mussels. Mussels are natural water filters, removing impurities as they draw in water. They are vital in maintaining stream water quality. Unfortunately, about 70 percent of them are extinct, endangered, or in need of special protection. To make things trickier, mussels also need more than the usual amount of luck to reproduce; the hatchery with its tight, happy-hour crowd of mussels can dramatically increase the little bivalves' odds. The female mussels' eggs are fertilized by sperm she draws inside her when she siphons water. For most species, if a male of her kind isn't nearby upstream sending out sperm, she can't reproduce.

Visitors to the hatchery can view trout in the pool beside the visitor center, in the raceways, and through the windows of the broodstock building. The mussels are in an earthen pond. Although the grounds are open all the time, the hatchery facilities and visitor center are open to visitors only Mon through Fri, 8 a.m. to 3 p.m. You have two tour options: self-guided with a brochure from the visitor center, or a free guided tour that must be arranged a week in advance by calling (304) 536-1361. In addition to its open houses, the hatchery hosts a May fishing derby and a free October Freshwater Folk Festival to raise environmental awareness. For information, visit wsshatcheryfriends.org.

If you'd like to try your hand at fishing in the wild, you have many choices. But **Summit Lake** on Route 39 north of Rainelle can give you an experience with four types of trout. Consisting of 43 acres of lake and 33 campsites, the public Lake Summit Recreational Area has an electric-motor boat ramp and accessible fishing piers. It's fully stocked with rainbow, brown, brook, and West Virginia golden trout. Hiking trails are nearby. Call (304) 846-2695 for more information.

Tours galore are available in historic **Lewisburg** (downtownLewisburg .com), the Greenbrier County seat. The 230-plus-year-old community, located about 10 miles west of White Sulphur Springs on US 60, has more than seventy 18th- and 19th-century historic sites (for public tours call North House Museum at 304-645-3398), not to mention Civil War battle reenactments, dozens of antiques and specialty shops, 8 art galleries, a fall ghost tour, and a chocolate festival.

Antiques shops in Lewisburg come in many forms—you'll see antiques and crafts combos, antiques in art galleries, even antiques and fabrics, as well as **Robert's Antiques,** touted as "Lewisburg's finest antiques, gourmet, and wine shop." Besides holding wine tastings, Robert's displays a gorgeous collection of hand-carved bars, podiums, confessionals, cabinets, and a "medical museum" full of medical antiques, as well as caviar, pâté, and specialty meats in its food section. Other not-to-miss stops on the 5-block tour of Lewisburg are **Brick House Antiques,** the contemporary **Harmony Ridge Gallery, Cooper**

Gallery, Lee Street Studios, A New Chapter Bookstore, and 2 upscale cloth-iers who also deal in art, *Wolf Creek Gallery* and *High Country Boutique.* *Antique Cabins and Barns,* across from the *Lewis Theatre* on Court Street, specializes in the recovery and restoration of 19th-century hand-hewn log and timberframe structures. They have a gallery of construction and decorating projects done with aged wood, antique wide-plank flooring, and hand-hewn beams that will have you viewing old barns in a new light. This wonderfully pedestrian-friendly town also offers two great bakeries, a kitchen store, and several of the Mountain State's best eateries, including the French Goat, Star-dust Cafe, and the General Lewis restaurant.

One of the best walking tours begins at 105 Church St. in the *Carnegie Hall building.* Yes, there is another Carnegie Hall, and most locals refer to the New York cultural institution as "the other one." Just like its Big Apple coun-terpart, Lewisburg's Carnegie Hall was funded entirely by the iconoclastic busi-ness tycoon Andrew Carnegie. Interestingly, it was the first electrically lighted public building in town and in this corner of West Virginia. Built in 1902, the ornate four-story building is the artistic nerve center of Lewisburg. It houses 11 classrooms and 3 art galleries. The centerpiece 500-seat auditorium stages drama, musical, and performance-art productions throughout the year and is now supported by local contributions. A free lunchtime piano concert second and third Tuesdays is popular around town. The building is open year-round Mon through Fri 9 a.m. to 4:30 p.m., Sat 10 a.m. to 1 p.m. Call (304) 645-7917, or visit carnegiehallwv.com.

Carnegie's neighbor across Church Street is the *Old Stone Presbyterian Church,* the oldest Protestant church building in continuous use west of the Alleghenies. On any weekday between 9 a.m. and 2 p.m., you can sit in one of the boxed pews or climb up to the balcony where slaves sat in ladderback chairs. Except for electricity and cushioned seats, the old church looks much the same as it did in 1796, when some parishioners walked 20 miles from places like Renick's Valley, Irish Corner, and Big Clear Creek for services. Guests are always welcome to join the congregation for the 11 a.m. service each Sunday.

North House Museum sits on the opposite side of a wide, green lawn from Carnegie Hall. A wing removed in the 20th century was recently restored to the 1820 former hotel, giving ample accommodations for the Greenbrier Historical Society's genealogical archives. These documents date from 1778 to the present and contain the signatures of Thomas Jefferson, George Wash-ington, and James Monroe. The museum also houses a fabulous collection of wedding gowns from 1820 to the mid-1900s, a Conestoga wagon, and an 1896 buggy used to deliver mail to the first RFD (rural free delivery) postal custom-ers in the nation. The postmaster general at that time hailed from the Mountain

State, so his first three pilot routes were in West Virginia—in Charles Town. The second-oldest quilt in the nation—a 1795 broderie perse design—shares museum space with Confederate general Robert E. Lee's saddle and a chair he willed to his servant. But the artifacts of the everyday life of the common citizen are most evident here—the tools, weapons, and kitchen implements of people who worked the soil and fought off marauding Shawnees. Hoop skirts, stiff hats, and teacups are part of the education here at North House. Children are encouraged to dress up in 1850 costumes supplied by the museum as they learn the customs and manners of the day while sipping afternoon tea. To participate, call ahead for reservations at (304) 654-3398. This is also the number to arrange for a stimulating guided tour of the museum—one that will explain the torture device in the nursery as well as the true story of the Greenbrier Ghost.

The museum has created a historical escape room with an appropriate historic storyline in its 1799 Barracks house downtown. The scenario involves using clues—many historical—to "escape" to freedom on the frontier within an hour. The *Barracks Escape Room* experience requires 2–6 participants and is available for $25 per person by reservation at 304-645-3398 (Mon through Sat 10 a.m. to 4 p.m.).

No matter when you visit, you can still pay your respects at the cross-shaped mass grave of 95 unknown soldiers at the *Confederate Cemetery* on McElhenny Street and view the cannonball that is still stuck in the southwest corner of John Wesley Methodist Church.

For a small town (population about 3,800), Lewisburg has a surprisingly vibrant night life. Besides performances at Carnegie Hall and weekend movies on the big screen of Lewis Theatre, Trillium Performing Arts dance offers performances at the Lewis Theatre. The downtown *Greenbrier Valley Theatre* offers more options. West Virginia's official state professional theater presents dramatic productions, concerts, high-definition broadcasts of New York's Metropolitan Opera, and literary events for children and adults almost every weekend. "The Greenbrier Ghost," an annual favorite, tells the local legend of a young woman who came back from the grave to convict her murderer. The venue can be reached at (304) 645-3838 or gvtheatre.org.

Musical offerings are served up at Carnegie Hall, *Wild Bean Coffee Shop* downtown, and on Tuesday nights as well as the fourth Saturday of the month at neighboring Ronceverte's *American Heritage Music Hall.* Local bluegrass and true-blue country musicians start gathering at 7 p.m. in the hall. Call (304) 645-4667 for info.

Given all there is to do, you'll probably want to spend at least one night in Lewisburg. Try the 1834 *General Lewis Inn*—from there you can walk to almost anyplace in this safe little town—and a night with the general is like stepping into your own friendly little museum. The inn is chock-full of antique glass, china, and antiques. An old stagecoach used on the mineral springs circuit is parked out front. You can wander through the open guest rooms and pick which one you want for the night—there are 26 to choose from, each furnished with a bed more than a hundred years old and other period antiques. An occasional ghost is rumored to haunt room 208 in the east wing, but most folks say the scent of sumptuous country cooking is the only thing wafting through these halls. The dining room serves modern gourmet fare as well as country classics like baked ham with a chef's touch.

For a jaunt that's really off the beaten path, go underground at *Lost World Caverns* (lostworldcaverns.com) on one of Steve Silverberg's wild cave expeditions. You'll be outfitted with a lantern on your helmet, kneepads, and gloves because you'll be doing a bit of crawling through subterranean chambers few others behold. You're guaranteed to see a few sleeping little brown bats and maybe a salamander or cricket, but mostly it's just your group and the formations. You'll hear water dripping off the walls and the echo of your footsteps

Dick Pointer: Enslaved Hero

One of Lewisburg's most celebrated war heroes is buried in an African-American cemetery beside Carnegie Hall. On May 29, 1778, in the last significant American Indian raid on the Greenbrier region, Dick Pointer almost single-handedly fought off a band of Shawnees attempting to storm Fort Donnally while the militia slept upstairs.

As the Shawnees battered the door with tomahawks and began to force it open, Pointer seized a musket. He fired through the cracked door into the crowd of American Indians. They fell back, and Pointer was able to secure the log door with help from a white comrade.

Troops from Camp Union commanded by Captain William Johnston drove the Shawnees out of the Greenbrier region the next day. Four white settlers and 12 American Indians died in the battle, 10 miles north of Lewisburg.

While all the men who slept upstairs in the attack were granted land as defenders of the country, Pointer continued to be enslaved for the next 23 years. In 1795 he petitioned for a pension. It was denied. When local citizens heard the news, they built Pointer a cabin. He was finally granted his freedom in 1801.

Pointer died in 1827 and was buried with full military honors in the African-American cemetery across the street from the white cemetery. Two plaques and a large monument topped with a stone cannonball mark Pointer's final resting place, and his musket is on permanent display a few hundred yards away at North House Museum. None of those other soldiers at Fort Donnally, even Pointer's former master, Colonel Andrew Donnally, is memorialized in this way.

on stone. This cave harbors the oldest known stalagmite in the world (500,000 years) and the nation's largest stalactite, a 30-ton chandelier of pure white calcite. If you prefer light and open spaces, you can opt for the standard 0.5-mile self-guided tour. *Lost World Natural History Museum* contains castings of almost a dozen dinosaurs, as well as petrified dinosaur eggs and dung. Rocks and artifacts in the gift shop will tempt junior (and senior) geologists.

Lost World is open daily, 10 a.m. to 4 p.m. from Thanksgiving until Dec. 31, 9 a.m. to 5 p.m. on weekends only till April, and 9 a.m. to 7 p.m. in the summer. Rates are $12 for adults and $6 for kids under 13. Wild caving tours and gear rental are $79. To make wild caving reservations, call (304) 645-6677 or (866) 228-3778.

Five miles down US 219 from Lewisburg is the quiet town of Ronceverte (French for "Greenbrier") and the provocative *Organ Cave* nearby. Pioneers discovered the cave in 1704 and used it for shelter. However, when Thomas Jefferson visited the site in 1791, members of his party found the remains of a large three-toed sloth.

During the Civil War, Organ Cave sheltered soldiers, and at one point it served as a chapel for a thousand of General Robert E. Lee's beleaguered Confederate troops. The cave provided them with much more than solace. Water collected inside the cave was laden with potassium nitrate, which, when evaporated, produced saltpeter, a main ingredient of gunpowder. The cave became a major Confederate saltpeter supply source, and today 37 of the original 52 wooden saltpeter hoppers are preserved here.

Visitors to the cave, named for its "rock organ" formation resembling the pipes of a church organ, will discover there are more than 40 miles of mapped passageways. A one-hour guided tour will take you through cathedral-size rooms along a well-lighted path past myriad calcite formations and relics of the Civil War (as well as some formerly female and rather scruffy mannequins depicting soldiers drafted to mine saltpeter).

Tours are available year-round 10 a.m. to 4 p.m. Mon through Sat. From Nov 15 through Apr 1, reservations are recommended. Be sure to bring a jacket; underground temperatures remain a constant 55°F. Admission is $17 for adults and $7 for children 6 to 12 years old. Military discounts offered. Wild tours and gear are available for a variety of skill and endurance levels. Prices range from $30 for an easy two-hour trek to $250 for a long "undernighter" camping trip. A special ladies-only caving trip departs every Tuesday morning and is always 50 percent off the regular price. For information on tours, call (304) 645-7600 or visit organcave.com.

Nearby is the southern terminus of the *Greenbrier River Trail* (www .greenbrierrailtrailstatepark.com), a 77-mile Rails-to-Trails project that presents

BEST ATTRACTIONS IN THE NEW RIVER/ GREENBRIER VALLEY REGION

Beckley Exhibition Coal Mine
Beckley
(304) 256-1747
beckley.org/coalmine

Greenbrier River Trail
Caldwell to Cass
(304) 799-7416
www.greenbrierrivertrail.com

New River Gorge National Park
Glen Jean
(304) 465-0508
www.nps.gov/neri

Organ Cave
Ronceverte
(304) 645-7600
organcave.com

Outdoor Theatre West Virginia at Grandview
Beaver
(304) 256-6800 or (800) 666-9142
theatrewestvirginia.com

Pipestem Resort State Park
Pipestem
(304) 466-1800 or (800) CALL-WVA
wvstateparks.com/park/pipestem-resort-state-park.com

Tamarack: The Best of West Virginia Crafts
I-77, exit 45, Beckley
(304) 256-6843
tamarack.com

excellent family outing options including hiking, biking, and horseback riding. For those who don't know, the Rails-to-Trails program converts abandoned rail lines into nonmotorized multiuse trails. This trail runs from Caldwell, in Greenbrier County, to Cass, in Pocahontas County, crossing 35 bridges along the way. The trail follows along the banks of the mild Greenbrier River, the longest free-flowing river in the eastern US through hamlets such as Clover Lick, Beard, and Stony Bottom. A wide, level, gravel-covered trail makes for excellent family bicycling. Several area businesses offer bicycle rentals, bicycle repairs, shuttles, and overnight accommodations. The trail features a relaxed cycling atmosphere through some of the state's most beautiful scenery. The trail links two state forests, Greenbrier and Seneca. It also links two of the state's more popular state parks, Watoga and Cass Scenic Railroad State Park. *Free Spirit Adventures,* in Caldwell, near Lewisburg, offers bike rentals, guided tours, shuttle services, personal training, cycling instruction, and cottage rental on the Greenbrier River. For more information, call (304) 536-0333, or check freespiritadventures.com.

For those who don't want to walk the whole 77-mile trail but enjoy a little relaxing leg-stretching, *Riverwise Labyrinth* at the trail's southern terminus is the place to go. Geography students might notice something familiar about the twists and turns of the intricate concrete pathway. Actually, the labyrinth represents the Greenbrier River, with the central path copying the entire river and each path offshoot representing a smaller portion of the Greenbrier. Volunteers spent two summers building the labyrinth, which was blessed upon completion in 2006 by a visiting Tibetan Buddhist monk. Riverwise Labyrinth is located at the Caldwell boat launch, off US 60 east of Lewisburg. A popular spot for river enthusiasts, the boat launch has a picnic shelter and native plant garden.

Unless you're an avid perennial gardener, you probably don't know a hellebore from a heliotrope. But if you can appreciate the fact that deer eat almost anything green except hellebores and that it takes a rugged flower to stay in blossom through three months of snow and rain, then you'll appreciate the hellebore for the truly exceptional flower it is.

Now you have to ask yourself if it is worth driving 10 miles over unpaved, mountain single-lane to see acres of hellebores blooming in the snow. Barry Glick, who owns the mountaintop **Sunshine Farm and Gardens** in northern Greenbrier County, will assure you it is. But if you go, use caution on his driveway, a mile-long vertical chute of mud and shale. A four-wheel-drive vehicle with high clearance is best.

Glick's 68,000 outdoor hellebores bloom maroon, black, white, yellow, and pink from February through June. On sunny days you'll see his crew dabbing paintbrushes into the flowers, doing the work of the hummingbirds and the bees and creating new varieties of the nodding, poppy-like flower.

Besides the outdoor gardens, Glick nurtures 4 greenhouses of plants, almost 10,000 varieties of hellebores, cyclamen, primroses, anemones, and other species, some unknown to anyone else (a flower described as a "hardy African violet on steroids," anyone?). Glick introduces them to the world through his wholesale business with nurseries around the globe. "You might say I have an obsessive love of plants," he says.

For information and directions to Sunshine Farms (subtitled "Uncommonly Rare and Exceptional Plants for the Discriminating Gardener"), call (304) 497-2208 or go to sunfarm.com.

If you happen to be in this section of the county in July through early October, you could stop by **White Oak Blueberry Farm** near the Renick post office to pick your own mouthwatering fruit. The blueberries are ready July through August and red raspberries ripen in late August until the first frost. Buckets are provided and the picking is easy. The farm is usually open Mon, Tues, Thurs, and Sat in season. Call first at (304) 497-3577 or check whiteoak berryfarm.com to confirm availability.

Other locally grown products, hard cider and mead from **Hawk Knob Cidery and Meadery,** can be found at the toe of Muddy Creek Mountain at

2245 Blue Sulphur Pike, 2 miles out of Lewisburg. Here you can sip fermented cider in seasoned whiskey barrels—dry cherry, elderberry-infused cider, and good old traditional hard cider are the favorites. Heirloom apple honey mead sells out fast as well. Tastings and tours are available Thurs through Sunday 3 to 7 p.m. or other times if you schedule in advance by calling (304) 651-4413.

Southeast West Virginia attracted visitors to its healing springs by droves some 150 years ago. White Sulphur Springs (now The Greenbrier) was one of the younger resorts. To see some of the older resorts, you can take a scenic drive south on Route 311 down to *Sweet Springs,* swinging back and forth over the Virginia state line. This 1790 resort looks like Versailles in West Virginia; the massive Georgian Colonial hotel designed by Jefferson, the classical bathhouse, and a ring of two-story guesthouses still stand grand against their Peters Mountain backdrop. George Washington did spend the night here, as did James Madison, Patrick Henry, and General Robert E. Lee; Virginia Governor John Floyd is still sleeping here, in the Sweet Spring Cemetery. A recent private attempt to revive the complex as a spa, golf resort, and conference center stalled and the resort stands idle, with Sweet Springs' 73-degree stream trickling under the highway west of the bathhouse. The 100,000-square-foot grand lodge stands empty while a nonprofit foundation started by visionary preservationist Ashby Berkley (who renovated Pence Springs hotel) raises the funds to save the structures and create a park to put the hotel back in business. Warm weather events include an outdoor concert, tours, car show, games, yoga, and a fall motorcycle rally.

"Old Sweet," as it was called, drew celebrities and noted statesmen before the Civil War, while nearby Salt Sulphur attracted the partiers and Red Sulphur Springs (of which nothing remains) the seriously ill.

"I could not stand the thought that this building was going to fall down," said Berkley, who thought he was retired until he bought the resort at auction in 2015.

The resort isn't Sweet Springs Valley's only historical property. Just down the road is a sign denoting the home of the first U.S. female journalist, Anne Royall. Royall came to the area as a servant for the wealthy Royall family and ended up marrying the patriarch. It wasn't until he died and his family left her nearly penniless that she became a traveling journalist and newspaper publisher.

Before Sweet Spring's lodge was built, guests who were innocent of any crime sometimes overnighted in the jail. Lodging was in short supply. Eager to see the region prosper, resort owner William Lewis built a courthouse and jail for the court system in 1795, using both as guest quarters in the off-season. The small stone building in the hayfield beside the resort is said to be the oldest jail building west of the Alleghenies.

Across the road stands the state's oldest Catholic church still in use. *St. John's Chapel* isn't used much—the occasional wedding, a few summer services, and Assumption Day mass—but it continues a tradition started around 1850 by chapel founder, Letitia Floyd Lewis. After Assumption Day mass, her family served homemade ice cream to the community—a tradition still sometimes honored following the mid-August mass.

Pretty Sweet Springs Valley has attracted a number of entrepreneurs and craftsmen. The resort's Mennonite neighbors on Route 3 near Gap Mills create oak chairs *(Valley Springs Furniture),* all manner of baked goods *(Kitchen Creek Bakery),* and cheeses, jellies, and jams *(Cheese 'N More Store).* Cheese 'N More is an especially good place to stock up on spices, preserves, and gifts, some made just down the road at *Yoder's Country Kettle.* The store is open 9 a.m. to 5:30 p.m. Mon through Sat. Call (304) 772-5211 for more information about the store or the community.

From near the bakery in Gap Mills, you can take the Mountain Shadow Trail scenic byway to CR 15, up to Peters Mountain to a small parking lot on the right side of the road. From there, follow the 1.5-mile footpath to *Hanging Rock Observatory.* The little house braces on a rock outcropping atop 3,800-foot Peters Mountain, the perfect vantage point to watch the hawk migrations or the unfolding of the seasons. Visitors from 43 states and several countries have recorded their observations of eagles, hawks, and falcons at the observatory's website: hangingrocktower.org.

Returning to the valley, you can follow Route 3 toward the little town of Union and its *Union National Historic District.* You'll pass the turnoff for *Moncove Lake State Park,* a secluded spot for bass and walleye fishing, boating, and camping. Just before you reach town, you'll see a sign for *Rehoboth Church.* For almost 230 years, Rehoboth Church has been sitting in a dimple in Monroe County, the state's rolling hills, hidden to road travelers. Built when the Shawnee raided the region, the log church is sited so that no one can slip within rifle-shot range unseen. Some say it was built to double as a fort, or at least a refuge. Rehoboth is the oldest Protestant church building west of the Allegheny Mountains, dedicated by the famed Methodist circuit rider Bishop Francis Asbury in 1786. An iron plaque declares it a place for worship "as long as the grass grows and water flows."

Although regular services are no longer held in the small, dim building, Rehoboth does open up its plank doors for special occasions, such as historical services. The original pulpit remains, but the old book-board is gone, split long ago by the fist of a rousing preacher. At barely 600 square feet, the structure's interior is too small to comfortably accommodate more than two dozen congregants. Still, it was larger than any of the homes where local Methodists had previously been meeting. The backless puncheon benches, still standing in the church, look to be a butt-numbing roost during the standard three-hour sermons. The tiny church is now a designated United Methodist shrine and appears on the National Register of Historic Places. Ironically, the church plot was donated by a Roman Catholic settler, Edward Keenan, who was sympathetic to the Methodists. Keenan's tombstone is located beside those of former Revolutionary War soldiers in the Rehoboth Church cemetery.

A small museum and conference center sits adjacent to the original church, 2 miles east of Union. The museum displays significant historical artifacts from the region, including Rehoboth's battered poplar communion table. The museum is open Fri, Sat, and Sun from 1 to 4 p.m., May through Oct. Visits can be arranged at other times by calling (304) 772-3518.

Despite the name of the town of Union, a large limestone Confederate monument stands alone in a pasture just outside town. Apparently, town fathers expected more development when they erected the memorial in 1901. Or, some say, the town's Union sympathizers didn't want that symbol of the Confederacy to dominate downtown. Sentiments were mixed here. Hugh Tiffany, captain of the Monroe Guards, was the first Confederate officer killed in the Civil War, and his neighbor from Salt Sulphur Springs, James Madison Harvey, served as captain with the Union forces and later became governor of Kansas.

Although both armies passed through this area repeatedly, they were kind to Union—29 antebellum structures still sit in Union's downtown area. The 1810 Wiseman House, furnished with local antiques, is part of the *Monroe County Historical Society Museum.* The adjacent museum on Main Street contains early tools, Confederate relics, ladies' Victorian clothing, and an exhibit on making linen from flax. The museum has built a Gothic Revival timber-frame building to house its adjoining *Monroe Co. Carriage Museum* (304-772-3003, monroewvhistory.org), The collection contains carriages, a John Deere wagon, and a sleigh, but the centerpiece is an omnibus, a1880s horse-drawn bus capable of carrying a dozen wealthy guests from the train station to Sweet Chalybeate Spring. It is the only known omnibus surviving in good original condition, hand painted with scrolls and country scenes. Every surface in this lightweight vehicle is curved like a boat. About 50 vehicle-related tools and images are also displayed, from spoke-making kits to wheel shrinkers, indicating earlier life was hardly simple. If you are lucky, your guide will be Fred Ziegler, who wrote the book on Monroe County carriages. The museums are open June through Sept, Tues through Sat 10 a.m. to 4 p.m.

Heading south on US 219 for 3 miles, you glimpse the great stone lodge, guesthouses, bathhouse, and spring house of *Salt Sulphur Springs.* Once hundreds guests from all over the South would revel in these sweetly sulfurous waters, but the Civil War reversed most Southern fortunes. Owner Betty Farmer still bottles water to treat her family's skin and hosts the occasional wedding on wide lawns Indian Creek.

From here you can follow Route 3 west to **Alderson,** home of the Alderson Federal Prison Camp where Martha Stewart was briefly imprisoned in 2004–2005. Although the media mogul and her hand-knit afghans are long gone, you can shop the long surviving **Alderson's Store** (aldersonsstore.com), which has been serving customers with grace and style since 1887. No general store with tinned meat and sprouted potatoes, Alderson's is as classy as its elegant Art Deco exterior. Inside you'll find tastefully organized collections of china, specialty books, women's clothing, and jewelry.

Sunset Berry Farm & Produce at the peak of Flat Mountain near Alderson, is a great place to stop and pick your own strawberries, asparagus, tomatoes, green beans, or peaches, depending on the season. Owners Kent and Jennifer Gilkerson grow more than 8,000 quarts of strawberries each year and won the sweetest strawberry award at the West Virginia Strawberry Festival in Buckhannon. At the end of summer, they celebrate sunflowers with a festival, photo sessions in the sunflower garden, and sunflower picking farm dinners. To find out what's ripe, call them at (304) 646-3784 or check sunsetberryfarm.net.

Following the riffling Greenbrier River southwest on Route 3, you come to another women's penitentiary. Actually, that's not quite fair, because the historic **Pence Springs Hotel,** now the **Greenbrier Academy for Girls** was a thriving resort long before it was used as a prison. Located in the hamlet of Pence Springs, the inn was first opened in 1897 by Andrew Pence, an entrepreneur who sought to capitalize on the idyllic location and famed spring waters of the region. (The village's water took the silver medal at the 1904 World's Fair.)

By 1926 the spacious 60-room Georgian mansion was considered the grandest and most expensive hotel in the state, commanding an unheard-of daily rate of $6, which included all meals. During its heyday, 14 trains stopped here daily, bringing in folks from as far away as New York. The day after the stock market crashed in 1929, however, the inn closed its doors, only to be reopened briefly as a girls' school, a dude ranch, and then finally as a state-run women's prison from 1947 to 1977.

Now the old hotel is a girls' school again and closed to the public. But on Sunday you can still visit the historic spring down the hill, sample the water, and pick up some bargains at the **Sunday Pence Springs Flea Market.**

There's an almost primeval quality to the smoky ravines and deep hollows here in southern West Virginia. It's easy to sense that this was a land of courageous pioneers and rugged American Indians, and nowhere is that feeling more acute than at nearby *Graham House.* It's an impressive log home dating from 1770, built for the express purpose of guarding Colonel James Graham's family from the Shawnee, who quite understandably weren't too terribly keen on European encroachment into their region. In 1777 Colonel Graham's estate was raided, resulting in the death of his 10-year-old son and the capture of his young daughter. For eight years the determined colonel searched for the girl, finally rescuing her more than 100 miles away in what is now Maysville, Kentucky. Today the two-story house, considered extravagant for the times with its thick reinforced log walls and beams, is a National Historic Site. You'll see firsthand that living on the frontier of 18th-century West Virginia was an egalitarian experience. Not even the wealthy, such as Graham, were immune from the hardships of isolated life.

Beside Graham House stands the *Saunders One Room School House Museum,* filled with reminders of days gone by, from the hickory stick to the potbellied stove, antique desks, and primer collections. The house and museum are just south of Pence Springs along the river road. They're open Memorial Day through Labor Day from 11 a.m. to 5 p.m. Sat and from 1 to 5 p.m. Sun. For more information, call (304) 466-5336.

"Well, John Henry was a steel-drivin' maaaan, oh yeah." This famous line, popularized by Johnny Cash, is from the "The Ballad of John Henry," a song immortalizing West Virginia's and perhaps the nation's most famous railroad worker. In Talcott, a tiny village snuggled between the hills and the Greenbrier River south of Pence Springs, the legend of John Henry lives on at a small park commemorating the man and the myth. It is a must-see, for the muscular John Henry sculpture as well as the ominous Big Bend railroad tunnel where legend says Henry died competing against a steam-powered drill. The men who tunneled through the shale mountain in the 1870s found it a monstrous undertaking. Recurring rockfalls killed many workers. A few months after first train passed through the tunnel, a massive rockfall killed an entire train crew. Rumors still abound about the ghosts in Big Bend Tunnel. Some say they've heard the eerie echo of Henry's hammer striking steel or seen his ghost just inside the tunnel.

According to both mountain storytellers and researchers, John Henry was an amiable, massively built man who could work a steel hammer like no one else. He was employed by the Chesapeake & Ohio Railroad, a company charged with clearing a tunnel through the concretelike red-clay shale of Big Bend Mountain. It was perilous work, to say the least. About 20 percent of the laborers lost their lives here, falling victim to all-too-frequent cave-ins or the more stealthy destroyer of lungs, silicosis from rock dust. One morning, one of the foremen bet John Henry $100, a huge sum of money in the early 1870s, that he couldn't beat a mechanized drill through one of the last stretches of the tunnel. Henry took the bet, grabbed his hammer, and won handily. As we all know, however, the extraordinary feat killed him soon after the race. (Most historians agree Henry's death was related to exhaustion, although some claim he died later in a cave-in.) In any event, Henry's hammer, bearing the initials J.H., was later found in the tunnel when a concrete floor was poured in 1932.

John Henry Park, containing a statue of the famous railroad man, was funded partly by a donation from Johnny Cash. The small roadside park is open year-round, dawn to dusk.

Just south on route 12 in Forest Hill, Marcia Springston-Dillon produces stunning stoneware in an old general store. Ironically, the renowned potter can't see the bowls, vases, and plates she generates. Blind since birth, Springston-Dillon creates with a delicate sense of touch. In fact, she can tell the color of a glaze by its feel. Green, she tells me, has a nice texture—not too slick and shiny. The shelves of her *Wake Robin Gallery* are lined with her work, including her specialty chili bowls with attached cracker platters. Handmade wooden gifts, local baskets, glass, and other crafts made by regional artisans also help stock the shop. The gallery is open Thursdays through Saturdays from 10 a.m. to 4 p.m.

Turn left (east) onto Route 122 in Forest Hill to see historic Cook's Mill, just before Greenville. This is also the site of Cook's Fort, which covered more than an acre and reputedly protected more than 300 settlers from an American Indian attack in 1778, but nothing remains of the fort today. Nearby, the 1867 *Cook's Mill* (cooksoldmill.com) stands on its old mill pond in perfectly restored working order. Construction elements include hand-hewn, mortise-and-tenon posts and beams. The original mill was built in this same spot in 1796. The present owner is developing the mills and surrounding buildings as a center for artisans using traditional techniques. The adjacent forge building contains blacksmithing equipment, and occasional demonstrations take place in the summer. Travelers are invited to wander around the grounds, take pictures, have a picnic, do some fishing in the mill pond, or just soak up some history. For more information, see cooksoldmill.com.

The waters some folks take in this area have been turned to wine—meads, ciders, and wine from *Old World Libations*. Even if you're not a big wine drinker, it's hard to resist a beverage described as having "the bold flavors of cherry and currants with subtle hints of vanilla." The winery is located off Rt. 219 eight miles south of Union on Route 122 at the edge of Greenville. The tasting room opens Friday evenings and Saturday and Sunday afternoons as well as other times by appointment (304) 992-8424.

In the opposite direction on Route 12 lies the little riverside community of **Hinton,** a picturesque railroad town that has escaped many of the urban trappings of the 21st century. The railroad arrived here in 1873, finding it the only practical route through the treacherous New River Gorge. The railroad brought prosperity and economic development. Today Hinton's beautifully restored courthouse, freight depot, 1890s passenger station, opera house, hotels, stores, warehouses, and gorgeous American Gothic, classical, and Greek Revival churches have been preserved. Even the original brick streets and gaslights have been saved from modernization. To reach it, go right (west) on Route 12 after Willow Wood Bridge.

The **Hinton Railroad Museum,** conveniently located in the same building as the Three Rivers Travel Council (206 Temple St.; threeriverswv.com), explains the railroad history of Hinton through vintage black-and-white photographs, recordings, documents, and train fixtures. Be sure to look for the old C&O Railroad baseball uniform worn by town resident Robert O. Murrell back in 1897. Murrell's team, perhaps the best company baseball club in the US at the time, actually took on the Cincinnati Reds in an exhibition game and won. The museum's collection features tools that would have been used by John Henry, as well as the 98-piece John Henry wood carving exhibit that took the carver Charles Pemelia three years and 20 types of wood to finish. It represents every 1870 railroad job that existed. The museum is open Mon through Sat from 10 a.m. to 4 p.m. The museum is closed for repairs and upkeep during Jan and Feb each year. Call (304) 466-5420 for more information.

Interestingly enough, the house Murrell lived in is now the town's oldest standing residential structure. You can visit the **Campbell-Flannagan-Murrell House Museum** at 422 Summers St. and get a feel for how a typical Hinton railroad family lived during the late 1800s. The three-story wooden Federal-style home was built in 1875; at the time, the basement level was used as a general store. Today it's used as a museum, with home furnishings dating from the golden years of the railroad. Visitors taking free Saturday tours can examine such 1875 artifacts as arsenic complexion wafers, Cristo Colas bottled in Hinton, and Lula, a doll dressed appropriately for a Victorian lady—covered from wrist and toe to chin. The house and shop are open Sat from 10 a.m. to 5 p.m. June through Aug only. Call (304) 466-0005 for more information.

The **Veterans Memorial Museum** in the old Carnegie library a few blocks away on Ballengee Street is another free attraction if you're visiting on a Saturday between 9 a.m. and 4 p.m. in May through November. It is a treasury of artifacts of every conflict Summers County natives participated in—from the French and Indian War to the Gulf War. Special artifacts are General Douglas MacArthur's footlocker and a vintage 151A2 jeep.

Other in-town diversions include the Ritz Theater for movies as well as *Otter and Oak*, where outdoorsy folk will want to explore Columbia, Birkenstock, Teva, and GoPro products. Enticing shops include *Grandma's House Antiques & Collectibles* and *Big Four Drug Store & Gift Shop*, which includes a soda fountain that makes coconut almond floats. A fine eatery at a reasonable price is *Market on Courthouse Square*, which specializes in brick-oven pizza and train-themed sandwiches.

A new city park for launching boats, kayaks and canoes on the New River opened in 2021. West Virginia University students helped create the park's innovative design and its picnic shelter. In addition to parking, restrooms, and the shelter, the park offers a boat dock and boat ramps.

When Paramount Pictures cast Lassie in a heroic whitewater scene in 1994, they took the canine classic to *Summers County's Sandstone Falls* in West Virginia's New River Gorge National Park and filmed along the 1,500-foot broad cascade. It was perfect. The roar, the mist, the water walloping over boulders all show a mighty river in charge of its course.

But it's a scene that few actually experience. Oh sure, a lot of motorists pull off at Sandstone Overlook on Route 20 for a remote viewing. But the real excitement lies in getting up close and personal with the New River's largest falls. And that involves driving to Hinton and taking a mostly one-lane, mostly unpaved CR 26 almost 9 miles along the western side of the river to the park.

Once you get there, the National Park Service has made things easy. They've constructed a 0.25-mile, wheelchair-accessible boardwalk to islands in the middle of river. On an observation deck below the island, you can admire the pounding, 25-foot waterfall. The site has other attractions: It's a popular fishing spot for smallmouth bass and catfish as well as home to some unusual plants, including the Virginia cup-plant, Kentucky coffeetree, hoptree, and toothache tree. (Yes, its berries numb your mouth, but don't try it—tasting unfamiliar berries is risky and in the park it's illegal.)

Maybe looking at all this water has activated your inner oarsman or -woman. You're in luck. *Cantrell Ultimate Rafting* has a base right in Hinton. The 40-year-old rafting company provides a range of water adventures from wild to mild; those who just like to cast a line and watch the scenery are also served. From the Hinton base, Cantrell sets up raft and ducky trips on the peaceful Lower New as well as bass fishing trips on the New and Greenbrier and a 7-mile tube float young children love. Cantrell also rents small rafts and duckies for private floats on a serene section of river and offers camping on a private island just outside of town. For more information or to make reservations, call (800) 470-RAFT (7238) or visit ultimaterafting.com.

Hinton lies in the shadow of the towering Bluestone Dam of the New River. The resulting lake is the focal point of **Bluestone Lake State Park.** If you like bass fishing, this is your place—the state record for striped bass was caught here—40.88 inches and 29.56 pounds. Boat and canoe rentals are available at the marina. In addition, special weekly programs, hikes, movies, and picnics are provided by the park naturalist. For further information, visit bluestonesp.com or call (304) 466-2805.

Wild critters outnumber humans in Summers County, and to glimpse life from their perspective, take a side trip to **Three Rivers Avian Center** in nearby Brooks. This private, nonprofit organization provides rehabilitative care for West Virginia's wild birds. Staffers give tours of the facility on the first Saturday of the month May through October in an effort to educate the public about conservation. At any given time, you're likely to meet Robbie the barred owl, Horton hawk, or Apex the kestrel. For information on tours, call (304) 466-4683, or check the website at tracwv.org.

As you head south of Hinton along Route 20, you'll pass over and through the beautiful **Pipestem Gorge.** Named for the native pipestem bush whose hollow, woody stems were used by Native American tribes to make pipes, the Pipestem is actually part of the much larger Bluestone River Gorge. On late summer mornings, fog slides out of Bluestone Gorge like a backward avalanche—first a few wisps tear off, then the whole cloud levitates and dissipates in minutes. Some visitors make a daily ritual of awaiting this spectacle, coffee in hand, on the balconies of **Pipestem Resort State Park's** McKeever Lodge—a grand way to start the day.

The fog rise is one of many reasons why the southeast West Virginia resort is a way cool place for a laidback getaway. Cool is the word here. Just minutes from Bluefield, West Virginia, "nature's air-conditioned city," Pipestem shares the climate of a town so certain of its low summer temperatures that the chamber dispenses free lemonade on rare days when the thermometer hits 90. Years can go by without the need to squeeze a lemon in downtown Bluefield. Pipestem, at a higher altitude, is even cooler. On a sweat-drenched lowland weekend, Pipestem guests could be grabbing their sweaters for the fog rise.

But there are many other reasons lowlanders love to escape here. Pipestem takes adventure up a notch with a slate of outdoor activities, including one of the longest zip line systems in the East. Participants soar over the Bluestone River three times at heights of more than 300 feet. Visitors can also try ax throwing, 3D archery, drone flying, skeet shooting, and motor assisted bicycles. Youngsters frolic in the park's splash park while teens and older folks can perfect fly fishing skills on guided tours. The 4,023-acre forested park has 3 golf courses—a full-length 18-hole, a par-3, and a miniature golf course. The

18-hole par 72 championship course designed by Geoffrey Cornish features views of the Bluestone Canyon and free-range deer. Rates are $28 weekdays; $34 weekends. The resort's Mountain Creek Lodge is so secluded, you can get there only by taking a tram down into Bluestone Canyon—all the better for that away-from-it-all feeling. The dangly ride in the gondolas lasts only 6 minutes, but descending some 1,100 feet takes you deep into the cool, breezy gorge. The Bluestone River is an ice-cold, splashing, wild thing, with slow backwaters for wading. Each room offers river views, and a restaurant serving breakfast is steps away. Have the lodge set you up with a horseback riding trip through the gorge; or, if you'd rather wet a hook, the Bluestone is famous for its small-mouth bass fishing. Long Branch Lake is stocked with catfish each spring, some tagged. An 18-hole disc-golf course sits near the Olympic outdoor swimming pool. The course is designed with good variety, from tightly wooded, technical fairways to long, open holes.

Lighted tennis courts and a minigolf course also are located within the 4,000-acre preserve. Concerts and storytelling events draw folks into the amphitheater each summer Saturday. Numerous interpretive programs covering subjects such as bats and snakes and including night hikes are held through-out the year. The park's visitor center regularly hosts arts-and-crafts sales and demonstrations by local artisans. When hunger pangs hit, the park has a nice buffet at McKeever Lodge and gourmet dinners at Mountain Creek. "Remote but hardly rustic" describes the experience here.

Pipestem's rooms start at $85 for two guests and are open year-round. Mountain Creek Lodge takes guests from May 15 to October 31 only. The rest of the park is open all year. Call (304) 466-1800, or view the website at wvstate parks.com/park/pipestem-resort-state-park.

New River Gorge

Sometimes there's no overstating the obvious—this is a gorgeous place. The natural beauty coupled with the man-made attractions makes for a not-to-be-missed West Virginia experience.

The natural drama of Sandstone Falls seems an appropriate primer to this region, considered by many outdoor enthusiasts to be among the most scenic natural areas east of the Mississippi.

The **New River** is ancient—it's been flowing on its present course for as long as 225 million years, making it second only to the Nile as the oldest river in the world. Glaciers in the Ice Age buried it and diverted much of the water flow into two other rivers, the Ohio and the Kanawha. Another indication of its age: The New River flows across the Appalachian Plateau, not around it or from it as do most other rivers in the East. The New River existed before the Appalachians did, and these are the world's oldest mountains.

The river was virtually inaccessible along its entire length until 1873, when the railroad opened up the isolated region. The railroad followed the river and made possible the shipment of coal to the outside world. Today more than 50 miles of the New River (between Fayetteville to the north and Hinton to the south) and 40 miles of its tributaries are preserved and protected as a national park, one of the nation's newest.

The best place to get acquainted with New River Gorge National Park is at the **Canyon Rim Visitor Center** on US 19, about a mile north of Fayetteville. The center's overlook offers the most impressive views of the gorge and the awe-inspiring **New River Gorge Bridge,** which is actually part of US 19. This is the world's longest single steel-arch bridge, with a central span of 1,700 feet and a total length of 3,030 feet. It rises 876 feet above the riverbed. If you want to take your time admiring the view, come back for **Bridge Day** the third Saturday in October, the one day of the year when the bridge highway is open to foot traffic. You will have to share the road with more than a quarter of a million other visitors who come to watch the rappellers and parachutists drop over the side. Music, food, crafts, and guided walks are part of the festivities. This gala affair has become West Virginia's largest festival.

Among the diverse lodging choices around the gorge, **Country Road Cabins** in Hico stands out. While some tree houses on stilts earn the moniker because they jut above the tree line, the treehouses at Country Road Cabins in Hico are actually built into trees. This is no easy undertaking. Former owner Paul Breuer, who built two such houses at the cabin resort, said everything had to tested and retested to ensure they were light enough to be supported by trees yet strong enough to withstand some flexing in a storm. He had to use a light heating and cooling system and have the steel main beams ziplined in place. No climbing is necessary here. Both Holly Rock and Tuscany treehouses are accessed by bridges from nearby hillsides. The houses feature deck hot tubs as well as kitchens and are open year-round. Prices range from $175 to $325 a night. The resort also features woodland cabins, yurts, and two safari-style glamping tents with floors, heat, electricity, and plumbing (Wvcabins .com).

Offered collaboratively between the park service and the highway department, New River Gorge Bridge Walk offers daily catwalk tours for about $70, and reservations are required. The two- to three-hour tours are open to participants who are at least 10 years old and can walk 1.5 miles. Bridge walkers are fastened onto a safety cable, securing them to the bridge.

West Virginia Rafting Is Running Hot

Long before you see the first big rapids of West Virginia's lower New River, you hear their ominous song—a crashing like rocks barreling through a bowling alley. Your guide is grinning like a demon from the back of the raft, and you feel your heart beating in rhythm with the chopping of the waves. Your arm muscles tense as you gear up for what feels like the fight of your life. All you can think of as the raft bucks are the walls of mad whitewater closing in on you.

Some 250,000 people come to West Virginia every year to do this for fun. It's a contest between a boisterous river spirit and a bunch of neoprene-clad riders with something to prove.

The contest started back in 1965, when young West Virginia paddlers looking for thrills repeatedly sacrificed their canoes on the rocks of the New. Luckily, they discovered the Czechoslovakian slalom canoe and began emerging intact at Fayetteville Station.

The pioneers of the West Virginia whitewater industry were made of the same stuff—college kids who really just wanted to have fun. Jon, Tom, and Chris Dragan began taking friends down the New in 1968 using army surplus rafts and asking everyone to chip in for food and shuttle gas. Rafting seemed like a pretty harebrained scheme to the bankers who turned down the Dragans' request for a $4,000 loan, so the young entrepreneurs borrowed money from their family for two used pickup trucks and two army rafts. The Dragans ran the river from the day they got out of school in June until classes started up again in September. Thus, Wildwater Unlimited was born.

These days the New is so busy April through October that a state advisory board has been set up to regulate raft traffic on the nationally protected river. You can choose among more than a dozen outfitters who operate state-of-the-art, self-bailing rafts, duckies, and kayaks in New River Gorge. For information, see newrivergorgecvb .com/play/whitewater or call (800) 927-0263.

The **Canyon Rim Visitor Center** (nps.gov/neri/planyourvisit/crvc.htm) is located just beyond the north end of the bridge. This visitor center contains a museum with exhibits on the history and natural features of the area. A boardwalk descends 100 feet into the gorge. A variety of trails start here, ranging from an easy loop along the rim of the trail to an arduous round-trip trek to the bottom of the gorge and back.

One of the area's best water attractions (at least in the warm-weather months) calls for a trip under the New River Gorge Bridge with **New River Jetboats.** Travelers climb aboard the 12-seat Miss M. Rocks at the **Hawk's Nest State Park Marina.** The trip is captained by a licensed river pilot, who'll take you upstream on the New River through shoals and small rapids for an up-close view from beneath the massive bridge. The jet-boat trip affords an unforgettable vantage point. Don't forget your camera. New River Jetboats is open from 11 a.m. to 4 p.m. daily except Wed from Memorial Day through Labor Day, and on weekends in May and Oct. For more information, call (304) 469-2525 or visit newriverjetboats.com.

The New River Gorge has received additional national exposure for its beauty and recreational opportunities when it beat out 80 other contenders for the *Summit Bechtel Family National Scout Reserve.* The national scouting center opened its 10,600-acre property in July 2013 to more than 40,000 young men attending the national Boy Scout Jamboree. In 2019 the site near Mount Hope hosted scouts from 160 countries for the 24th World Scout Jamboree.

Outdoor recreation is plentiful here, to say the least. *Whitewater rafting* is among the popular sports on the river. The water churns and tosses as it begins its 750-foot descent along the 50 miles from Bluestone Dam to Gauley Bridge. (By comparison, the mighty Mississippi falls less than twice that over the entire course of its 2,300-mile journey from northern Minnesota to the Gulf of Mexico.) The New boasts some of the best whitewater conditions in the US and is certainly among the top three rivers in the East for rafting. (The neighboring Gauley River and Tennessee's Ocoee River are in the same league.)

If you decide to take the plunge, nearly a dozen rafting companies, all certified and well trained, are eager for your business. Trips run the gamut from gentle, mostly flat-water affairs to gut-wrenching, heart-stopping rapids. Length and degree of difficulty are planned around participants' age and skill levels.

Adventures on the Gorge (an amalgam of the former Mountain River Tours, Class VI, Rivermen, and Songer Whitewater outfitters) runs family paddling adventure travel on the mild rapids of the Upper New River in "duckies," inflatable kayaks children as young as 8 can paddle. Running the river with kids has its benefits—no iPods, text messages, or even cell phones get in the way of the fun. It's quality time with built-in natural thrills. For more information, call (304) 574-4909 or visit class-vi.com. Many outfitters also piggyback the water experience with a combination of camping, fishing, mountain biking, ATV riding, horseback riding, rock climbing, llama trekking, river ecology, and bed-and-breakfast trips. ACE rafting has even added a mud obstacle course—or team building! Participants crawl through the gloppy stuff, balance on logs, and swing from ropes in team competitions. They also have low- and high-challenge courses, paintball wars, and adventure races that combine hiking, climbing, and orienteering. For more information, call *ACE Adventure Resort* at (800) 787-3982 or visit aceraft.com.

One popular add-on, really a destination in its own right, is the canopy tour. Harness up, close your eyes, lift your feet, lean back, and feel the adrenaline. The zipline really does go *zzzziiiipp* as the trolley carries you down the cable. The 3.5-hour adventure called the ***TreeTops Canopy tour*** is as close to flying as you can get. You soar from one tree platform to another over Mill Creek's rhododendron canyon near the New River Gorge. The guided long zipline tour offered by Class VI Mountain River is a mile long (which is good—it may take a few zips to gain trust in your harness and cables even though they're perfectly safe). You move from tree to tree via a network of platforms and sky bridges, allowing you to actually look down on warblers and other wildlife. You start out by testing your skills with the guides on a trial zipline a few feet above the ground, and before long you're zipping along the course at speeds up to 30 miles an hour. You cross 5 sky bridges and end with a 35-foot rappel. TreeTops Canopy tour is recommended for people over 10 who weigh between 70 and 250 pounds. The cost is $99 for adults and $55 for youth. For reservations or information, visit adventurewestvirginia.com or call (855) 379-8738.

Rafting prices vary widely—$65 and up—depending on the length and type of trip, the number of people in the group, and other factors. Most have base camps with camping facilities; some include luxury cabins and bed-and-breakfast accommodations. Trips are held from early spring through late fall. For more information on rafting companies in the region, call (800) CALL-WVA.

If your adrenaline is still running, why not try ***climbing*** the gorge walls? Some of the finest climbing rock in the East can be found here—solid, hard, mostly straight up. The ***New River Gorge National Park*** (nps.gov/neri) claims 1,500 climbing routes up its rock cliffs within a 10-mile stretch. To set up your vertical adventure, contact the Southern West Virginia Visitor Center (800-847-4898) to get information on the half dozen outfitters offering climbing expeditions.

Next to rafting, ***hiking*** is the second most popular activity in the gorge. Not only are there many trails for hiking, but the National Park Service offers several guided hikes. Guided by park rangers, these hikes may have either a nature or a history theme. Special hikes may be arranged with park service officials. For more information, call (304) 465-0508. Nearby, the 8-mile White Oak Rail-Trail runs through the town of Oak Hill, connecting the communities of Summerlee and Carlisle at either end. The mostly paved trail passes two abandoned company stores and other relics of coal mining communities.

Several once-booming but now-abandoned mining communities await the inquisitive hiker all along the river. In the ghost town of ***Silo Rapids,*** you'll come across remains of silica sand storage vessels, while in ***Claremont*** vestiges remain of a giant coal preparation plant. In ***Beury,*** you can get a glimpse of a now abandoned but once spectacular 23-room mansion owned by a local coal baron.

There aren't many towns with populations of 5 people that have such colorful and sordid pasts as does *Thurmond,* which sits in about the geographic center of the gorge. The town grew up with the railroad and coal operators that opened the gorge in the early 1900s. In fact, the C&O Railroad was about the only way into town since Thurmond had no streets—the only such town in America with that distinction. Nevertheless, it became a commercial and social hub and a prosperous shipping center during its heyday. More freight tonnage was generated here than in Cincinnati and Richmond combined.

westvirginia
southerners

Confederate flags wave from several roadside shops on eastern US 52. West Virginia became a Union state after it broke away from the rest of Virginia in 1861. But the story down here is different. When the Civil War first began, Mercer County sent 10 full companies to the field under the Confederate flag—the highest proportional recruitment of any Virginia county.

Thurmond also cultivated quite a reputation as a rough-and-tumble outlaw town. A common joke heard during the 1920s and 1930s was "the only difference between Thurmond and Hell is that a river runs through Thurmond." The town also had the distinction of hosting the longest-running poker game in history. The game began in the lively Dun Glen Hotel and ended 14 years later, but only after the hotel burned down. Thurmond's demise came with the advent of the automobile, and its population dwindled to its present tiny state. It is now one of the smallest incorporated towns in West Virginia. As you hike through, notice the small wooden homes (some still occupied) that cling precariously to the hillside. Many of these were built by coal operators as company housing. Take a quick scan of this hardscrabble village, and it's easy to understand why director John Sayles chose Thurmond as the setting for his film *Matewan,* about the 1920s miners' uprising in southern West Virginia.

With only 5 year-round residents, Thurmond has become the smallest incorporated town in West Virginia. Thurmond may be five breaths away from being a ghost town, but it's not lonely in the warm weather. Hikers, mountain bikers, motorbikers, cavers, and anglers make the serpentine downhill journey in great numbers. And Thurmond is changing. A multimillion-dollar restoration, including a face-lift to the railroad depot, by the National Park Service has perked up the old burgh. A small museum greets tourists, many of whom come in via the Amtrak Cardinal. Now might be the best time to visit the state's most off-the-beaten-path town—before the commercialization sets in. You can float into Thurmond by hooking up with a rafting company, hike in on the 3.5-mile Thurmond-Minden Trail, or drive down the county road leading into the gorge from the Glen Jean exit off US 19 north of Beckley, and follow the signs to Thurmond. If you elect to drive, park on the west side of the river and walk the bridge into Thurmond. Bring a camera, because you'll certainly want to document your trip to the "end of the earth." The Thurmond visitor center is open 9 a.m. to 5 p.m. daily from Memorial Day to Labor Day and 9 a.m. to 5 p.m. weekends May through Oct. Phone (304) 465-8550 for information.

The old Midland Trail became part of the first transcontinental motor route. Now designated a national scenic highway, the trail chases along the New River after crossing US 19 near Canyon Rim. The village of **Ansted** is steeped in history: A coal baron's mansion, the PageVawter House (page-vawterhouse.com); Civil War trail markers; and Contentment House Museum, an 1830 home sheltering the Fayette County Historical Society are all right off the highway. West Ansted nestles up to *Hawks Nest State Park* (www.wvstateparks.com/park/hawks-nest-state-park), a Civilian Conservation Corps park with trails, nature programs, and dramatic views from the rim of the New River Gorge. A tramway descends into the gorge where, in summer, you can take a jet-boat ride upstream almost to the base of the New River Gorge Bridge, 976 feet above the water. Those feeling more energetic can follow several trails along the rim or to the bottom of the gorge. An exceptionally lovely rail trail leads from the gorge floor up to Ansted, past an old mine and several small waterfalls. The lodge and restaurant allow you to watch the sunset over the New River from your table or room. If you look west, you'll see a large dam. In an engineering feat, more than 3,000 men drilled through Gauley Mountain in the 1930s. They diverted part of the New River into a conduit to turbines that generate electricity. Drilling the tunnel resulted in one of the worst industrial disasters in US history. The project took the lives of at least 476 workers, many of them migrant African Americans, who died from lung disease after inhaling silica dust in the tunnel.

If you look below the dam, you'll see what is known as "the Dries," a 5.5-mile rocky river bottom dotted with small pools of water—what is left after perhaps 90 percent of the river is diverted through the tunnel under Gauley Mountain. The diverted water reemerges at Hawks Nest hydroelectric plant near Gauley Bridge. You can park in a small lot here and walk down to stairs that lead along the side of the plant and over the reemerging river. This scenic area is a popular fishing spot.

Just west of Ansted on US 60 sits the antithesis of New River Gorge's natural beauty—an outlandish manmade attraction called *Mystery Hole.* Every road trip begs for at least one stop at a zany, hyped-up roadside attraction, and in West Virginia, the mysterious, gravity-defying Mystery Hole wins hands-down in the weird, offbeat attraction category. The enigmatic hole is hidden under a garishly painted Quonset hut with a VW bug smashed into its side. The tiny roadside gift shop is littered with signs urging you inside. After you pay your $8 admission ($7 if you're under 12), you descend a staircase past eccentric art and fun-house mirrors to a tilted room where gravity has gone berserk. It will confuse you, frustrate you, entertain you, and alter your perception of reality. It's probably good for your brain, but watch your step. Some people say it made their vacation. Step right up. Come right in.

The Mystery Hole is open June through Aug, Thurs through Mon from 10:30 a.m. to 5 p.m. and on weekends in May, Sept and Oct. Call (304) 658-9101 for more information or to join their fan club.

Continuing on US 60, you'll pass the turnoff for the Hawks Nest hydro-electric plant. At the edge of the village of Gauley Bridge, look to the north for the cascading Cathedral Falls. A small parking area and path allow you a closer look at the moss-covered rocks and pool. At Gauley Bridge, the New and Gauley Rivers unite to form the wide Kanawha River, which you follow on US 60 almost to the Ohio border. The ***Glen Ferris Inn,*** built in 1810 as a home, was the first permanent building constructed in the village of Glen Ferris. In 1839 it became the Stockton Inn and received such famous guests as Andrew Jackson, John Tyler, Henry Clay, and John James Audubon. During the Civil War, it hosted officers from both sides. The Federal-style inn offers meals and lodging overlooking the wide Kanawha Falls; a small park below the falls is a favorite fishing and picnic area.

Southern Coalfields

Seven rugged counties—Boone, Logan, McDowell, Mingo, Wyoming, Raleigh, and Mercer—represent a large share of West Virginia's coal industry. Although coal is found in other parts of the state, these counties cumulatively produce huge quantities of the stuff—as much as 60 percent of the state's total output in 1998.

In 1742 German immigrant John Peter Salley discovered coal along the Coal River in what became Boone County. The next century saw the introduction of railroads and coal mining to the area. By 1900 the combined coal output of Mingo, McDowell, and Mercer Counties alone was almost more than the entire state's production just a decade earlier. McDowell and Logan Counties were producing 5 million tons each by 1914, and to date over 4.1 billion tons have been produced in these historic coalfields.

The story of coal mining and the hard life of miners might not sound like the stuff of tourism, but West Virginia has done a good job promoting the cultural heritage of the region. And it's a heritage that's every bit as different and fascinating as those of the Cajuns of Louisiana and the watermen of the Chesapeake Bay.

The gateway to the state's most productive coalfields is **Beckley,** located at the intersection of I-77 and I-64, about an hour south of Summersville. The city (population 18,000 and the region's largest) was founded and later named for General Alfred Beckley, the first Clerk of Congress during the administrations of Presidents Washington, Adams, and Jefferson. Beckley's home, **Wildwood,** a two-story log cabin on South Kanawha Street, is preserved as a museum and is open to visitors Memorial Day through Labor Day on Saturday afternoons. Call Wildwood House Museum at (304) 252-3730 for more information. Also of interest is the city's preserved uptown section, with its boutiques and restaurants situated around the town square.

Beckley is, as the slogan goes, a town with a mine of its own. The **Beckley Exhibition Coal Mine** offers daily summer tours into a former 1880s working mine 1,500 feet beneath the town park. Ride aboard a clanking "man trip" car guided through the mine for a look at how low-seam coal mining developed from its earliest manual stages to modern mechanized operation. The retired miners who pilot the cars, men who may have hand loaded coal carts, are your teachers. Some of their anecdotes alone are worth the trip. One guide insisted that rats were a miner's friend, and said he always left part of his lunch for them, claiming they had a sixth sense about danger. "If you see a lot of rats running by, you'd better run the same way," he said. "You were probably minutes, maybe seconds, from disaster." Luckily, no rats appeared in this old and stable mine.

Outside of the mine, you can tour a restored coal camp including a company house, single miner's shanty, superintendent's home, church, and school. The visitor center replicates a company store and includes exhibits and a gift shop with legendary homemade fudge.

The **Youth Museum of Southern West Virginia,** made up of railroad boxcars, is just footsteps away. Step back in time as you enter the one-room school and experience "readin', writin', and 'rithmetic" as it used to be. The barn, blacksmith shop, and general store all help to complete this rich historical journey of the late 19th century. Its changing exhibit has featured a castle, where kids donned costumes and played roles, as well as opportunities to interact virtually with dinosaurs and a host of authors of children's books. A puzzle gallery enhances the mental acuity and creativity of visitors of all ages, but generally allows the young to show up their elders. Group tours include a visit to the planetarium, where seasonal programs highlight special celestial events. The museum has also re-created a settlement on the Appalachian frontier. Trained interpreters explain the importance of each reconstructed historical building, such as the weaver's shed with its loom. The adjoining park offers swimming, camping, and a skateboard park. RV and tent camping are available on-site. The facilities are located right off Harper Road (Route 13) and are open daily Apr 1 through Nov 1 from 10 a.m. to 6 p.m. Rates are $22 for adults, $16 for seniors, and $12.50 for children under 13. For more information, call (304) 252-3730.

newriver/ greenbrier valleytrivia

The late Senator Robert C. Byrd, a native of Sophia, West Virginia, at 50 years, was the longest serving member in the history of the US Senate. He was also the only congressman to put himself through law school while in office.

Before you leave Beckley, you owe yourself a visit to **Tamarack.** This star-shaped building, just off exit 45 of I-77, is West Virginia's showplace for high-quality arts and crafts, food, and entertainment year-round. Not only can you observe West Virginia glassblowers and carvers working in the studio, but you can hear mountain fiddle players or watch West Virginia's Swiss folk dancers in the auditorium. Juried West Virginia artists display art in various media each month in the gallery; recent themes have included recycled art, environmental beauty, and coal-related art.

Locals line up early at Tamarack's quilt-theme cafeteria for economical meals developed by Greenbrier chefs. Here you can sample ramps, the legendary mountain onion, with your salad or try a colonial bread pudding. Tamarack's retail area stocks books, pottery, wearable arts, and more. Tamarack is open 8 a.m. to 8 p.m. daily. For information on upcoming events, call 88-TAMARACK (888-262-7225) or check tamarackwv.com.

Just 15 minutes south of Beckley, you pass the exit for **Winterplace Ski Resort** (800-607-SNOW; winterplace.com) and **Glade Springs Resort** (866-562-8054; gladesprings.com), a 4,100-acre, 200-room, all-season resort with 3 golf courses. Glade and Winterplace offer combined ski/lodging packages in winter. Winterplace boasts the longest skiing day in southeast West Virginia and the largest tubing park. To warm up, guests can soak in Glade Springs' heated pool, even in January, or enjoy a session of hot rock therapy at the spa. Glade's sophisticated spa offers specialized treatments for rejuvenating skin, including chocolate sugar body polishes and rose-petal wraps.

In summer Glade offers horseback riding, mountain biking, and all manner of off-resort expeditions, including a team-building rafting and climbing outing. And you don't have to work up an appetite to enjoy four-diamond clubhouse food.

Taking to the Tubes

Snow tubing is a democratic sport. At Winterplace Ski Resort's tubing park, the young, the old, the unskilled, and the underimplemented are reclaiming the slopes.

I grew up snow-tubing in a snow-packed pasture, sharing the run with other kids on sleds, plastic trays, and even an old Pontiac hood. We didn't wear color-coordinated outfits or have much technique. But we loved speed and the jolt of hitting the knolls at screaming velocities.

Now folks are tubing in droves in West Virginia's tubing parks, where they pay a fee for canvas-covered tubes they ride up and down the slopes. Straddling the tube, they're pulled up the mountain on a tow lift, then released at the top to blast down an icy chute at speeds up to 30 miles per hour.

It's all perfectly safe, of course. But tubing can be an exercise in relinquishing control as your tube spins down the slope, backward, forward, all perspectives rushing together into a dizzying blur until force peters out at the end of the carefully banked lane.

At Winterplace, where skiers practice feline cool, negotiating clifflike precipices with nonchalance and maintaining silence through close calls, the tubing park is the emotional hot spot. Kids whoop; teens cheer; grandmoms yodel bloodcurdling screams the entire run.

Technique and skill aren't factors here. You can ride the tube butt-down in the doughnut or lie on your stomach; you start the tube down the incline with a shove, then jump on or get someone to push you off. The rest is up to gravity.

Tubing runs are open when the ski resorts are, usually early Dec through late Mar. Besides Winterplace, Canaan Valley Resort, Snowshoe Mountain Resort, Alpine Lake Resort, and Oglebay Resort have tubing parks.

Nestled in the rolling hills of a Flat Top in southern West Virginia, **Blueberry Hill** is the state's largest u-pick blueberry farm. With 15 acres of northern highbush blueberry bushes growing in 100 manicured rows, finding enough blueberries for your pie is easy. Pack a lunch to enjoy at the shaded picnic area. Berry season runs from late June through early August. For specifics, visit blueberryhillWV.com or call (304) 787-3930.

An hour south of Beckley on the West Virginia Turnpike puts you in Princeton, a recovering coal-belt city with the huge **Chuck Mathena Center for the Performing Arts** (877-425-5128; chuckmathenacenter.org) near the center of town; the center has hosted West Virginian Kathy Mattea as well as Ralph Stanley, Sha Na Na, and the Preservation Hall Jazz Band. Go another mile on Route 20/104 (Mercer Street), turn on Main, and you'll come to **Sisters Coffee House**—at least that's its cover by day; on Friday and sometimes Saturday nights Sisters lets down its hair to become a blues cafe featuring some locals and some masters of the national circuit. By day, Sisters serves great coffee, mix-and-match sandwiches, and luscious desserts. Look over the murals and other art by local outsider artists. Call (304) 487-8701. The Sisters' artsy cousin on Mercer Street is the ***RiffRaff Arts Collective*** (304-425-6425; theriffraff.net), a drop-in kind of place for art exhibitions and acoustic, eclectic, and electric music, as well as social drumming, free dance workshops, and occasional open-mike nights. A turn-of-the-20th-century ballroom creates an elegant ambience for live events.

While in Princeton, you may notice a number of restaurants and sports bars with "club" entrances. This is code for "slot machines"—video games that no one under 21 is allowed to play. West Virginia differs from its neighboring states in that gambling is legal here.

In 2001, West Virginia lawmakers set out to control illegal gambling by creating a state-run industry that allows bars, restaurants, and clubs to operate video lottery machines. About 2,000 establishments statewide hold licenses

Disaster

In Maybeury, just over the McDowell County line, company houses radiate up the narrow hollows. This town was the site of the worst railway disaster in the history of the Pocahontas coalfields. On the evening of June 30, 1937, westbound Norfolk & Western freight No. 85 plunged off the east end of the Maybeury trestle, killing three crewmen and a pedestrian and creating an inferno that tied up rail and road traffic for weeks. Fifty-three boxcars spilled liquor, canned pineapple, and Vicks VapoRub over the site, and the explosions shattered windows a quarter mile away. Today the foundations of the old bridge are visible on the left side of the Maybeury curve.

Disaster seemed to lurk around these turns. A mile north on US 52 at Switchback, a deadly combination of coal dust and ignited methane at the Lick Branch Mine killed 50 miners on December 29, 1908. Less than two weeks later, 67 miners died in another explosion, likely caused when an experienced miner overcharged his shot.

"I would hear the sirens going off and people screaming up and down the hollow when there was a mining accident," says Jim Bishop, who grew up in a Mercer County mining town. "Everybody would run to the mine entrance and wait for them to carry out the casualties."

In 1907, 361 miners died in an explosion in Monongah. In 1914–1915, more than 400 miners died in separate incidents in Benwood, Leland, and Eccles. In fact, during World War I, West Virginia miners had a higher casualty rate than the American Expeditionary Force in Europe. While the dangers have subsided dramatically since the 1950s, risk still looms. In 1973, for example, a collapsed slag dam resulted in 175 deaths near Buffalo Creek.

to host such video games as slots, poker, blackjack, and keno. If you'd like to donate money to send West Virginia students to college, try your hand in these glittering arcades. You can find gaming machines in every West Virginia county but Webster—and the closer to the state border you are, the more slots you'll see.

Just south of Princeton is *Bluefield,* a little city that resonates with coal-mining history. Here you should make time to visit the *Eastern Regional Coal Archives,* housed in the Craft Memorial Library (600 Commerce St.; craft-memorial.lib.wv.us). The late archivist Stuart McGehee masterfully assembled a collection of coal-mining memorabilia, including company records, company store account books, correspondence, diaries, films, ledgers, maps, miners' tools, newspapers, and oral history tapes. Black-and-white photographs, some dating from 1919, capture the pain and pride of the miners.

The center is open on a variable schedule Mon through Fri. There is no admission charge. Call (304) 325-3943 for more information.

Bluefield itself makes for an interesting afternoon of touring. The city straddles the Virginia border and is incorporated in both states. It's known as "nature's air-conditioned city" on account of the unusually cool summers. Plays and dinner theater are presented regularly in the elegantly renovated *Summit Theatre* of the old town hall, now the *Bluefield Arts Center.* For information on upcoming events, call (304) 325-9000 or see summitplayers.com.

Like most towns in the coalfields, Bluefield blossomed with the arrival of the railroad. In the 1880s, when the Norfolk & Western Railroad began hauling coal out of the Pocahontas seam, Bluefield consisted of two large farms; six years later, the population topped 1,770, and it doubled every 10 years thereafter for its first three decades. The Norfolk & Western hauled the world's finest coal out of this area for more than 100 years, and the city has long been the industrial, financial, administrative, medical, and corporate center of the region. Its grand 1920s architecture is striking even today and is evident in a host of classical revival, neoclassical, and second–Renaissance revival buildings and homes. One of the most impressive is the elaborate West Virginia Hotel at Federal and Scott Streets. Twelve stories high, it's still the tallest building in southern West Virginia. The hotel once boasted a huge ballroom, dances, and a Paris-trained chef who was stolen away from the Greenbrier Resort. Today the building houses office space, and pawn shops are its neighbors. The Ramsey School, once listed by *Ripley's Believe It or Not* as having the most multilevel entrances, it's now the home of *Gary Bowling's House of Art* as well as the *One Thin Dime Museum*, whose admission is always 10 cents.

Bluefield: Lemonade City

Bluefield is deceptive. A city of imposing commercial buildings and marble-facade storefronts, it seems very much at loose ends, serving a population of barely 12,000. Once a thriving city that boasted the nation's highest per capita ownership of automobiles, Bluefield now counts tire recapping and shoe repair prominent among its downtown businesses. But the edifices of the gilded era still dominate the skyline: the old Elks Lodge with its opera house; the Law and Commerce Building, which once housed a full bowling alley for lunching railroad men; and the Ramsey School, listed in *Ripley's Believe It or Not* for its seven entrances on seven levels. Old City Hall, now the Bluefield Arts Center, houses an art gallery as well as a theater for the town's own Summit Players as well as gallery space. Now the city's claim to fame is tied to its geography rather than its geology. At 2,612 feet, Bluefield is the highest city east of Denver, although with a population of 9,500, it no longer seems like a city. In 1939 the chamber of commerce voted to serve free lemonade on the day following any day when temperatures reached 90°F. Servers had to wait two years to offer their first glass and hit another dry spell between 1960 and 1982. In 2007, however, the Lemonade Lassies passed out free lemonade on 18 days, breaking all records. People have said modern Bluefield is depressed. If its call was a vigorous whoop in its heyday, it would be a loud sigh today. But the city is coming back in little ways. One indication is *Gary Bowling's House of Art* in the Old Ramsey School at 300 Ramsey Street. For starts, artist Bowling vowed to make every door is this building unique, and they are—every one a work of art. Bowling, now past 70, was born in Bluefield and has returned from assignments in Hollywood to make his gallery/studio/performance space/cafe the heartbeat of the community.

He and friends have crafted an artistic, offbeat wild dream of a go-to place for culture with an edge in this rundown coal city. It's a trippy sanctuary for outrageous art packed into every corner and swimming across the ceiling. The House of Art currently represents 20-some West Virginia artists who are becoming known way outside of Bluefield for their outrageous creativity. Bowling's own work includes a life-size, cigar-smoking sculpture of himself draped in Mardi Gras beads. He's also made an Egyptian sarcophagus from an actual shipping coffin. "It was fixin' to be destroyed, so I asked for it," Bowling said. "Since it was a girl, I put a lady pharaoh on top. I hope I did her proud."

Bowling leans heavily on found objects for his art and has been accepting pieces salvaged from Bluefield buildings, including a dozen jail beds as the foundation for his stage and a swooping vulture from a louvered door. All-you-can-eat spaghetti nights and local music raise just enough money to keep his center going.

The House of Art is becoming a zany backdrop for a host of events including bridal showers, kids' parties, and a Harley-Davidson Christmas party. The House of Art is open 10 a.m. to 4 p.m. Saturdays or other days by appointment. Call (304) 324-4242 or see facebook.com/pages/Gary-Bowlings-House-of-Art.

The treehouses at **Buffalo Trail Cabins** near Bluefield offer a surprising extra—a resident buffalo herd that visitors can enjoy watching. Four of the stilted cabins come equipped with the modern amenities such as kitchens, Wi-Fi, cable, heat, AC, and bathrooms. The 11 rustic treehouses are a fun way to go camping and still sleep in a bed. They rely on a nearby bathhouse for showers and toilets. Each comes with a firepit, picnic table, two bunk beds, and an outdoor water source.

The Buffalo Trail resort makes hunkering down in the woods easy with its restaurant, brewery, and camping areas. It is especially popular with ATV riders and is located 3 miles from a Hatfield-McCoy trailhead. Prices are generally $45 a night for the rustic treehouses and $145 for full-service treehouses. (Buffalotrailcabins.com)

West Palm Beach, Newport, Beverly Hills, and Palm Springs: These cities are famous today for their affluence. About 100 years ago, however, tiny **Bramwell,** West Virginia, was undeniably the richest town of its size in the US. Located on a bend of the Bluestone River, about 7 miles northwest of Bluefield on US 52, Bramwell (current population 650) was home to most of the major coal barons of southern West Virginia. In the early part of the 20th century, 14 millionaires lived within a 2-block radius. Their homes, needless to say, are spectacular. Perhaps the most opulent is the **Thomas House,** on Duhring Street. The revival Tudor-style home was built by coal operator W. H. Thomas between 1909 and 1912. Thomas actually had Italian masons brought over to do the stonework on the house and the retaining wall. It's estimated the house cost nearly $100,000 to build, an amazing sum of money at the time.

The nearby **Cooper House,** right on Main Street directly across from the downtown storefronts, is equally impressive. It was built in 1910 with orange bricks sent over from England. The compound contains an indoor swimming pool, among the first found in West Virginia. **Perry House,** located two houses up from Cooper House, was built in 1902 by the bank for the cashier of the Bank of Bramwell, an institution that had the highest per capita deposits in the US at the time. (This powerful little bank helped finance the construction of the Washington, DC, area's famous Burning Tree Country Club.)

If you'd like to try out the small-town life for few days, Bramwell's **Hewitt House B&B** on River and Main Streets puts you right in the middle of things. Take your morning walk along the Bluestone River. Eat lunch at the Corner Shop, an old-fashioned soda fountain with strawberry spinach salad and chicken croissants. The Hewitt House, built in 1914, was the last of the coal baron mansions and featured an early security system, Tiffany lights, and glass roof panels directing sunlight into a skylight. The carriage house, where guests stay, once housed the butler. For reservations, call (304) 248-8385 or visit hewit-thousebedandbreakfast.com.

Bramwell's reconstructed train depot houses the ***Southern Interpretive Center of the Coal Heritage Trail,*** a national historic byway with exhibits depicting life during the coal boom. Private tours can be organized by contacting Bramwell's Town Hall, or you can go it alone by simply picking up a brochure at the interpretive center—more affectionately referred to as the depot—to use on a self-guided walking or driving tour. Sweet-talk Betty Goins, Bramwell tour coordinator, and you may be able to arrange a private tour of the mansions. (You will need to do this a few days ahead.) The little town of Bramwell has a full schedule of festivals and food events during May through October, so check the website at bramwellwv.com or call (304) 325-8438 to find out what's going on or arrange a group tour with Goins. The newest addition to the Hatfield-McCoy ATV trail system, the ***Pocahontas Trail,*** enters Bramwell from Indian Ridge. ***Liberty Station Lodge*** & Tavern has been created in the old Bluestone school near the trail's Pocahontas trailhead. The bar and 14 lodging suites opened in 2021. For info see Liberty-Station-Lodge-Tavern-WV at Facebook.com.

Pinnacle Rock State Park just east of Bramwell on US 52 is a dramatic pointy crag of sandstone that looks a bit like Rapunzel's tower in fairy tales. You can scramble up a short path to the observation deck, but you can't safely go up top to let down your hair. A compact wayside park with a 2-mile trail down to 15-acre Jimmy Lewis Lake, Pinnacle is a product of the Works Progress Administration (WPA). Its stone walkways, fireplaces, and green shelters were constructed in 1938. Pinnacle Rock's peak effectively marks the end of sandstone/limestone topography and the beginning of shaley coal country—to the east you're likely to see farms; to the west, mines and mined-over hills.

As you pass the Bramwell turnoff, look into the forest for the crumbling remains of a line of old beehive-shaped brick coke ovens. These coal-processing kilns are on the left as you climb the US 52 hill west toward Welch.

Continue west on US 52 to get deeper into Appalachian coal country. About five minutes out of Bramwell, you'll cross into McDowell County, or as some locals call it, the Free State of McDowell (in reference to its stormy political history and independent nature). Almost immediately you'll notice how the mountains begin to close in on one another; the valleys narrow to small canyons, and the sky disappears under heavily canopied forests. It's a claustrophobic feeling that's common to this part of the world. You start wondering how folks got into this remote country, let alone exploited it with coal operations.

Coal towns border US 52 through the coalfields—once 132 separate communities. The architecture varies with the distance from Bluefield; the older

Coal Camps

Clusters of houses keep the US 52 coal camps of Simmons and Freeman alive in name, if not in activity. Englishmen John Freeman and Jenkin Jones opened Simmons Creek Mine with only one mule, one mine car, a few shovels, and their bare hands.

In 1889 the pair formed Caswell Creek Coal and Coke Company and made a huge fortune. Their story was not unusual in the southern West Virginia coalfields at the turn of the 20th century, when mines could be opened with relatively little money.

All that was required were houses for miners, a store to supply them, and a tipple to dump coal into the railroad cars. Miners furnished their own tools—picks, shovels, breast augers, tamping bars, needles, and axes. Because of the low cost, many small companies were formed throughout the Pocahontas coalfield.

villages, built first in the railway's westward expansion, have a Victorian look. The wee town of Elkhorn is anchored by a gabled white clapboard home and matching schoolhouse, but Keystone and Kimball are composed of decidedly industrial redbrick row houses. The arched, brick **Elkhorn Inn** (elkhorninnwv .com) hugs a tight curve between US 52 and the Elkhorn Creek in Landgraff. The site began life as a clubhouse for Empire Coal and Coke Company officials. When the original clubhouse burned, Empire erected a reinforced concrete and brick structure built to last till doomsday. And last it did—through years as a rooming house, three floods, and the widening of US 52 to its doorstep. Now an inn, the Elkhorn is especially popular with rail fans, who sit on the balcony watching for some of the 20 or more trains passing the inn daily.

More than 100,000 miners toiled in West Virginia's coalfields during the boom years. Miners came from all over, including African Americans fleeing the Deep South and Eastern European immigrants seeking a better life in the New World. A century ago coal mining was hard, dangerous hand work. Highly mechanized mining today requires fewer workers for more output. Some 500 small company camps have been recognized along the Coal Heritage Trail, many of them just remnants and a few only marks on the map. Isolated as they were, miners were part of tight communities, with scant attention paid to racial or ethnic differences.

As you pass into Kimball, the first thing you notice is the three-story classic Greek temple on the right, its yellow bricks shining like the sun in this dingy coal town. The restored **World War I Memorial Building** stands honorably as tribute to the 400,000 African-American soldiers who defended America. It is reportedly the nation's first monument honoring Black soldiers. As many as 1,500 Black McDowell Countians, all coal miners, volunteered.

Captain G. E. Ferguson, the state's only Black officer of his rank to serve in World War I, dedicated the building in 1928. The building is also the site of the first African-American American Legion post and is on the National Historic Register. It has been the center of community life for Black and white people alike in Kimball and has hosted Cab Calloway's band and other notables. After years of neglect and a devastating fire, the War Memorial has been fully restored, thanks to a $1.6 million renovation and an interactive museum exhibit prepared by West Virginia University students and faculty. It can be visited most weekday mornings, but you might want to call first at (304) 436-3096.

In the town of **Welch,** in the southern end of the Tug Fork Valley, US 52 takes you close to the stately McDowell County Courthouse. It was here on August 1, 1921, on the front steps of the building, that detectives hired by coal-company officials gunned down Matewan chief of police Sid Hatfield and union activist Ed Chambers in retaliation for the deaths of two of their colleagues during the Matewan Massacre a year earlier. The courthouse killings touched off a series of events that led to the Battle of Blair Mountain in neighboring Logan County, in which 10,000 miners took up arms against coal-company officials. It was the largest insurrection in the US since the Civil War, and it was put down only after federal troops were called in and several lives were lost.

Every year in July and August, West Virginia thespians gather to put on performances of *"Terror of the Tug,"* a dramatization of the Baldwin-Felts coal company murders of Hatfield and Chambers outside the Welch courthouse

FOR MORE INFORMATION

New River Gorge Convention and Visitors Bureau
(800) 927-0263
newrivergorgecvb.com

Southern West Virginia Convention and Visitors Bureau
(304) 252-2244 or (800) VISIT–WV
visitwv.com

Summers County Convention and Visitors Bureau
(304) 466-5420
exploresummerscounty.com

Mercer County Convention and Visitors Bureau
Bluefield/Princeton
(800) 221-3206
visitmercercounty.com

Greenbrier County Convention and Visitors Bureau
(800) 833-2068
greenbrierwv.com

in 1921. The play, written by local playwright Jean Battlo, is presented at the McArts Amphitheater on Toms Mountain Road off US 52 between Kimball and Welch. Story characters provide their opinions of what happened and attendees can draw their own conclusions. On the afternoon of August 1, there is usually a reenactment of the shootings outside Welch Courthouse. For information, call (304) 888-2057.

Places to Stay in the New River/ Greenbrier Valley Region

ANSTED

Hawks Nest State Park Lodge
US 60
(304) 658-5212
wvstateparks.com/park/
hawks-nest-state-park
moderate

BLUEFIELD

Bluefield Inn
2109 Jefferson St.
(304) 323-2200
bluefieldinn.com
Moderate to expensive

DANIELS

Resort at Glade Springs
255 Resort Dr.
(866) 671-5892
gladesprings.com
Moderate to expensive

FAYETTEVILLE

Morris Harvey House B&B
201 W. Maple Ave.
(304) 646-7561
morrisharveyhouse.com
Moderate to expensive

HICO

Country Road Cabins
1508 Sunday Rd.
(304) 658-5267
Wvcabins.com
Moderate to Expensive

HINTON

Guest House Inn on Courthouse Square
419 Second St.
(304) 466-8100
guesthousewv.com
Moderate to expensive

LEWISBURG

General Lewis Inn
301 E. Washington St.
(304) 645-2600
generallewisinn.com
Moderate to expensive

PIPESTEM

Pipestem Resort State Park
Route 20
(304) 466-1800
wvstateparks.com/park/
pipestem-resort-state-park
Inexpensive to moderate

Places to Eat in the New River/ Greenbrier Valley Region

BLUEFIELD

The Vault Downtown
401 Federal St.
(304) 308-6601
Moderate to expensive

DANIELS

Glade's Grill at Glade Springs Resort
255 Club Dr.
(304) 763-3033
gladesprings.com
Expensive

FAYETTEVILLE

Cathedral Café
134 S. Court St.
(304) 574-0202
thecathedralcafe.com
Moderate

KIMBALL

Ya'Sou Greek Restaurant
138 Main St.
(304) 585-7959
Budget

LEWISBURG

**The General Lewis Inn
and Restaurant**
301 E. Washington St.
(304) 645-2600
Moderate to expensive

Stardust Cafe
102 E. Washington St.
(304) 647-3663
stardustcafewv.com
Moderate

MULLENS

**Twin Falls Resort
State Park**
Route 16
(304) 294-4000
Moderate

PIPESTEM

Pipestem Resort
State Park
Route 20
(304) 466-1800
Moderate

PRINCETON

Tudor's Biscuit World
1218 Stafford Dr.
(304) 487-8010
Budget

**WHITE SULPHUR
SPRINGS**

The Greenbrier Resort
Route 92
(304) 536-1110
(800) 624-6070
Very expensive

Metro Valley

Named for the population center stretching from the capital city of Charleston west to Huntington, the Metro Valley region is the most populated in the state. The area boasts large museums and an abundance of restaurants and theaters, but there are many places to get off the beaten path—especially along the byways of the southern counties.

Steeped in Appalachian history is the Mingo County town of *Matewan,* site of the Hatfield-McCoy feud (yes, it really happened) and the Matewan Massacre. Matewan is located on the Tug Fork River, a twisty two-hour-plus drive from Charleston along WV 65 US 119 (that is, if there's not a coal truck in front of you).

Vestiges of the Hatfield-McCoy years surround you here. Snuggled into the hillside above Mate Street and the Norfolk & Southern Railroad is *Warm Hollow,* site of the Anderson Ferrell House, where Ellison Hatfield died in 1882 after an attack by three McCoy brothers. The retaliatory violence came on Election Day in August 1882 just across the river in Kentucky. After the young Hatfield died, "Devil" Anse Hatfield executed the McCoys in Kentucky. The killings went on for eight more years, but the sensationalism surrounding the feud continues.

METRO VALLEY

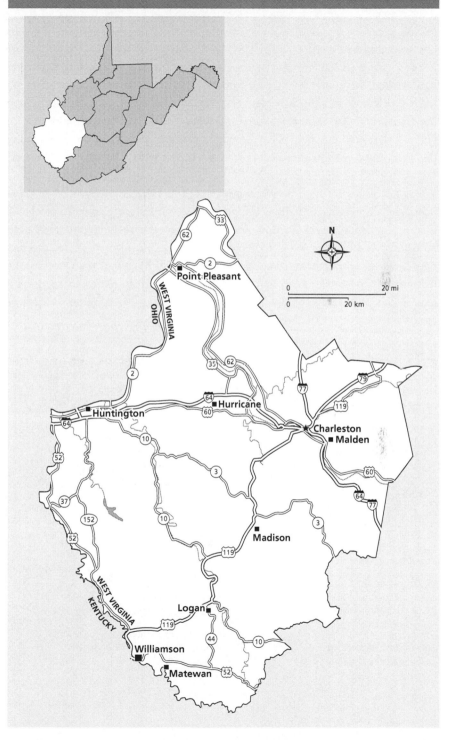

today. Some accounts in major eastern newspapers of the time cited death tolls in excess of 100 people. In reality, the ongoing feud resulted in 12 deaths and probably had its roots in the Civil War; "Devil" Hatfield had fought for the Confederacy and Randall McCoy took up arms for the Union. The Civil War had divided this community, with rumors running rampant about who might have shot whom in various battles. The fight over the runaway pig that started the Hatfield-McCoy conflict stoked a fire whose coals had been smoldering for years. Today Hatfield and McCoy descendants meet peacefully on the banks of the Tug outside Matewan each June for a reunion with a Hatfield-McCoy rope tug as their most aggressive act.

A fire swept through downtown Matewan in 1992 and destroyed or damaged several historic buildings. A massive revitalization program produced a new but familiar-looking downtown. Some of the historic buildings have received face-lifts, green spaces have been created, and a museum/interpretive center was constructed in a replica of the old Matewan train depot. The historical-minded restoration has had the result of giving Matewan the look it had in the 1920s. The whole downtown was designated a National Historic Landmark by the US Department of the Interior in 1997.

BEST ANNUAL EVENTS IN THE METRO VALLEY REGION

Annual WV Hunting and Fishing Show
Charleston; late January
(304) 767-4466
wvtrophyhunters.com

St. Patrick's Day Celebration
Huntington; mid-March
(304) 525-7333
visithuntingtonwv.org

Dogwood Arts and Crafts Festival
Huntington; late April
(304) 696-5990
bigsandyarena.com

Vandalia Gathering
Charleston; late May
(304) 558-0220
wvculture.org/vandalia

West Virginia Coal Festival
Madison; mid-June
(304) 369-5180
wvcoalmuseum.org

FestivALL
Charleston; mid-June
(304) 470-0489
festivallcharleston.com

Hatfield & McCoy Reunion Festival
Williamson/Matewan; June
(304) 235-5240
hatfieldmccoyreunion at Facebook.com

Mothman Festival
Point Pleasant; mid-September
(304) 812-5211
Mothmanfestival.com

The stories of the region's bloody past, as well as its proud coal-mining traditions, unfold in the *Matewan Depot Museum* through fascinating photographs and exhibits. The exhibition area is open 10 a.m. to 5 p.m. Tues through Sun. Call (304) 426-5744 for more information. If you're approaching town from the west, look for the floodwall murals, which start at the depot and extend along the town, keeping the Tug River in its bed.

Over the past 20-some years, interest in Matewan and its past has undoubtedly been rekindled because of the award-winning 1987 film *Matewan,* a historical drama that featured James Earl Jones. The actual confrontation took place on May 19, 1920. At the time, the United Mine Workers of America (UMWA) was trying to organize the area's coal miners, but those who joined soon found themselves fired and evicted from their company-owned homes by Baldwin-Felts guards hired by the mining company. When chief of police Sid Hatfield encountered coal-company detectives hired to evict miners, shots were fired, resulting in the deaths of the town's mayor, seven detectives, and two miners. Hatfield emerged as a hero, both before and after the tragic events a year later in McDowell County. Among many other great treats, the depot has the actual gun and badge of Al Felts, who was killed while leading the Baldwin-Felts guards during the Matewan Massacre.

As you walk through Matewan, head to the *Old Matewan National Bank Building* on the northeast corner of Mate Street and a small alley leading back to the railroad tracks. It is now the *Mine Wars Museum*. The massacre began in the alley here, and bullet holes from the confrontation are still visible on the side of the former bank building. The building located next door once housed Chambers Hardware, where the first shots of the massacre were fired. Down the street at the corner of Mate and Hatfield is the Buskirk Building, whose second-floor Urias Hotel served as headquarters for the coal-company detectives. The UMWA, interestingly, was headquartered almost directly across the street in the Nenni Building, adjacent to the Hatfield Building The Mine Wars Museum explores this tragic event as well as the machine gun battle during the Cabin Creek strikes and the Battle of Blair Mountain, in which thousands of armed miners marched into Logan County. The resulting guerilla warfare claimed the lives of about 100 and only ended when 2,500 federal troops were sent in by President Warren Harding. Outside the Civil War, Blair Mountain is the largest armed insurrection in American history. The museum uses historical artifacts, photos, film, and art to tell the stories. In West Virginia, it's always a good idea to toss your fishing rod into the car. Matewan has a nice waterfront area on the Tug River with good fishing spots. While you're there, you can study the sculpted floodwall that depicts Matewan's history.

Using the Hatfield-McCoy names in an endeavor of unusual cooperation and community spirit, a group of southern West Virginia citizens, politicians, and corporations is building a multiuse trail system. The user-fee-supported Hatfield-McCoy Trails have opened more than 1,000 miles of track in Logan, Lincoln, McDowell, Mercer, Mingo, Wyoming, and Boone Counties, with plans for an eventual 1,500 more miles. Right now the system is open to motorcycles, ATVs, mountain bikes, and hikers. The unique part is that the trail system exists totally on private land, mostly resurfaced mining and logging roads. Already the trails are providing both recreational and economic opportunities for the area; several cabins and ATV and motorcycle repair shops have opened in Logan, Gilbert, and Delbarton near the trailheads. Annual activities on the trail include a summer hike, a dirt bike rally, a national ATV rally, and an October Hatfield-McCoy Trail Fest. Trail use fees are $26.50 annually for state residents and $50 for out-of-state visitors. For more information and detailed trail maps, call (800) 592-2217 or (304) 752-3255 or consult the website at TrailsHeaven.com.

Lodging possibilities are growing in this corner of West Virginia, but you might want to start heading toward Charleston, the state capital and West Virginia's largest city, about two hours north, for the more extensive nightlife. On your way up US 119, you'll pass through the town of Logan and by Chief Logan State Park. The lodge (chiefloganlodge .com) features 75 modern rooms, an indoor swimming pool, a fitness room, and complimentary breakfast. If you have children, the park is a good place to stop and acquaint them with several West Virginia animals they aren't likely to see outside of the park's wildlife exhibit: the wild boar and the bobcat. During the summer months the park stages productions of *The Aracoma Story,* an outdoor play depicting the struggle of the Shawnee to survive in a changing land. It's based on both historical fact and local legend and tells the story of Chief Cornstalk's daughter Aracoma and her lover Boling Baker, a British soldier captured by her father. The Chief Logan Amphitheater also houses other dramatic productions, such as *Coal*, a drama inspired by true events and the Battle of Blair Mountain, as well as the Aunt Jenny Wilson Music Festival. A lodge and restaurant serve guests in style year-round; Sunday buffets are especially popular. The Museum at the Park showcases the region's coal and railroad heritage along with a rotating art exhibit. It is open Wed through Sat 10 a.m. to 5 p.m. and Sun 1 to 5 p.m.

metrovalley trivia

The Tug Fork River, which meanders along the Kentucky–West Virginia border, is the longest free-flowing river in central Appalachia.

For more information on the shows, call (304) 792-7229, or visit www.chief loganstatepark.com.

Madison is a required stop on US 119 if you're at all interested in coal history. The **Bituminous Coal Heritage Museum,** located at 347 Main St., features an interactive display offering a glimpse of how coal was mined in the early days of the mining industry. The 2,000-square-foot display includes a simulated company store, a miner's home, and a locker room where miners changed for work. There's also a dark, tight area where visitors can get the sensory experience of underground mining without the coal dust. You can even try your hand with the pick, auger, drill, and shovel of an old-fashioned craftsman miner. The exhibit covers mining methods, company stores, coal camps, unions, disasters, and the legacy of the coal industry. It's no surprise that the annual **West Virginia Coal Festival** is held here in June. The event features music, crafts, parades, and a memorial to lost miners. The museum is open Thurs through Sat and Mon afternoons. For more information about the museum or the festival, call (304) 369-5180 or visit wvcoalmuseum.org.

In the summer Julian, 15 minutes up US 119, offers a great water stop. **Water Ways,** operated by Boone County Parks and Recreation, features 2 giant downhill water slides, a floating chute, a junior-Olympic-size pool, 18-hole miniature golf, and a playground—recreation challenging enough for even a bored teenager. Water Ways is open 11 a.m. to 6 p.m. daily June through late Aug. General admission to the pool, slides, and golf is $12 per person; $5 for children under 44 inches tall, and free for children under 3 when accompanied by a paying adult. For more information, call (304) 369-1235 or see waterwayspark.net.

The Capital Region

West Virginia is graced with one of the most beautiful state capitals in the US. **Charleston** (population about 50,000) fans out along the banks of the Kanawha River, a major transport link to the Ohio Valley and the industrial Midwest. Charleston is actually a good five to six hours from the nearest major population centers of Pittsburgh and Cincinnati and as such has maintained a certain rugged "big small-town" charm. The relative remoteness of the capital city probably explains why so much of its beautiful architecture has been so well preserved.

There's a lot to see and do in Charleston, starting with the **Capitol Complex,** located just off Washington Street 2 blocks up from the Kanawha River. The gold-domed Capitol Building and Governor's Mansion are both worth the hour you'll spend on the tour, not only for the beauty of the architecture, but for the inside stories you'll get. Call (304) 558-4839 for reservations. The first two capitol buildings in Charleston burned down, but this marble and limestone edifice was built to last in 1932. While the Capitol Building and Governor's Mansion are among the city's most on-the-beaten-path sites, few folks wander over to the impressive *West Virginia Cultural Center,* the $17.6 million facility that reopened in the summer of 2009 after being closed for five years for renovations. And it was worth the wait. Rather than simply displaying artifacts behind glass, the museum offers a total sensory experience. Its focal point is a show path winding between scenes in the 24,000-square-foot facility, beginning in prehistoric coal forests 300 million years ago. Highlights include a re-creation of the courtroom in Wheeling's Independence Hall where the state's founding fathers give their case for West Virginia's separation from Virginia, and a display of frontier life featuring Daniel Boone's rifle and George Washington's sword.

Visitors also enter an eerie coal shaft, witness the beginning of the Great Depression, and experience a scale model of the view from New River Gorge Bridge, complete with 9,500 tiny trees. The tour doesn't shy away from the negative elements of the state's history, including the deaths of hundreds of workers building Hawk's Nest Tunnel, the 1920s mine wars, and the ongoing controversy over mountaintop removal mining methods. Touring the show path typically takes about an hour, but if you stopped to view every display and watch every documentary video, the tour would require 26 hours. That's reason for a few return visits.

BEST ATTRACTIONS IN THE METRO VALLEY REGION

Avampato Discovery Museum
Charleston
(304) 561-3575
theclaycenter.org

Blenko Glass
Milton
(304) 743-9081
blenko.com

Heritage Farm Museum & Village
Huntington
(304) 522-1244
heritagefarmmuseum.com

Huntington Museum of Art
Huntington
(304) 592-2701
hmoa.org

West Virginia State Capitol Complex
Charleston
(304) 558-4839
wvculture.org

West Virginia State Museum and Cultural Center
Charleston
(304) 558-0220
wvculture.org

The museum is open year-round from 9 a.m. to 5 p.m. Tues through Sat. Check wvculture.org or call (304) 558-0220. Don't miss the craft shop adjacent to the Great Hall, with its wide assortment of mountain arts, crafts, historical books, novels, and music. There's also a gallery displaying everything from quilts to photos to oil paintings.

World Music from West Virginia

West Virginia's live public radio show may be called *Mountain Stage,* but the music doesn't always come from the hills of West Virginia. You could hear a bluegrass musician from Japan or a Hungarian ensemble teamed up with Jerry Jeff Walker and a traditional Irish band.

"We have a show that is radically eclectic," says host Larry Groce

Mountain Stage gives airtime to folks who don't necessarily fit neatly into today's radio formats, particularly in the singer/songwriter and Americana genres. Groce, who is best known for his 1976 pop hit "Junk Food Junkie," is the mix master who has blended the music of the known and not so well known for more than two decades. "We've been able to feature people who aren't famous yet, but who become famous later," he says. Some of those who have taken the stage of the West Virginia Cultural Center before they were stars were Mary Chapin Carpenter, Kathy Mattea, and Sheryl Crow.

In fact, West Virginia native and country singer Kathy Mattea took over Groce's reins as host of *Mountain Stage* in late 2021. Mattea, a two-time Grammy winner from Cross Lanes, has performed on the show more than any other artist except fellow West Virginia native Tim O'Brien.

Each week more than a quarter of a million people worldwide listen to the show on more than 300 radio stations in the US, in Ireland, and on the Voice of America. It's public radio's longest-running live musical variety show, on the air since December 1983.

On Sunday at 6 p.m., Groce ambles on stage at the intimate theater in his faded blue jeans to introduce the show to his live audience. It takes a minute for the band to saunter in—Ron Sowell, Bob Thompson, Julie Adams, Michael Lipton, Steve Hill, Ryan Kennedy, and Ammed Solomon—mostly 60-ish folks who started playing together in the days of tape decks.

"If you only listened to *Mountain Stage* on radio and had illusions about us, this could be sad," Groce says to the live audience. Then the Mountain Stage Band kicks off and nobody cares about anything but music.

"We're relaxed because we're like family," Groce explains, "and because it's the West Virginia way. We're an international show, but the pressure is off because we're in West Virginia. Artists relax. You hear music here you won't hear on their recordings. There's just something magical about live music."

The West Virginia Petroglyph Mystery

Just south of Oceana in Wyoming County, a little roadside marker makes a bold claim: Celtic explorers were here in the heart of southern West Virginia at least 700 years before Columbus visited America. A petroglyph, or rock carving, on a nearby sandstone outcropping supposedly corroborates that statement.

The little path beside the railroad could lead to one of continent's most important historical sites—or just to an interesting archaeological find left by American Indians perfecting their carving techniques. No one really knows for sure.

The hundreds of short vertical lines and turkey-foot symbols, known as the Lynco petroglyph, are similar to some of the other petroglyphs found at about two dozen sites in West Virginia—and attributed to the Woodland-era American Indians. But these and a few others in Wyoming County were written in an old Irish alphabet called ogham, according to the late Barry Fell, a controversial Harvard marine biology professor who studied ancient languages. He and some others thought the carvings told the story of Christ's birth. They hypothesized these petroglyphs were at least 1,300 years old, bearing out Fell's belief that prehistoric America was visited by European explorers, possibly a sixth-century Irish missionary named St. Brendan. Never mind that another scholar who studied Basque languages said the story was about a buffalo stampede. Others read something about a supernova, while still others dismissed the markings as the more recent work of American Indians.

And then there is the question of why a European would be slogging through impenetrable West Virginia, when even mounted soldiers 1,100 years later turned back exhausted before reaching Wyoming County during the French and Indian War. How would these Europeans cross all the rivers?

A few years later, the West Virginia researcher who first began advancing the idea of the Irish alphabet found human remains at another Wyoming County petroglyph site, bones that DNA indicates are likely European and dating to AD 700. Still the archaeological society is not yet convinced of the message, nor of the language of the petroglyphs. The West Virginia petroglyphs remain a mystery.

To see the Wyoming County petroglyphs for yourself, take Route 971 from Oceana toward Lynco and look for the roadside marker on the right. It's on a bank just above the railroad. You can also visit the Dingess Petroglyphs, removed for a strip-mining site in nearby Mingo County, at Laurel Lake Wildlife Management Area near Lenore. The Ceredo Museum (townofceredo.com) near Huntington contains a large petroglyph pulled from the edge of the Ohio River during bridge work.

If you love authentic old-time or bluegrass music, the cultural center is the place to be every Memorial Day weekend when the *Vandalia Gathering* comes to town. In addition to two full days of music featuring West Virginia musicians—many of whom are world renowned—Vandalia is spiced with plenty of food and folklife demonstrations. You'll also hear some feats of imaginational gymnastics at West Virginia's biggest-liar contest. If you missed the show, head back into the cultural center shop and get a copy of *The Music Never Dies: A Vandalia Sampler,* a CD of some of the festival's finest musical performances over the years.

Also found in the cultural center is a concert theater that offers a variety of performances, including **Mountain Stage,** the eclectic music program produced by West Virginia Public Radio. The two-hour live show is taped every Sunday from 7 to 9 p.m., except when *Mountain Stage* is touring around the state. The show regularly hosts nationally and internationally recognized musicians and features some of the best jazz, folk, blues, and new music in America. Past shows have included the likes of R.E.M., Buckwheat Zydeco, Steve Earle, Kathy Mattea, Robin & Linda Williams, and the Flatlanders, to name a few.

Tickets are available for $25 to $45 through their website at mountainstage.org or by calling (304) 556-4900. The cultural center, meanwhile, is open Mon through Sat from 9 a.m. to 5 p.m.

From the Capitol Complex, hop a trolley that'll take you through Charleston's **East End Historic District.** Here you'll find more than 20 historic buildings and mansions, most dating from the 1890s, Charleston's gilded age. The grand homes give way to downtown, with modern hotels, fine restaurants, a large civic center, and interesting shops.

Charleston has been called one of the most northern of the southern cities and the most southern of the northern cities. Its past is just as full of contradictions and contrasts, but now that just means many things are possible. You can cruise the Kanawha on a stern-wheeler or play the slot machines in nearby Cross Lanes. You may spend an evening with the **Charleston Light Opera Guild** (charlestonlightoperaguild.org) or participate in the state turkey-calling contest at the WV Hunting and Fishing Show. You might go virtual caving or play in the ball pond at Avampato Discovery Museum's ElectricSky theater or taste pawpaw ice cream or jalapeño poppers a few blocks away.

metrovalley trivia

Contemporary country music star Kathy Mattea is a native of Cross Lanes.

Charleston may be a small capital, but it's the hub of business, industry, and government for a surrounding metropolitan area that consists of more than 6,000 businesses and 250,000 people. However, taking care of business is not the only priority of this sweet city. Embracing a sense of community, Charleston has maintained one of the lowest crime rates in the nation.

The downtown *Clay Center for the Arts & Sciences* (399 Leon Sullivan Way) combines a first-class performing arts center and concert hall with the high-tech *Avampato Discovery Museum,* complete with planetarium and hands-on educational programs for children of all ages. Whether it's exploring earth science through a series of water troughs, learning about health by stretching a giant intestine, or making music with a spider, kids have fun learning. The art gallery showcases West Virginia and international artists and has cultivated a permanent collection of nearly 800 works. The Avampato is open Mon through Sat 10 a.m. to 5 p.m. and noon to 5 p.m. on Sun. For more information call (304) 561-3570 or see theclaycenter.org.

A night at the *Charleston Ballet* (thecharlestonballet.com), *Chamber Music Society* (charlestonchambermusic.org), or *Charleston Symphony Orchestra* (wvsymphony.org) is the perfect complement to delectable fare at one of Charleston's fine restaurants. You can enjoy a spectacular view of the river and city while sampling dishes at Laury's fine restaurant in a restored C&O Railroad depot. *Playa Bowls, Los Agaves, Little Indian, Best of Crete,* and *Sahara* will satisfy a range of cravings. Top off the evening with some original live music at the *Empty Glass,* where Mountain Stage performers and guests sometimes let their hair down after the radio show.

Other downtown attractions include the Charleston Civic Center and one of the largest downtown malls in the East, encompassing 140 stores on 3 levels, 18 eateries, and shops dedicated to tea, lingerie, baseball caps, and games. *Taylor Books* (226 Capitol St.; 304-342-1461; taylorbooks.com) manages to blend book readings, an art gallery, live music, and a cafe all in one bookstore. Taylor is the place to find work by your favorite West Virginia artist, whether it's Mountain Stage violinist Julie Adams or West Virginia–born author Jayne Anne Phillips. Across the street is *Ellen's Homemade Ice Cream,* a favorite for its cappuccinos, light lunches, and super-premium ice cream in flavors both beloved or as offbeat as pawpaw and mulberry.

metrovalley trivia

Charleston's Craik-Patton House, a 166-year-old Greek Revival home, was once owned by Colonel George S. Patton, grandfather of General Patton of World War II fame.

Ten minutes east of downtown on US 60 is the boyhood home of African-American educator Booker T. Washington. The riverside village of *Malden* seems dedicated to his history, from the life-size replica of *Booker T. Washington's cabin* to the *Women's Park* dedicated to his sister, Amanda Johnson, who lived there in a house he purchased.

"Kick a rock in Malden, and you wonder if Booker T. kicked that same rock," says West Virginia attorney and former senator Larry Rowe, whose office stands near Washington's homesite. "I tell kids they could be the next world leader to come out of Malden."

In 1865, 9-year-old Washington walked 225 miles with his family from the Virginia farm where he had been enslaved to his freedom home in Malden. Here he labored in the saltworks with his stepfather, eventually becoming a garden helper for the wealthy Ruffner family, who encouraged his education. By the time of his death in 1915, he was called "the most important leader of any race to come out of the South after the Civil War" by his arch-critic, W. E. B. Du Bois.

metrovalley trivia

African-American educational pioneer Booker T. Washington is one of three West Virginians elected to the Hall of Fame for Great Americans.

A replica of Washington's small cabin and the schoolhouse he attended has been built behind the church where he learned to read. *African Zion Baptist Church* was organized in the 1850s as the first Black Baptist church in western Virginia. After his graduation from Hampton Institute, Washington taught Sunday school here and also got married in the sanctuary. The original pulpit and pews remain. *West Virginia State University's Booker T. Washington Institute* is creating a museum in the nearby *Norton House,* home of the Norman Jordan African-American history collection. The Malden site interprets Washington's life as well as early industry in Malden, where young Washington worked in a salt mine while teaching himself to read. Nearby is a park dedicated to the women of Malden, built on the site where the home of Washington's half-sister, Amanda, once stood. Visitors can arrange tours through the Booker T. Washington Institute at West Virginia State University (304-766-5736) or inquire at WV Delegate Larry Rowe's adjacent law office (304-925-1333) about the tour schedule.

On the western side of Charleston, look for a high spot. A huge earthen blister at the end of D Street, *Criel Mound* rises 35 feet out of Staunton Park in a knoll the length of two tennis courts. Once it contained 13 skeletons. That was before West Virginia residents built a horse-racing track around its base and lopped off the top for a judge's stand, back in 1840. The mound, created by Adena people between 250 and 150 BC, was excavated by the US Bureau of Ethnology in 1883–1884 and restored with a walking path spiraling up to its summit. The view from the top is the best orientation to South Charleston.

Glass Dancing at Blenko

Cajoling screaming-hot, molten glass into art is an intense dance. This is not something you realize right away when you first step into the observation area with a tour group at **Blenko Glass**. The terse moves of the glass crafters are so carefully orchestrated, the duties so precisely configured and intuitive for these relaxed masters in tennis shoes, that you don't realize a second's delay will turn the glass unworkably sluggish; a second more heat will melt it into amorphousness. Too much pressure cracks the molding glass; too little produces weak stems.

Heat is life for glass. The craftsmen work when the glass is about 1800°F. When they lose the heat, the glass goes brittle.

So these master craftspeople step lively as they work—from the gatherer, winding a gob of fiery taffy on the end of his punty rod; to the gaffer, who straightens stemware with a wooden paddle; or the swinger, twirling glowing glass to give it shape.

Water breaks are important here, where temperatures routinely hit 100°F. Sunglasses and even shorts are de rigueur for folks who face red-hot furnaces all day. Once "snowbird" glassworkers picked up work in the warm factories during the winter but set out hunting or fishing with the first warm breezes of spring. Now workers toil year-round, serving an apprenticeship of two to 12 years to become a skilled member of the glassworkers' union.

During excavation, scientists found the fragments of two skeletons near the top and an earlier burial of 11 people in the bottom. A giant skeleton almost 8 feet tall lay at the center of the base. The remains, which fragmented when exposed to air, were removed to Washington, DC. The place to learn the story of the mound and the Adena people is the **South Charleston Interpretive Center** (313 D St.; 304-720-9847; southcharlestonwv.org/interpretivecenter), 4 blocks down D Street. The little museum contains a trove of arrowheads, stone tools, and Adena jewelry, as well as a relief model of the Criel Mound and images of its sibling mounds near Charleston. South Charleston Interpretive Center is open 10 a.m. to 5 p.m. Mon through Fri and 11 a.m. to 4 p.m. Sat.

The Tri-State Area

The Tri-State Area begins just west of Charleston and extends westward about 60 miles to Huntington and the confluence of the Big Sandy and Ohio Rivers, the point where the states of Ohio, Kentucky, and West Virginia meet. It contains portions of Putnam, Cabell, and Wayne Counties, and it's among the most densely populated and industrialized parts of the state. Of course, comparatively speaking, what's considered densely populated in West Virginia would be thought of as largely rural in most other states.

The Tri-State is marked by low rolling hills that don't seem all that intimidating until you try driving the back roads over and around them. Most of the secondary roads here aren't going to take you anywhere particularly fast. But because they're so close to the population corridors of Charleston and Huntington, you can ramble off the beaten path without ever worrying about getting totally lost—a claim that could never be made in the more mountainous and isolated parts of the state.

If you ever thought of going to the dog track, you probably had South Florida and swaying palm trees in mind. The Sunshine State comes to the Mountain State via the ***Mardi Gras Casino & Resort*** in Cross Lanes, about 13 miles west of Charleston off I-64. You can expect to watch some of the best dog racing in the US right here in West Virginia, as well as simulcasts of races at other locations. Casual seating is available in the 3,000-seat grandstand; more formal viewing is offered in the clubhouse area, which seats 1,200 and includes the rather nice ***French Quarter Restaurant.*** Motown, R&B, jazz, and country bands play some Friday and Saturday—no cover charge. Clubhouse patrons can also watch and bet on simulcast horse racing from around the country. For resort information and reservations, call (888) 789-7829. The center also features 1,200 slot machines in its 90,000-square-foot casino, and 30 table games—blackjack, roulette, poker, and craps. It all makes for a fun afternoon or evening.

The park is open from 11 a.m. to 5 p.m., with races beginning at 7 p.m. Live races run from the second week of April through mid-October, Tues through Sat. Another facet of the center is ***Friends of Greyhounds Adoption Services*** (304-776-1000; friendsofgreyhounds.org/fog), which finds homes for retiring dogs. For specific information about the track and gaming center or how to place a wager, see the website at mardigrascasinowv.com.

Head west on I-64 from Charleston and you'll venture into the heart of what was once West Virginia's ***glass country.*** The area, along with the Mid-Ohio Valley, was once dotted with dozens of companies that specialized in the difficult and beautiful art of glassmaking. West Virginia's prized sandstones and sands have been used over the years in a variety of ways, from extracting silica and minerals to oil and natural gas production to the making of some of the world's finest glassware.

The small community of ***Hurricane*** was named by George Washington when, as a young surveyor, he came across a spot near the Kanawha River where all the trees were bent in the same direction. Legend had it that a hurricane, or at least a strong windstorm, must have come through just prior to

Washington's arrival. The town existed as a stagecoach stop and livestock center for another century before the railroad arrived in 1873 and the community began to thrive in earnest.

If you stroll along Main Street in Hurricane, you'll spot several historic items—a Victorian gazebo, a restored CSX caboose, and a large chunk of rock carved with a primitive drawing of what looks like an indignant woman. The rock, West Virginia's most controversial petroglyph, is known as "Maiden of the Rock," "Water Monster's Daughter," or "Prom Queen," depending upon who's talking. The 77-inch sandstone carving represents a woman standing with her arms akimbo and her hair sticking straight out all over her head. She looks pretty scary, frankly. Before being moved downtown, the petroglyph was part of the roof of a natural stone shelter overlooking a nearby valley. Although authentic arrowheads and stone tools lay around the site and the figure's head resembles others carved by Native Americans in the 1500s, most archaeologists

"Mad Anne" Bailey Was Here

The exploits of *"Mad Anne" Trotter Bailey* are legendary in the Kanawha Valley. Not only did the frontierswoman evade the American Indians as a colonial spy, but tales of her fighting prowess have added to the intrigue of Point Pleasant. You can visit her grave at Point Pleasant Battle Monument State Park (also known as Tu-Endie-Wei State Park), where the museum contains her hair and other memorabilia.

Anne didn't start out mad. Anne Hennis came from Liverpool, England, and married fellow indentured servant Richard Trotter when their servitude expired. They settled in the mountains near Covington, Virginia, and were raising a family when Richard enlisted with Colonel Andrew Lewis's forces to fight the Shawnees in 1774. He was killed in the fight against Chief Cornstalk at the Battle of Point Pleasant.

When Anne heard of her husband's death, she became obsessed with revenge. She immediately put on leggings, armed herself with a tomahawk and rifle, and left her son in the care of others as she rode about attending every muster she could find.

In a few years she married an army ranger named John Bailey and went off to serve with him at Fort Lee in Clendennin's Settlement, where Charleston now stands. When the officers saw her skill with the rifle, they offered Anne a career as a spy and messenger.

Soon after the murder of Cornstalk at Point Pleasant, American Indians surrounded Fort Lee. The colonials were almost out of gunpowder, and not a man would risk his life to ride to a distant warehouse. Anne mounted her steed, Liverpool, and took off alone. She rode day and night for 100 miles, often pursued by American Indians, until she arrived at Fort Savannah (Lewisburg). Anne loaded up two horses with ammunition and stole back to Charleston, saving the fort.

who examined the Putnam County petroglyph immediately suspected its body was chipped out more recently—"with a coal chisel," suggested Virginia Commonwealth University art historian Reinaldo Morales after visiting Hurricane.

In Hurricane, they call her **Water Monster's Daughter.** Locals say the state historical society believes she is partially authentic. An amateur archaeologist who lived here all his life admitted to adding the skirt when he was a teenager. Dean Braley, the budding archaeologist who embellished the Water Monster's Daughter, lived to regret his adolescent actions. As an adult, he studied the religious significance of petroglyphs and published a book, *Shaman's Story: West Virginia Petroglyphs* in 1993.

Most often, historians say, petroglyphs were a form of prewriting communication and may have embodied magical techniques in a coded symbolic language. Petroglyphs have been identified at 27 sites in West Virginia, mostly in the western and southern sections. Images range from birds and serpents to suns and abstract symbols.

Visitors to Hurricane can pay their respects to the Water Monster's Daughter 24 hours a day, 7 days a week. She's located in second block of downtown Hurricane beside the fire station. For more information about the Water Monster's Daughter or Hurricane, call (304) 562-5896 or see hurricanewv.com.

Although strip malls do lure travelers from I-64 in other towns, downtown Hurricane has managed a comeback by attracting small specialty shops. Across from the Victorian bandstand on Main Street, you'll see a coffee shop, wood-fired pizzeria, gift shop, jewelry boutique, the amazing Dale Morton custom mask and costume studio, and—across the tracks—a curio shop run by the Humane Society and staffed by a calico cat. **Bear Wood Company**, also in this block, repurposes wood from barns into attractive home furnishings. On the street, the scent of fresh baked pepperoni rolls and cheddar biscuits emanates from **Old Mill Bakery**, where Saturdays are celebrated with cinnamon rolls. Not far away, sit a farmer's market and the artisan Commons Marketplace. Hurricane's popular community events include the West Virginia Food Truck Festival, West Virginia JeepFest, the Putnam County Fair and challenging fitness events.

West Virginia may be landlocked, but you can still catch a wave in Hurricane. If you're traveling with young children, start your day here at Valley Park Sports Complex and **Waves of Fun wave pool,** located off I-64 on Route 34. This county-operated water park is complete with a gigantic wave pool, an aqua tube slide, and a giant slide. If the natural whitewater of West Virginia's raging rivers seems too intimidating, try the park's equally fun—and markedly safer—whitewater tube run. This is a great place to cool off and wind down in the summer months, when the lower elevations of the Ohio River Valley can turn a bit sultry, to say the least. The park is open Mon through Sat, Memorial Day through Labor Day from 11 a.m. to 7 p.m., and Sun from noon to 6 p.m. General admission is $10 for adults, and children ages 5 to 11 get in for $8, as do senior citizens. Call (304) 562-2355 or visit wavesoffunwv at Facebook .com for more information.

Back on I-64 and heading west from Hurricane, detour into another delightful little town, *Milton.* Take exit 28 and when you hit downtown, take a left on US 60 and head to the city's most impressive attraction, the ***Blenko Glass Factory,*** founded in 1922 by William Blenko, a British glassmaker. Today it's recognized worldwide for its exquisite handblown stained glass, some of which is found in the great museums and art galleries of the world. Blenko's art glass Flatwoods Monster decanter sold out in 2021in a matter of weeks.

The factory is run by the fourth generation of Blenkos, who beam with pride over their most notable creations, including the colorful windows found in the chapel at the US Air Force Academy in Colorado, in St. Patrick's Cathedral in New York City, in Washington Cathedral in the nation's capital, and at Riyadh Airport in Saudi Arabia. These folks are also responsible for making the beautiful, clear, rocket-shaped trophies of the Country Music Awards and were the original manufacturers of Williamsburg reproduction glassware. The lighting globes in the US Capitol were created here.

The factory offers a free tour, which includes a stop at an observation deck for a how-do-they-do-that, up-close view of the glassblowers and other craftspeople. There's also an attached eclectic visitor center, with a factory outlet on the lower level and a small glass museum and stained-glass showcase upstairs. Outside in a riverside park, visitors can observe mallards, geese, swans, and other waterbirds, although no one is allowed within the fenced area during nesting season—for the safety of the humans, not of the fowl.

The fascinating complex can consume the better part of a day. And beware, you could fall in love with the sparkling glass and be compelled to return for the early February clearance sales. Other items are water pitchers, glass jewelry, and other glass items bearing licensed collegiate logos.

Observation deck tours are available from 9:30 to 1 p.m. Mon, Tues, Thurs, and Fri, except for a week or so around July 1 and the week between Christmas and New Year's Day. The visitor center is open from 9 a.m. to 5 p.m. Mon through Sat and noon to 4 p.m. on Sun. Both the plant and the visitor center close for holidays and have closed for short furloughs. Blenko is the last large glass company left in a state that once harbored more than 500 glass plants. High energy costs, the use of plastics, and overseas competition are putting a strain on the homegrown glass companies. For more information about Blenko, call (304) 793-9081.

If you're spending the weekend in Milton, don't miss a visit to the ***Mountaineer Opry House,*** a nationally known venue for country and bluegrass music stars. Performers Ricky Skaggs, Doyle Lawson, Rhonda Vincent, and others come here to play on Saturday nights year-round. Many nationally known acts play the Opry House every year. The cinder-block theater, just off I-64, is nothing fancy to look at, but you're not here for the visuals. This is all about old-time and country music with a West Virginia twang. Grab a goody at the concession stand (no alcohol allowed) and let the good times roll. Shows begin at 7:30 p.m. Admission is $15 for adults and $5 for children. Call (304) 743-5749 or visit mountaineeropry.com for more information.

If you're ready for some fresh air and a picnic lunch, head over to Woody Williams Bridge in ***Barboursville,*** on Route 60 where the Mud and Guyandotte Rivers converge, and take a hike on the beautiful ***Kanawha Trace.*** The 32-mile trail (you don't have to walk the entire length—a short stroll provides plenty of beautiful scenery) runs from Merritts Creek Road, Barboursville to Fraziers Bottom on the Kanawha River. The trail was created by the Boy Scouts for hiking and is open year-round. Check theKanawhaTrace at Facebook.com for more information. A major footrace is held on the trail each July.

Beech Fork State Park (wvstateparks.com/park/beech-fork-state-park), 12 miles south of Barboursville, is one of West Virginia's newest parks, which means its 6 deluxe vacation cottages still smell a bit like new wood and have air-conditioning and modern kitchens. The park offers boating, fishing, biking, and camping, as well as a 50-meter swimming pool. Swimming is prohibited in the Beech Fork Lakes, and you won't want to step foot in the water after seeing the groundhog-size carp in a feeding frenzy at the marina. Purchase fish chow at the marina shop, but don't join these big guys in the water.

Back on I-64 and heading west toward Kentucky, plan to spend a few hours—or better yet, a few days—in the charming but often overlooked town of ***Huntington,*** West Virginia's second-largest city. Nestled right up against the Kentucky and Ohio borders, this historic riverside community offers a number of interesting diversions. Here you'll find ***Marshall University,*** whose football team, the Thunderin' Herd, is a perennial NCAA powerhouse, The November 14, 1970, plane crash that killed 37 members of the Thundering Herd football team was depicted in the 2006 Warner Brothers movie *We Are Marshall,* starring Matthew McConaughey and Matthew Fox.

Marshall hosts regular concerts in its jazz center with its digital recording studio. Huntington is also home to the Huntington Railroad Museum and a beautiful downtown.

A good place to start is at the ***Huntington Museum of Art*** (hmoa.org), located on a wooded hilltop near downtown. The museum was started by the benevolent Herbert L. Fitzpatrick, who donated the land on which it sits as well as his own art collection. Several other wealthy local art patrons have since given generously to the museum, including Henry and Grace Rardin Doherty, who helped fund the 300-seat **Doberty Auditorium,** former home of the Huntington Symphony Orchestra (huntingtonsymphony.org). Additions and studios were designed by Walter Gropius, founder of the Bauhaus school of architecture. Clerestory windows flood the rooms with natural light.

Here, at the largest fine arts museum in the state, you'll discover room after room of 18th-century European and American paintings, contemporary graphics, Georgian silver, Oriental prayer rugs, American furniture, 1,000-year-old Near Eastern pottery, Appalachian folk art, and 4,000 pieces of historical and contemporary glass. The **Herman Dean Firearms Collection** includes 18th-century powder horns inscribed with maps, breech-loading rifles, and a Kentucky flintlock with "Dan'l Boone" and "Kantuckee" carved on the buttstock.

metrovalley trivia

Huntington, one of the largest cities in West Virginia, is also the westernmost city in the state.

The Huntington Museum of Art has West Virginia's only plant conservatory. It features tropical and subtropical plants, including fragrant, unusual, agriculturally important, and beautiful varieties. The orchid collection is especially stupendous, containing 100 varieties of the showy flowers, which are brought into the conservatory when blooming, but otherwise grow in the museum's greenhouses. The conservatory also contains food plants we in North America don't usually see: cashews, cocoa beans, bananas, papayas, and a coffee tree. Orange jasmine, white ginger, and stephanotis give the conservatory a perfumery air.

Green always, the conservatory takes a green approach to plant care. Predatory insects and mites are used in conjunction with oil and soap sprays to control plant pests such as whiteflies and aphids. Large insect pests are controlled by free-ranging tree frogs and tokay geckos. In fact, the conservatory is a little artificial ecosystem where plants and animals live together in mutually beneficial relationships.

The plants and sculptures in the conservatory can be viewed at any time during regular museum hours. Admission is free to everyone on Tuesday, $5 per person otherwise. Hours are noon to 5 p.m. Wed through Sat, 10 a.m. to 8 p.m. Tues, and noon to 5 p.m. Sun. Closed Mon and most major holidays. Call (304) 529-2701 or visit hmoa.org.

Huntington is also home to another museum, the *Museum of Radio and Technology,* the largest of its kind in the eastern US. It seems rather appropriate to honor such technology here, since radio has long helped open up remote areas of the state with national and global information and entertainment.

This museum has got to be an electronics geek's heaven. The technophile can examine radio schematics, try the working crystal radio set, look over a 5,000-watt AM radio transmitter, and view old test equipment. On display are hundreds of old radios from the 1920s to the 1950s, telegraph items, and early televisions and computers—lots of wood around these electronics. There are vintage and modern ham radio stations, plus a "geek toy" area full of erector sets, chemistry sets, lead-casting kits, a cloud chamber, and other Gilbert toys baby boomers wish they could find today. For the rest of us, there's the *West Virginia Radio Hall of Fame* featuring Don Knotts, Soupy Sales, Little Jimmy Dickens, Bob Denver, and other native sons and daughters. A favorite stop is a re-creation of a radio station studio from the 1950s. Listen closely and you'll hear the sounds of the King himself, Elvis Presley. An adjoining gift shop features new books of radio technology, collecting, and early radio memorabilia reproductions. The museum is open from 10 a.m. to 4 p.m. Sat, and Sun from 1 to 4 p.m. Admission is free, but donations are encouraged. The museum, in a former elementary school at 1640 Florence Ave., is very close to the city's antiques district, just off I-64. For more information call (304) 525-8890 or visit radiomuseum.org.

While in Huntington, don't miss *Pullman Square,* an award-winning shopping and entertainment complex clustered downtown near the river around Heritage Station, a former B&O Railway Station that now houses an art venue/coffee shop as well as the Cabell Huntington Convention & Visitors Bureau. There's much activity here, with Pullman Square's two parking garages, plaza and movie theater, comedy club, bookstores, restaurants, a local-foods store, and a renovated Pullman car. Also take note of one of the quieter attractions—the statue of city founder Collis B. Huntington, sculpted by Gutzon Borglum, the same man who created Mount Rushmore. For information, see pullman-square.com or call (304) 522-3203.

The *Heritage Farm Museum and Village,* set in a hollow 10 minutes away, is a place where you can get lost in another era. Stop by an old log church, visit the village smithy shop, tour a broom-making workshop, drop by a one-room schoolhouse, and shop a general store, then head over to the kitchen-through-the-ages exhibit to revel in how lucky we are that washing and food preparation don't monopolize our time. Children will especially love the petting zoo (May through Sept) and find vicarious terror in the 19th-century dentist's office.

The village now consists of 7 separate museums (Progress, Transportation, Country Store, Heritage, Coal, Doll & Carriage, and Children's Activity Museum). The Transportation Building includes a 1908 electric truck. (Yes, we've known about electric vehicles for more than a century.) Named West Virginia's first Smithsonian Affiliate Institution, the property has than 30 structures, including five log cabin inns and overnight train-caboose accommodations. Artisans and reenactors bring Appalachian history to life during special Way Back Weekend Saturdays May through December. With over 500 acres, 5 miles of hiking trails, artisan workshops, aerial adventure courses, and a rock climbing wall, the site pays homage to the physical spirit of its Appalachian ancestors in many ways.

Heritage Farm is the 30-year project of the late Mike Perry, former lawyer and bank CEO, and his wife, Henriella, who started out with a burned-out log cabin that they envisioned as their family home. They became fascinated with the craftsmanship and the ingenuity of isolated mountain people. That led the couple to a collecting hobby and began a mission to show how life was lived in early West Virginia.

The Perrys' mission was to show that being a "hillbilly" is nothing to be ashamed about.

Ironically the award-winning museum site has seen an uptick in visitors because of the *Hatfields and McCoys* History Channel miniseries, which shot a dozen scenes of the famous feud on the farm. Another History Channel show, *American Pickers,* was set at Heritage Farm. The Perrys are pleased with the publicity, but they are resolute in their decision to leave TVs out of their rental cabins so that families can experience a little of what life was like 150 years ago.

The Heritage Farm Museum is open May through Oct variable days of the week depending upon the season, but always Saturdays and often Thursdays and Fridays, 10 a.m. to 3 p.m. Admission is $15 per adult and $10 per child. The 5 two- to four-bedroom log homes rent for $175 to $225 a night, year-round. For more information visit heritagefarmmuseum.com or call (304) 522-1244.

The existence of North America's largest English-speaking Orthodox monastery about 45 minutes south of Huntington is one of the area's best-kept secrets. Since May 2000, about three dozen monks have been living, working, and praying at Holy Cross Monastery, tucked in a remote mountain bowl at the end of a labyrinth of very narrow roads. Their black cassocks and veil-draped cylindrical hats are a familiar sight in the village of Wayne, where they shop for supplies. To support themselves, they produce Athonite-style, granular incense. The heavy scent of frankincense, roses, and lavender rolls out of the monastery gift shop each time the door opens.

Although the monastery can't accommodate curious tourists, the monks do welcome visitors to their gift shop. The shop sells incense, honey, candles, icons, liturgical items, lip balms, and goat's milk soap produced from the monastery's herd. The shop is usually open Mon through Sat 9:15 to 11:30 a.m. and weekday afternoons from 1:30 to 4:30 p.m., but call first at (304) 849-4726 to make sure.

All visitors are asked to respect the monks' privacy and to honor the dress code, which for women is rather severe—long skirts, long sleeves, a head covering, and no makeup. For men accommodation is less rigorous—long-sleeve shirts and pants. Guests may be invited to attend the evening vespers, a beautiful service filled with incense, scripture reading, and song, but be prepared: You are expected to stand for an hour or more, except for periods when you "reverence the icons." In the Orthodox church, one is expected to kiss things regarded as holy, so a part of the service involves making one's way through the chapel, kissing dozens of icons including some set calisthenically high and low. This service is for the devoted and not for the casual spectator. For information, visit holycross.org.

As you travel south from Wayne, the county becomes more sparsely populated, the restaurants and gas stations scarce. You see signs of clear-cutting and strip-mining. If you're thinking about overnighting, there's no better place to hole up in these parts than within the 8,123 wooded acres of Cabwaylingo State Forest. During the 1930s, the hardworking members of the Civilian Conservation Corps built log cabins with stone fireplaces, picnic pavilions, stone staircases, hiking trails, and a fire tower. The log cabins, dome-shaped springhouse, trails, and stone and log picnic shelters are still in use today, testimony to the skills these young men learned during the Great Depression. Several of the smaller picnic shelters, set high in the forest above Twelvepole Creek, would make perfect settings for marriage proposals. To see a map of the trails, book a cabin, or get more information, call (304) 385-4255 or see cabwaylingo.com.

If you love green landscapes, river vistas, and city views, there are at least three in Huntington that you shouldn't miss. At Tenth Street and Veterans Memorial Boulevard (directly across from the visitor center) is the **David Harris Riverfront Park,** deemed one of the nation's most beautiful urban green spaces. It sits on a wide expanse of the Ohio River and is the base for several sightseeing cruise boats and a popular riverfront amphitheater (complete with a floating stage). Call (304) 696-5954 for a park schedule.

Huntington's premier family park lies up against the mountain. At 70-acre **Ritter Park,** it's almost mandatory to stop and smell the roses. Ritter's nationally acclaimed rose garden contains more than 3,000 bushes. June is an especially fragrant month to visit. The park's second must-see stop, especially if 'you're toting children, is the playground—and not just any playground. This one was voted one of the 10 best children's playgrounds in America by *Child* magazine. The fairy-tale-like play area features bigger-than-life stone columns, arches, and tunnels to climb on and hide in. Add the small zipline, the cord bridge, and the parents' hammock, and you've got a few hours' entertainment. Another Huntington park, Memorial Park, is home to the free outdoor **Huntington Railroad Museum**. The park includes a Baldwin H-6 steam locomotive, 2 cabooses, and a Porter steam tank engine, like Thomas the Tank.

The Mountain State's only remaining amusement park, the **Camden,** just west of Huntington, claims not one but two vintage wooden roller coasters and authentic old bumper cars, a pendulum rattler ride, Tilt-A-Whirl, and many more, as well as the state's third-largest American Indian burial mound. The 20-foot conical mound is right beside the Big Dipper roller coaster and was once used as a bandstand. The Little Dipper coaster has the distinction of being the only wooden kiddy coaster still operating in the US, while the Big Dipper has been voted into the American Coaster Enthusiasts' Hall of Fame. Camden's carousel has been spinning each summer since the park opened in 1903. Camden Park added 18-hole miniature golf a few summers ago.

Camden has also earned a reputation for its superlative corn dogs. The 26-acre park has 30 rides, as well as games, paddleboats, a haunted house, a sit-down restaurant, restroom facilities, and a petting zoo. It's open weekends only in May and August, Saturdays only in September, and from 11 a.m. to 7 p.m. Thursday—Sunday in June and July. In October it reopens weekend evenings for Spooktacular events. Admission is $21 ($17 online at camdenpark .com) for adults, $15 for children under 4 feet tall. For more information, check the website, camdenpark.com, or call (304) 429-4321.

Don't leave Huntington without taking a look at the **East End Bridge,** a mile-long steel spiderweb of a bridge connecting Huntington's 31st Street to Ohio's Route 7 in Proctorville. It's the second concrete cable-stayed bridge built in the US and the first to use triple-strength concrete. It cost $38 million and took 20 years to plan, 10 years to build. It was completed in 1985.

A 45-minute drive north of Huntington, along the lazy Ohio, puts you in **Point Pleasant,** which is also the terminus of the Kanawha River. **Tu-Endie-Wei State Park** (Point Pleasant Battle Monument State Park), at the south end of town, memorializes a battle fought here on October 10, 1774. The name was officially changed in early 2000 from Battle Monument to Tu-Endie-Wei, a Native American term meaning "the mingling of the waters." More than 1,000 Virginia militiamen fought against as many Shawnee, keeping them from forming an alliance with the British. The fighting allowed white settlers to push farther west into the frontier of Ohio and beyond. The 4-acre park's centerpiece is an 84-foot granite obelisk that honors the Virginia militiamen who fell here. Another interesting marker rests on the spot where Pierre Joseph de Celoron de Blainville, a French explorer, buried a leaden plate in 1749, claiming the land for his country.

A larger marker commemorates Shawnee Chief Cornstalk, whose remains are buried here. Though his warriors were defeated here in 1774, Cornstalk tried to make peace with his former adversaries and told them of British plans to ally with American Indian tribes against the colonies. Cornstalk was taken hostage and then murdered when he met with the commander at Fort Randolph in Point Pleasant. The story has it that he cursed the white community on the land, "blighted in its hopes and paralyzed by the stain of our blood."

Another tablet in the park is dedicated to "Mad" Anne Bailey, whose "mad" exploits in thwarting the Shawnee earned her the nickname. The park's Mansion House, built in 1796 as a tavern, is the oldest hewn-log house in the Kanawha Valley. It was so large for its day, with two stories and real glass windows, that the settlers felt justified in giving it such a grandiose name. It now houses battle artifacts, as well as period antiques. The park is open year-round, and donations are appreciated in lieu of an admission fee. Mansion House is open May through Oct, 10 a.m. to 4:30 p.m. Mon through Sat and 1 to 4 p.m. Sun. Call (304) 675-0869 for more information.

Krodel Park, on the southern edge of Point Pleasant, offers fishing, miniature golf, and camping along its 22-acre fishing lake. A walking path leads to **Fort Randolph,** a replica of the 1774 fort built here against American Indian attack. The structure includes 2 blockhouses and a log blacksmith shop. Demonstrations and reenactments are held here many summer weekends. Colonial crafts portrayed at these events include carpentry, broom making, candle dipping, basket weaving, soap making, yarn spinning, flintlock riflery, flint knapping, and blacksmithing. The fort is open weekend afternoons Memorial Day though Labor Day. For more information call (304) 675-2366 or see fortrandolph.org.

For more recent history, head downtown and look for an antebellum mercantile within splashing distance of the Ohio River. The **Point Pleasant River Museum** uses displays and demonstrations to highlight topics such as major floods in history, boat construction, local river industries, and the collapse of the Silver Bridge. Fish and other creatures common to the Ohio River swim in a 2,400-gallon aquarium. Although a fire gutted the historic building in 2018, the building plans to reopen in early 2022 in a new structure up the street. Visiting hours will be Tues through Sat 10:30 a.m. to 3 p.m. and from 1 to 5 p.m. on Sun. Admission is $5 for adults and $2 for children. For information, visit pprivermuseum.com.

At your next stop you'll learn a lot about what farm life in West Virginia was like in the 1800s. Just 4 miles north of Point Pleasant is the **West Virginia State Farm Museum,** with more than 50 acres of grounds and 31 period buildings demonstrating the hardy lifestyle of West Virginia farmers past and present. This is a working museum where crops are grown, harvested, and processed using 19th-century equipment and methods. On your tour take particular note of *General,* a Belgian gelding (now stuffed) on record as the third-largest horse ever to have lived. The museum is open April 1 through November 15, from 9 a.m. to 5 p.m. Tues through Sat and from 1 to 5 p.m. Sun. Admission is free. Call (304) 675-5737 or see wvfarmmuseum.org for information.

From a Main Street vantage point, Point Pleasant's most famous resident appears to be a winged, red-eyed being called Mothman. His statue stands in the center of town and there's even a museum devoted to the winged wonder. Every September, Point Pleasant hosts a Mothman Festival (mothmanfestival .com). Visitors take tours, hug the statue for photos, sup on Mothman pizza, and look over the Mothman Museum's props from the 2002 Richard Gere movie *The Mothman Prophecies.* Sightings of the 7-foot winged creature occurred in 1966 and 1967, ending on December 15, 1967, when the town's Silver Bridge collapsed into the Ohio River, killing 46 motorists. People have been speculating on Mothman's possible involvement ever since.

Located at 411 Main St., the **Mothman Museum** is open daily from noon to 6 p.m. Admission is $4.50 for ages 11 and up and $1.50 for children under 11. For information, see mothmanmuseum.com or call (304) 812-5211.

Places to Stay in the Metro Valley Region

CHARLESTON

Brass Pineapple Bed and Breakfast
1611 Virginia St. East
(304) 344-0748
brasspineapple.com
Moderate to expensive

Charleston Marriott Town Center
200 Lee St. East
(304) 345-6500
(800) 228-9290
charlestonmarriott.com
Expensive

Sleep Inn
2772 Pennsylvania Ave.
(I-79, exit 1)
(304) 345-5111
sleepinnwv.com
Moderate

CROSS LANES

Mardi Gras Casino & Resort
1 Greyhound Dr.
(304) 776-1000
mardigrascasinowv.com
Moderate to Expensive

DUNLOW

Cabwaylingo State Forest Cabins
4279 Cabwaylingo Park Rd.
(304) 385-4255
wvstateparks.com/
places-to-stay/cabins/
cabwaylingo-cabins
Inexpensive

HUNTINGTON

Heritage Farm Village
3300 Harvey Rd.
(304) 522-1244
heritagefarmmuseum.com
Moderate

LOGAN

Chief Logan Lodge
1000 Conference
Center Dr.
(304) 792-7125
chiefloganlodge.com
Moderate

WILLIAMSON

Mountaineer Hotel
31 E. Second Ave.
(304) 235-2222
mountaineerhotel.com
Moderate

Places to Eat in the Metro Valley Region

CHARLESTON

Bridge Road Bistro
915 Bridge Rd.
(304) 720-3500
Moderate to expensive

Chin's Restaurant
4114 MacCorkle Ave. SE
(304) 925-1080
chinsrestaurant at
Facebook
Moderate

Ellen's Homemade Ice Cream
225 Capitol St.
(304) 343-6488
Ellensicecream.com
Moderate

Harding's Family Restaurant
2772 Pennsylvania Ave
(304) 344-5044
hardingsfamilyrestaurant at
Facebook
Inexpensive

HUNTINGTON

Bahnhof WVrsthaus
745 7th Ave
(681) 204-3837
Bahnhofwv.com
Moderate

Savannah's Bistro
1208 Sixth St.
(304) 529-0919
Moderate

FOR MORE INFORMATION

Cabell-Huntington Convention and Visitors Bureau
(800) 635-6329
wvvisit.org

Charleston Convention and Visitors Bureau
(800) 733-5469 or (304) 344-5075
charlestonwv.com

South Charleston Convention and Visitors Bureau
(304) 746-5552
visitsouthcharlestonwv.com

Putnam County Convention and Visitors Bureau
(304) 757-7282
putnamcountycvb.com

Mid-Ohio Valley

The Ohio River Valley sits at the western edge of the Mountain State, extending northward along the namesake river from Huntington to the Northern Panhandle.

The valley was the site of some of the first western expansion movements in the US as settlers came down from Pennsylvania on the Ohio River, and as such it was open to attack from American Indians, backed by the British, who still held frontier outposts. Today this area of sloping hills, small riverside towns, and a few remaining glass factories and glass museums is gaining ground as a tourist mecca, with many visitors coming from Ohio and Kentucky to shop, fish, hunt, and spend weekends in out-of-the-way bed-and-breakfasts.

Of course, the mighty Ohio River is the defining feature here, and there is plenty to do on or near the water. But there are also numerous treasures to be found away from the riverbank, in the rich green folds and ravines of the Appalachian foothills.

Sharing qualities of both the Midwest and the upper South, the valley is a warm, friendly place where no one is about to get in a hurry or demand that you do, either.

MID-OHIO VALLEY

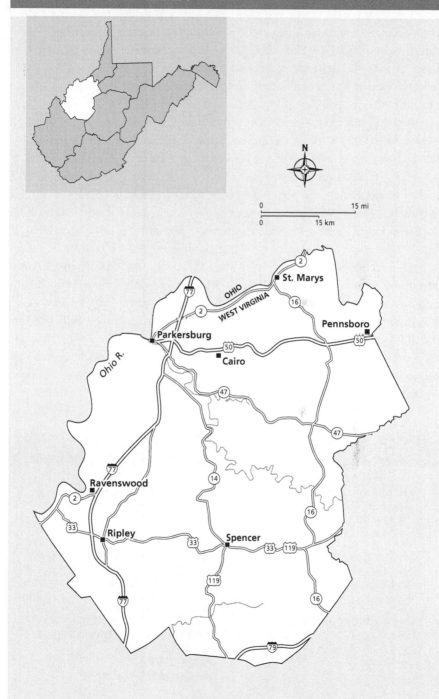

The slow-paced, easygoing Mid-Ohio Valley includes the large swath of country extending north along the Ohio from the Jackson County line, below Ravenswood, up to the Pleasants County line, north of St. Marys. It's a patchwork of forests, farmland, and serene river roads. It's also among the state's least-traveled tourist destinations; hence, virtually everything here is off the beaten path.

Heading east from Point Pleasant on Route 2 will take travelers "round the bend" of the Ohio River—that is, to the small community of **Ravenswood.** The village bears the distinction of hosting West Virginia's only naval battle. On July 19, 1863, US Navy armored steamers fought Confederates in the Battle of Buffington Island. Earlier, the site of the future town received accolades from none other than George Washington when he made his living as a land surveyor. He surveyed much of the Ohio Valley and wrote about the area in his journal. In fact, he once owned a tract of land that became this town. That bit of history is preserved, along with many other artifacts, at **Washington Western Lands Museum,** found in the upper two floors of a converted river-lock building and a restored log cabin. Land-grant documents signed by Patrick Henry, a log house furnished in 1840s style, and the trappings of an old country store are the highlights here. Take the Ravenswood exit to Route 2, then follow the signs to the Ritchie Bridge over the Ohio south of town. The museum is riverside. Hours are 1 to 5 p.m. Sat and Sun, Memorial Day through Labor Day; otherwise by appointment. Call (304) 532-0327.

BEST ANNUAL EVENTS IN THE MID-OHIO VALLEY

Taste of Parkersburg
Parkersburg; Memorial Day weekend
(304) 428-1130
downtownpkb.com

Mid-Ohio Valley Multi-Cultural Festival
Parkersburg; mid-June
(304) 428-5554
movmcf.org

Mountain State Arts and Crafts Fair
Ripley; early July
(304) 372-3247
msacf.com

West Virginia Honey Festival
Parkersburg; late August
(304) 481-6941
wvhoneyfestival at Facebook

Nature Wonder Wild Food Weekend
North Bend State Park
Cairo; mid-September
(304) 558-2754
northbendsp.com

West Virginia Black Walnut Festival
Spencer; mid-October
(304) 927-5616
wvblackwalnutfestival.org

If you're in an artsy frame of mind, head south on I-77 to the **Cedar Lakes Craft Center** in Ripley. The center stages the annual **Mountain State Arts and Crafts Fair,** a prestigious showcase for more than 250 of West Virginia's best artisans and mountain musicians held annually the first weekend in July. At the festival you're likely to find wood-carvers making ladderback chairs or mountain dulcimers (many of which are played on the spot) and specialty craftspeople churning out intricate quilts, dried-flower wreaths, sweaters, and jewelry. A big hit at one recent festival was a line of ladies' accessories woven out of pine straw.

If you're passing through at another time of year, there's still plenty to see and do at Cedar Lakes. From April through October, some of the country's best artisans teach others new ideas, designs, and techniques for handcrafted art. People come from all over the US to spend a week at the center (you can stay in a dormitory, in the campus hotel, in cottages, or off campus), learning pottery making, woodworking, knife forging, fly-tying, quilting, watercolor painting, blacksmithing, twig furniture making, and more. The center also participates in the Road Scholar program, an international network of colleges and other institutions that offers special classes for senior citizens. Whether you're taking a class or not, it's a fine place to retreat: affordable with hiking trails, swimming, tennis courts, and fishing. For information about the center, call (304) 372-7860, or check the website at cedarlakes.com.

The Western Frontier

The northern Ohio Valley counties of Wood, Pleasants, Ritchie, and Wirt were once considered outposts of the western frontier, a wild and woolly region of hardscrabble farms and some of the nation's earliest oil wells. In the towns, Victorian mansions and museums recall a tumultuous era, the oil and gas boom of the late 1800s. Collectors make pilgrimages to watch master artisans make glass, and antiques shoppers carry off treasures. The region offers plentiful opportunities for fishing the rivers and streams, hiking and biking along miles of trails, hunting in thousands of acres of wildlife areas and driving through quiet mountains.

Plan to spend at least two days in **Parkersburg,** for this friendly community of 29,000 on the banks of the Ohio has much to offer. The best place to start, naturally, is the **Convention and Visitors Bureau,** downtown at 350 Seventh St. Here you can pick up loads of information on local points of interest. The bureau is open Mon through Fri from 9 a.m. to 5 p.m. One interesting site is just down the street. Point Park is where local residents built a floodwall after a series of devastating floods. Marks on the wall show where the river crested each of the last three times; the most recent, in 1913, was 38 feet above normal.

Point Park is where visitors to *Blennerhassett Island State Park* catch the stern-wheeler to the island. The Blennerhassett story is a unique and tragic one. Wealthy Irish immigrant Harman Blennerhassett was an edgy sort of guy—he was ostracized in Ireland for marrying his young niece as well as for lambasting the British government. He and his young wife, Margaret, bought an island in the Ohio River, built "the most beautiful private residence in the Ohio Valley," and lived in unsurpassed splendor for several years.

mid-ohio valleytrivia

The Ohio Valley was the site of West Virginia's first oil boom; the region still contains some active wells.

Their downfall came when a prominent figure in American history, *Aaron Burr,* arrived in their lives. Burr, already notorious for killing Alexander Hamilton in a duel, had just lost the presidency to Thomas Jefferson and was very bitter. He hatched a scheme to set up his own country by seizing Spanish territory in the Southwest. He enlisted Harman Blennerhassett's help, but local officials discovered the plot and arrested the pair for treason. Though both were eventually acquitted, the Blennerhassetts were ruined financially and politically after the ordeal (the mansion had already burned to the ground in an accident). No one knew the Blennerhassetts' personal motives for supporting Burr. Was he planning to join Burr as ruler? At any rate, the Blennerhassetts were ruined financially and politically. They tried briefly to resurrect their lifestyle in Mississippi by running a cotton plantation, but it failed and they moved to England. Harman died there, and Margaret returned to the US seeking financial aid from her sons. One son disappeared; she and the other son died in poverty.

BEST ATTRACTIONS IN THE MID-OHIO VALLEY

**Blennerhassett Island
State Park**
Parkersburg
(304) 420-4800
www.blennerhassettislandsp.com

Cedar Lakes Craft Center
Ripley
(304) 372-7860
cedarlakes.com

Henderson Hall
Williamstown
(304) 375-2129
hendersonhallwv.com

North Bend State Park
Cairo
(304) 643-2931 or (800) CALL-WVA
wvstateparks.com/park/north-bend-state-park.com

Despite the tragic tale, there's much to see on Blennerhassett Island (www .blennerhassettislandsp.com), now on the National Register of Historic Places.

As the stern-wheeler heads down the Ohio, zigzagging when Captain Gary Kitchen lets child navigators take the wheel, visitors begin to see what the Blennerhassett family lost when their estate was seized and its contents auctioned off. Many years later, West Virginia reconstructed the Italian Palladian–style mansion on the original site using research and information from archaeological excavations. Resembling George Washington's Mount Vernon, the mansion has more than 7,000 square feet of space and is resplendent with oil paintings, opulent antiques, Italian sculptures, and other treasures. The park celebrates the Blennerhassetts' happy years of music and parties, when the throngs of guests strolling over the oriental rugs included Charles X, the future king of France. Costumed docents wait in the lawn to dazzle visitors with the particulars of the mansion's early 19th-century decorating and cooking. The main quarters are a marvel of black walnut panels, gold trim, and silver doorknobs. The kitchen is stocked with ingenious devices, such as a bread-toasting contraption and glass-globe flycatchers.

Beyond the mansion, the island offers horse-drawn covered-wagon rides and rents out bicycles for more island exploration. It's a rare day that you don't spot a raccoon, a turkey, or one of the more than 100 deer living here. South of the mansion, the 1802 Putnam-Houser sheltered generations of Putnams on the Ohio shore. After the last heir died, Shell Chemical had the building barged out to the island. On weekends, a host points out architectural details through windows cut into the walls to reveal peg joinery and horsehair plaster.

Sunday Sundae cruises, nature walks, dinners, and craft demonstrations are featured from June through August. Margaret Blennerhassett herself returns to socialize and entertain visitors over brunch on occasional Thursdays and Saturdays in August, September, and October. Call (304) 420-4800 for reservations.

The park's **stern-wheelers** leave the mainland for the island every hour between 10 a.m. and 3 p.m., Tues through Sun, May through Oct (Thurs through Sun only in Sept and Oct). The trip on a steam-driven paddle-wheel boat, once a common sight on the Ohio River, and tours of the mansion and museum cost $17 for adults, $11 for children ages 3 to 12. Horse-drawn-wagon tours of the island are available for $6 a person, a wonderful way to absorb more of the island's history.

The **Blennerhassett Museum,** Second and Julianna Streets, is where you can begin with a 12-minute video about the Blennerhassetts and view some of their most valuable possessions. The museum also houses some of the Ohio Valley's oldest manuscripts, maps, and a mourning fan, an item with a story to tell. The island itself is believed to have been inhabited as early as 11,000 years ago. So before boarding check out the glass-encased displays of ancient relics found there (don't miss the mastodon bones) as well as other exhibits unrelated to the Blennerhassetts. The museum is open 10 a.m. to 5 p.m. Tues through Sun, May through Oct, and from 11 a.m. to 5 p.m. Tues through Sat, Jan through April, Nov, and Dec. Admission is $5 adults and $3 for children. Call (304) 420-4800 or (800) CALL-WVA for information.

After you return from the island (or before you go), there's still lots to see and do. If you remain in a Blennerhas-

savingsbond capital

Parkersburg is the savings bond capital of the nation. Since 1957, every US bond bought or redeemed has passed through the US Treasury's Bureau of Public Debt in Parkersburg. If you want to know the amount of the debt or who owns it, you can write to the Bureau of the Public Debt, PO Box 2188, Parkersburg, WV 26106-2188, or visit publicdebt.treas.gov.

sett frame of mind, head over to the hotel bearing the family's name. The redbrick turrets and Palladian windows of the *Blennerhassett Hotel* (now on the National Register of Historic Places), Fourth and Market Streets, take visitors back to another time, when horses galloped by and gunshots sometimes rang in the rowdy Parkersburg streets. It remains the showcase today that it was when it was built in 1889 by banker Colonel William Chancellor. It was also one of the first hotels in the country to boast a bank branch in its lobby. Its elegance and sophistication made it the grandest hotel in the state, and those qualities are still evident. The elegant guest rooms are decorated with Chippendale reproductions and offer Wi-Fi and plush bathrobes. Its restaurant, Spat's, has a reputation for fine continental cuisine of the sort you might imagine being served in heaven—rich and saturated with flavor. Sunday jazz and Friday and Saturday dance music add extra bliss. For reservations or information, call (304) 422-3131 or (800) 262-2536.

The Blennerhassett is the starting point for spooky evenings on late September and October weekends. In a *Haunted Parkersburg* ghost tour ranked among the top 10 in the nation by Haunted America Tours, the tour guide dons her black cape and leads a throng to Parkersburg's most haunted places. She doesn't have to go far to start the tour—the historic Blennerhassett Hotel is reported to be haunted by its late builder, William Chancellor, who has been known to sit on occupied beds. Chancellor reportedly has calmed down considerably since his portrait was reinstated in the hotel library. Other ghosts reportedly break glasses in a restaurant during the wee hours, whistle Irish tunes on the site of a Civil War tent camp, and call for help over a nonexistent Kmart intercom. The guides know all their stories and are not afraid to

Victoriana

Probably the residents of Parkersburg's Julia-Ann Square Historical District know they're living in the 21st century—they have a website, juliannsquare.org, after all.

But those who live in the 126 homes of this elegant historic district—West Virginia's largest—seem to have immersed themselves in the ambience and trappings of the Victorian era, when these homes were built. It's not enough that residents spend their time researching 19th-century gas streetlights, Irwin and Russell hardware, brass newel posts, and pocket doors. Now the avid homeowners' association organizes an event almost every season in which they can indulge their zeal for all things Victorian.

The whimsy of the Easter Parade is fun for residents and tourists alike. As they did at the turn of the 20th century, the wealthy turn out in their newest hats and dress to parade down the avenue for all to admire. The hat contest is the biggest draw.

The year continues with Victorian garden tours, teas, historic street fairs, craft demonstrations, yard sales of the rich and not-so-famous, and a Christmas home tour. But any time of year, a walking tour of the mansions yields a visual feast of Second Empire, Gothic Revival, Italianate, Queen Anne, and Federal styles, occasionally all in one home.

For more information about the district, call (304) 422-9861 or visit juliannsquare.org.

share them in particularly frightening ways. Tickets can be purchased online, but participants with cash can just show up in the Blennerhassett lobby at 7:30 p.m. on Friday or Saturday on late September or October weekends. Tours are $15 for adults, $10 for seniors and students, and $6 for children under 13. The ghost tour is not advised for children under 6. For specifics, visit haunted parkersburgtours.com.

While you're still downtown, check out Parkersburg's *Oil and Gas Museum.* Not interested? Don't be so hasty. This exhibit offers a fascinating look at what could be a dry subject, no pun intended. Housed in a turn-of-the-20th-century hardware store is an impressive collection of engines, pumps, tools, models, documents, maps, photos, and more. Visitors can trace the development of West Virginia's oil and gas industry, from the American Indians (yes, the first Americans used oil, which was so abundant that it rose to the surface and oozed into the river) to the 1870s, when Standard Oil arrived, to the present day. In fact, Parkersburg is still known as "the town that oil built." Be sure to catch the video story of the birth of West Virginia's oil and gas industry. It examines the links between the accumulation of wealth in this section of the state and West Virginia's separation from Virginia. Confederate soldiers enraged citizens in 1863 by burning one of the area's largest oil fields in an inferno lasting days. To find the museum, look for the pumpjack and other oil field equipment in the second block of Third Street. The museum is open 7 days a week, 11 a.m. to 5 p.m., Apr through Nov. Admission is $7 for adults, $5 for children. Call (304) 485-5446 or visit oilandgasmuseum.org for information.

Perhaps the trip to Blennerhassett just whetted your appetite for a river cruise. **Valley Gem Sternwheeler** (valleygemsternwheeler.com; 740-373-7862), headquartered across the river in Marietta, Ohio, sends out several rear paddle-wheel ships each summer day on narrated sightseeing trips, as well as dinner and dessert cruises into the fall. Groups can charter cruises along the islands and river locks.

Now on to the more fanciful. Parkersburg's **Smoot Theatre,** 5 blocks from the floodwall, is a restored movie house and the city's most popular venue for performing arts. The original, glitzy theater was built in 1926 at the height of vaudeville, and for a while it was home to some of the most colorful acts of the era. That changed when vaudeville died. It then served as a movie house for half a century—promising nurses and smelling salts for *Frankenstein* showings during the Depression—but eventually lost out to new competition. Today, after a renovation largely completed by local contributions and elbow grease, the theater stages jazz, ragtime, opera, bluegrass, old favorites, and rock performances. Call the visitor bureau at (800) 752-4982 or the theater at (304) 422-7529. Prices per person range from $3 to $40.

African Americans hold a proud heritage in the Mid-Ohio region. It was here in Parkersburg that a small group of Black citizens founded the first free public school for African-American children south of the Mason-Dixon Line. When the Sumner School was established in January 1862, West Virginia was not yet formally a state of the Union, though it had severed its ties to Confederate Virginia. The Sumner School continued on into the 20th century to become the first West Virginia high school to racially integrate. Although the original building has been razed, its 1926 gymnasium remains, now reincarnated as the **Sumnerite First Free School.** Here you can browse through photographs and documents of the school's early years, as well as community artifacts that include a "beaten biscuit machine" used by an early caterer. The museum holds an annual September Jazz & Ribs Fest and is open by appointment. For information call (304) 422-0985 or visit sumner7.com.

Parkersburg's shopping possibilities are enticing, but none more than **Holl's Chocolates.** The chocolatier beckons from nearby Vienna, where you can sometimes spot Dominique Holl making truffles in the demonstration area. His father, Fritz, learned the fine art of candy making in his native Switzerland as an apprentice to the masters in Zurich and passed down the techniques and recipes to his son. Although Fritz supervised a research kitchen for many years in the US, the elder Holl kept on making chocolates, selling them through a local wineshop. In retirement, this activity blossomed into a full-time job, and Dominique came into the business, using his college education to blend old recipes with new automation. Holl's continues to use the traditional recipes, as well as fine Caillier chocolate from Switzerland and real cream, in their handcrafted, always fresh chocolates. They've added dessert sauces, cocoa mix, fresh roasted coffee, and a line of sugar-free chocolates, just as tasty but without the guilt.

The shop at 2001 Grand Central Ave. in Vienna is the main outlet, but Holl's chocolates can be ordered through their website, holls.com. They also have a shop on Smith Street in downtown Charleston.

While you're in Vienna, check out **Stephens Outdoor Railways** at 33 Sandstone Dr. Whether you're in the market for a model railroad or not, you'll be charmed by the miniature villages, intricate landscapes, and seasonal decorations at this year-round display. Stephens specializes in Z- to G-gauge trains and accessories. It can also be reached at (304) 295-4403.

Parkersburg also boasts a woodworkers' mecca, the **Woodcraft** shop, with its specialized tools, demonstrations, and classes. In any given season, woodcrafters can choose among such offerings as Federal-period inlay techniques, basic hand planing, carving a walking stick, building Windsor chairs, and box making for women. If you know what to do but don't have the equipment, you may rent workshop time for an hour or several days. The store is located at 4420 Emerson Ave. and is open 9 a.m. to 6 p.m. 6 days a week and Sunday afternoons. Call (304) 485-4050 for information.

Mountwood Park is 12 miles east of Parkersburg on US Route 50. The county-owned park's 30 miles of single-track biking trails are considered among the best of eastern United States' single-park mountain biking destinations. Meticulously designed according to International Mountain Bicycling Association standards, these trails have a high fun factor.

Within the wooded park, you can also find miles of hiking trails, campgrounds, primitive cabins, a 50-acre lake with fishing, ATV trails, and a disc golf course. Mountwood Park land has a rich history in the oil and gas industry. In the late 1800s, the third oil field in the United States was discovered here in the village of Volcano, which became boomtown of hotels and opera houses. After fire destroyed Volcano in 1879, it was never rebuilt.

Mountwood Park celebrates its annual Volcano Days the last week of September. The park visitors' center/museum displays artifacts and a brief history of Volcano. The museum is open May through Oct on Fri, Sat, and Sun afternoons.

A bit farther north on I-77 is *Williamstown,* within waving distance of the Ohio border. It was named for Pennsylvania backwoodsman Isaac Williams, who helped to settle the area. A few miles south of town sits lovely *Henderson Hall.* Talk about curb appeal! This redbrick, Italian villa–style manor house is jaw-dropping, so imposing as it sits on a hilltop amid gentle rolling hills looking down on the Ohio River. The three-story house has been called the most significant historic site in the Mid-Ohio Valley, and it is awesome. Today the estate, built beginning in 1836, sits on 65 acres, though the Henderson estate once held more than 2,000 acres.

Stepping across its threshold into the giant great hall is like a step back in time. Both the structure and its contents are intact and preserved in pristine condition. All the original furnishings, right down to the parlor wallpaper, are still there. The Hendersons, aside from being very wealthy, also apparently never threw anything away—even a letter from an escaped slaved asking to return. (He escaped again, this time with nine other slaves from the plantation.) All the Hendersons' personal papers, from daily shopping lists to the original grant to the land signed by Virginia governor Patrick Henry, are still in the house—two centuries of memorabilia.

The home was bequeathed to the Oil and Gas Museum in 2008 and is open Tues through Sun afternoons, March till Dec. Admission is $10 for adults and $5 for children. Call the museum at (304) 375-2129 for specifics.

Williamson is also home to a top-10 quilt shop (*Better Homes & Gardens,* 2007), which also happens to sell rughooking supplies and antiques. The *Woolen Willow* is located at 901 Highland Ave., where it offers classes and companionship for needleworkers of all levels. The one-day workshops are generally priced at $20 and range from rug braiding and weaving to beaded bracelet making and quilting by hand or machine. Open Mon through Sat 10 a.m. to 5 p.m. For more information, call (304) 375-WOOL.

Don't leave Williamstown without a visit to the *Williamstown Antique Mall* on Highland Avenue, where several dealers display beautiful collections in a two-story mall. Lustrous glassware and tableware, stoneware, flow blue china, dolls, clocks, quilts, furniture, and more are a delight to both the educated and the novice collector. Hours are 10 a.m. to 6 p.m. Mon through Sat and noon to 6 p.m. Sun. The antiques mall can be reached at (304) 375-6315.

If you're craving a little outdoor activity, head north on Route 2 to *St. Marys,* where the natives claim "the livin' is easy and the fishing is great." They're probably right on both counts. Here the deceptively named Middle Island Creek, wide and rolling, joins the Ohio River, creating one of the state's best spots for sport fishing. Trophy muskie are common in these waters, and the bass fishing is so good that the town holds a Bassmasters tournament each

A Vision of St. Marys

Legend has it that the town of St. Marys got its start from a vision of the Virgin by an eastern Virginia businessman. It seems Alexander Creel was traveling by steamer to Wheeling one night around 1834 when he was awakened by a vision of the Virgin Mary, who told him to look upon the Virginia (now West Virginia) side of the river.

"There," she said, "you will behold the site of what someday will be a happy and prosperous city." Creel looked out the door of his stateroom and saw the lower end of Middle Island illuminated in the moonlight. Beyond it was a large cove surrounded by wooded hills. Creel returned to buy the land and eventually devoted his energies to fulfilling his dream. In 1849 the town was named in honor of the mother of Jesus.

June. A few miles south the waters are still ripe. **Willow Island Locks and Dam** off Route 2 boasts largemouth bass, striped bass, white bass, northern pike, channel catfish, and a few more species that regularly bite hooks.

Running from New Martinsville down to Parkersburg, the **Ohio River Islands National Wildlife Refuge** has been a haven for fishermen and birders since it was created in 1992. The area's 3,300 acres are spread across 18 islands on the Ohio. Eleven of the refuge islands are clustered in a 20-mile stretch of river between New Martinsville and St. Marys. Most of them are accessible only by boat, but at St. Marys a short bridge gives you the opportunity to visit Middle Island, one of the most beautiful islands in the refuge. Turn right on George Street to reach the bridge. The pristine setting is home to more than 130 species of birds, including all kinds of waterfowl, wading birds, and the occasional pair of bald eagles. Rare plants and freshwater mussels (more than 30 species) are resplendent in the Ohio around this group of islands.

After a busy afternoon of exploring, you'll need a place to rest up and call it a night. You have a choice. You can head north on Route 2 about 30 miles to **Sistersville,** a collection of Italianate villas and other Victorian period mansions on the Ohio. The restored but still modestly priced **Wells Inn** (304-652-1312) serves guests comfortably in three stories with an indoor pool, dining room, and tavern. The surrounding National Historic Register district pays tribute to a city once at the heart of America's first oil boom. At one point during the 1890s, at least 20 millionaires lived here, more than any city its size in the US. More than 100 oil companies located in the county, and the new wealth prompted a flurry of construction, resulting in ornate Victorian mansions and a trolley line. By 1915 the oil was played out. The townspeople who remained had mostly prospered from the boom and were able to maintain their fashionable homes. You can obtain a free map of the historic district at the distinctive diamond-shaped city hall, which straddles the intersection of Main and Diamond. Visitors also enjoy antiquing, golfing, or taking West Virginia's last surviving ferry over to Ohio for dinner. The *Sistersville Ferry,* really a barge and a tug, has been in continuous operation in some form for 200 years and still transports nearly 100 cars daily, Thurs through Sun between early May and October when the river is not flooding. Without the 15-minute ferry commute, many people would have to loop south to St. Marys Bridge, 20 minutes away. The town-owned ferry charges $5 a trip for cars, $4 for motorcycles, and $1 for pedestrians and bicyclists.

Within spitting distance of the ferry are the *Little Sister oil well* and derrick towers along the Ohio shoreline, among the last remnants of the hundreds of wells that once covered the landscape. No mere decoration, this well is operational. Each September it pumps up some souvenir black gold during the West Virginia Oil & Gas Festival.

If you want modern accommodations, drive to *North Bend State Park* (www.northbendsp.com), near Cairo. This family-oriented, 1,405-acre park stretches along the banks of the Hughes River and has a beautiful 29-room lodge, with a restaurant as well as 9 deluxe cottages. West Virginia's 72-mile North Bend Rail Trail runs along the edge of the park, passing through a tunnel. The park offers the usual array of outdoor amenities, with one special surprise: the Extra Mile trail for wheelchair users and an adjoining playground designed for visually impaired and physically challenged children. Each July the park hosts a sports jamboree for blind and wheelchair-using competitors in such events as horseshoes, bicycle racing, basketball, and softball. Visually impaired participants pitch horseshoes or shoot basketballs at a beeping target.

Another lodging option is Mystic Manor in Pennsboro, a 1900 bed-and-breakfast that advertises itself as haunted by two ghosts. Although it's in a perpetual state of renovation, the home's restored rooms are gorgeous and the owner loves to cook. The inn serves guests just off the *North Bend Trail,* which runs along the old B&O Railroad line between Parkersburg and Wolf Summit near Clarksburg. It's part of the larger American Discovery Trail, which runs clear across the nation. This gravel section of the path passes through wooded park, farmland, and 13 tunnels. Call (304) 377-2121 for reservations and information.

You can make it a nostalgia day if you head south to Harrisville on Route

mid-ohio valleytrivia

Throughout the late 18th and early 19th centuries, the mighty Ohio River was the single busiest waterway in North America.

16. ***Berndine's Five and Dime*** at 106 N. Court St., is the nation's oldest dime store—a treasure. Berndine's has all the old tin wind-up toys, marbles, paper dolls, notions, salves, and inexpensive bling you'd have expected to find 50 years ago. This is the real thing—pressed tin ceilings, bins of novelties, and candies sold by the ounce out of great big oak cases. Since 1908 it has been the place where people come for gifts for children and adults. Berndine's is open year-round, 9 a.m. to 5 p.m. Mon through Sat. Call (304) 643-2217 or see berndinesdimestore.com for more information.

Another bit of local color is the ***Phantom of Silver Run ghost story walk*** that departs from the old 1902 Marshall Hardware store in Cairo along the adjacent North Bend Rail Trail some Saturday evenings in October. The tale involves the ghostly appearance of a beautiful young woman who reputedly disappeared along the railroad line shortly before she was to be married. For more information the ghost walk, call (304) 628-3321.

If you have time, head south for some oil history—this area was ground zero for an oil boom 150 years ago. Take CR 15 southwest to Route 47 west. Turn right and go about a mile to the hamlet of California. The Oil and Gas Museum recently opened its ***California Park*** here, on the site of one of the world's first two commercial oil wells. The community got its name from the California House hotel, where travelers rested on their way to the gold rush in California. The hotel burned in 1901, but its barn still stands. Bushrod Washington Creel named his hotel the California House because of the onrush of customers stopping while traveling to the state of California in hopes of finding gold. Creel's true gold, however, was black—he developed the oil field in California, WV. Oil production in California dates to the early 1800s. It was

The Last West Virginia Ferry

For almost 200 years, a ferry has operated on the banks of the broad Ohio River between historic Sistersville, West Virginia, and Fly, Ohio. The *City of Sistersville ferry boat* is still the fastest way for residents on the Ohio side to reach a hospital, so the town police chief occasionally gets calls from expectant parents who need transport across the Ohio after the ferry's 6 p.m. closing.

Until 1889 the boat was powered by paddles driven by a horse on a treadmill. A steamboat took its place for the next four decades. Now the pilot takes about six minutes to make the crossing on a calm day. The diesel craft normally transports 100 vehicles in a 12-hour day. Each car is charged $5 to cross the river. Pedestrians are charged $1 each way. It's a break-even venture for the town during the ferry's operating season, May through September, but no one wants to put an end to the last West Virginia ferry operating on the Ohio.

used to lubricate machinery in Cincinnati as early as 1819. At that time, crude oil bubbled to the surface and property owners simply dug trenches to collect it. When the world's first oil well was dug in Pennsylvania in 1859, crude oil was already being harvested in West Virginia. The California well was drilled the next year, starting an oil boom that was cut short by the Civil War. A historical display about the California is wells stands along Route 47 near its intersection with California House Road.

> ## mid-ohio
> ## valleytrivia
>
> The North Bend Rail Trail, which begins just east of Parkersburg and runs nearly 72 miles east to Clarksburg, was considered an engineering marvel when it was completed as the Baltimore & Ohio railroad line in 1857. Today it guides cyclists through 13 tunnels and over 36 bridges.

Burning Springs is perhaps 3 miles away as the crow flies, but closer to 8 over winding Routes 47, 53, and 5. This circuitous route through the rolling countryside takes you to the banks of the Little Kanawha River and the site where Confederate soldiers burned what was in 1863 one of the three major oil fields in the world. Nestled in the green hollows of Wirt County, this spot, because of its value to federal troops (it provided oil for machinery and illumination), was burned on the direction of General Robert E. Lee. It burned with such ferocity that the river became, as locals described, "a sheet of fire." More than 300,000 barrels of oil were destroyed, as well as every sawmill, business, and private dwelling in Burning Springs, a city with 10,000 residents at the time. The Oil and Gas Museum in Parkersburg is developing a 31-acre riverfront park on the site. Its on-site museum celebrates the oldest producing well in the world at what became the first American oil-field boomtown. The museum has restored an antique oil derrick at the site of the Rathbone Well.

Bluegrass Heartland

The moniker here applies to both the predominant music and the landscape of pastoral Calhoun and Roane Counties—agricultural areas rich in timber, pastureland, and old-time musicians.

The routes given here take a bit of pioneer spirit if you are to discover the treasures of life hidden off the interstates. So grab a cup of coffee and a road map and give yourself some time, for there's much to see in this quiet and pretty corner of West Virginia.

After you leave Burning Springs on Route 5, jump over onto Route 14 and head into Roane County to *Spencer,* where in the middle of October the locals celebrate their black walnut harvest in grand style. They host a four-day festival complete with singing, dancing, fiddling, turkey calling, flea markets, black walnut bake-offs, and the nuttiest parade you've ever seen. If you need a break, check what's playing at the old ***Robey Theatre,*** one of the nation's most economical spots for movies and movie food. The Robey opened in 1907 as a vaudeville house, making it one of the oldest continuously operating theaters in the nation. For its 100th birthday, the Robey restored its red, blue, and yellow neon sign and opened up the outdoor balcony. For its 105th, it

The Longest-Running Picture House in America: The Robey

You won't get surround sound or a selection of movies, but the old *Robey Theatre* in downtown Spencer has the charm of soda fountain drinks, a wide screen, and a history you won't find at other movie houses. The theater, which opened in June 1907, lays claim to being the oldest continuously running movie theater in the nation.

When Hamond Robey opened the theater during Spencer's oil and gas boom days, people had read about moving pictures, but most had never seen one. They turned out two or three times a week to see the same movie (for 10 cents), and it wasn't uncommon for the theater to run a show four or five times a day to accommodate the crowds.

Compared to other movie theaters, the Robey is still a few dollars cheaper. To stay afloat in this small town, owner Mike Burch rents videos from the backstage area by day.

The theater went through five name changes—Dreamland, Wonderland, Lyric, Auditorium, and the Robey—and traded locations on Main Street three times. It was one of the first theaters in the state to install sound equipment for the "talkies."

During its 1926 renovations, the Robey temporarily set up as a "Tentatorium," showing movies in a tent on the high school athletic field for a few months. During that time, actor Hoo Ray of *Our Gang* fame dropped by to do a live dance performance.

Although innovations have transformed some parts of the Robey's operations, the artifacts remain. The projection room still has the fireproof doors from the days when film was made with flammable nitrate, and a toilet still sits in the corner from the days before projectionists had automatic film systems.

Although the Robey's 400 seats are seldom filled in this small town, owner Burch is proud to own the nation's oldest theater and celebrated its 100th birthday by restoring the Robey's neon sign, broken for the past 40 years. General admission tickets at the Robey are now $8, children get in for $6, as are the Sunday matinees; for 3D movie tickets, add $2 all around. For current movies, call (304) 927-1390 or see robeytheatre.com.

purchased a 3D projection system. Movies show at 7 p.m. daily and at 9:15 on Fri and Sat nights.

Nearby **Arnoldsburg,** in Calhoun County, is also busy in late September celebrating the **West Virginia Molasses Festival,** an event dripping with homegrown mountain music and delicious food. On the first day of the festival cane stalks are ground through the mill, releasing the juice. For three days, workers stand over the heat, skimming off proteins and anything that isn't sugar. Gradually (slow as molasses) the amber color appears and the liquid thickens. Each batch sells out within minutes.

In this part of the state, there are many wonderful places to shop, but don't look for any malls. Stores and open-air markets are tucked away—small gems just waiting for the adventurous shopper. One of them is found just south of Arnoldsburg on Route 16 in the town of **Chloe.** Look for the Wednesday morning Calhoun County Farmers Market at the community center at West Fork Park. You'll find artisan breads and pastries, organic produce, crafts, even live animals. If you're lucky, Connie and Tom McColley might have some of their famed jewelry and woven wooden baskets for sale. The market is open May through Oct, 9 a.m. to 1 p.m. Call (304) 655-7429 for information.

Places to Stay in the Mid-Ohio Valley

CAIRO

Log House Homestead B&B
Homestead Cove Lane
(304) 628-3249
loghousehomestead.com
Moderate to expensive

North Bend State Park
Exit 176 off US 50
(304) 643-2931
wvstateparks.com/park/
north-bend-state-park
Moderate

PARKERSBURG

Blennerhassett Hotel
Fourth and Market Streets
(304) 422-3131
(800) 262-2536
Moderate to expensive

Comfort Suites
I-77 and Route 14 South,
exit 170
(304) 489-9600
Moderate to expensive

Mountwood Park Cabins
1014 Volcano Rd.
(304) 679 3611
mountwoodpark.org
Inexpensive

SPENCER

Arnott House B&B
103 Locust Ave.
(304) 634-5036
thearnotthouse.com
Inexpensive to moderate

Places to Eat in the Mid-Ohio Valley

PARKERSBURG

Spat's at the Blennerhassett
Fourth and Market Streets
(304) 422-3131
Moderate to expensive

Third Street Deli
403 Third St.
(304) 422-0003
Moderate

PENNSBORO

P&H Family Restaurant
206 Kimball Ave.
(304) 659-3241
Budget

WILLIAMSTOWN

Da Vinci's Restaurant
215 Highland Ave.
(304) 375-3633
villadavinci.com
Moderate

FOR MORE INFORMATION

Greater Parkersburg Convention & Visitors Bureau
(304) 428-1130
greaterparkersburg.com

Jackson County Chamber of Commerce
(304) 273-1060
jacksonchamberwv.org

Roane County Chamber of Commerce
(304) 927-1750
roanechamberwv.org

Northern Panhandle

Like neighboring Pennsylvania, the Northern Panhandle of West Virginia is a region of intensive mining, industry, and agriculture. It's an oddly shaped region whose northernmost point is actually closer to Canada than it is to the southern border of West Virginia. The four "Yankee" counties of West Virginia—Marshall, Ohio, Brooke, and Hancock—plus Tyler and Wetzel Counties collectively make up the Northern Panhandle region. All of the Northern Panhandle proper lies north of the Mason-Dixon Line (Tyler and Wetzel Counties are south of the line), and the residents here tend to have strong affiliations with such nearby northeastern industrial cities as Pittsburgh and Cleveland. Although industrial, the Northern Panhandle is also surprisingly green, with heavy forests, gentle hills, and fertile pastureland found along the Ohio River. The city of Wheeling is the industrial hub of the region.

Prehistoric people left their imprint on West Virginia in a grand fashion at *Grave Creek Mound,* a massive burial site located in the village of Moundsville. The Adena people, a native Indian tribe, were common to this part of West Virginia and what is now Indiana, Kentucky, Ohio, and Pennsylvania during the Woodland Period, an era lasting from about 1000

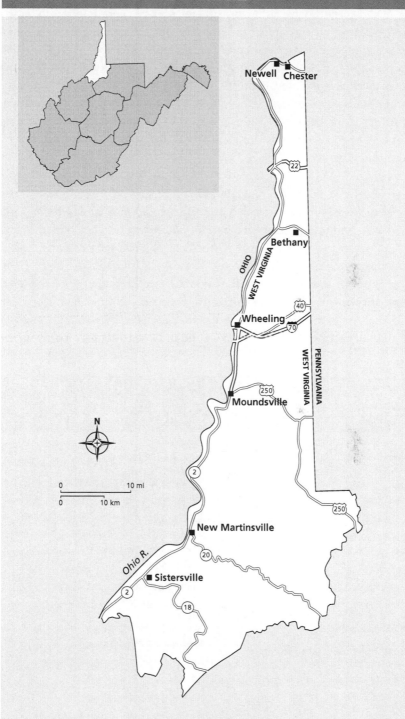

Newell   Chester

22

Bethany

OHIO

WEST VIRGINIA

40

Wheeling

70

PENNSYLVANIA

WEST VIRGINIA

250

Moundsville

N

2

0   10 mi

0   10 km

250

New Martinsville

20

Ohio R.

Sistersville

2

18

BC to AD 700. The Adena, a hunter-gatherer society, were referred to as the "mound builders" on account of their passion for constructing earthen burial mounds and other earthworks. Grave Creek Mound Archaeological Complex, now a historic site with the West Virginia Division of Culture and History, is the largest and certainly the most impressive of the Adena mounds and is probably the largest conical type of mound ever built. The mound measures 69 feet high; the diameter at the base is 295 feet. The mound was also once encircled by a 40-foot-wide, 5-foot-deep moat. In all, about 60,000 tons of earth were moved in the building of the burial place.

Grave Creek Mound, which dates from 250 BC, took more than 100 years to build, as evidenced by the multiple burial levels found here. Most of those buried here were probably cremated at death, placed in small log tombs, and covered with earth. Important members of society were often buried in the flesh and laid to rest with valuable personal belongings such as flints, beads, mica, copper ornaments, and pipes.

The story of the Adena and the mounds is told at the adjoining *Delf Norona Museum,* which has an exhaustive collection of Adena and Hopewell culture artifacts, including an inscribed sandstone tablet (whose meaning has been guessed at by a number of amateurs and professionals) found in the

BEST ANNUAL EVENTS IN THE NORTHERN PANHANDLE REGION

Celtic Celebration
Wheeling; first weekend in March
(304) 232-3087
wheelingheritage.org

New Vrindaban Festival of Colors
Moundsville; mid-Sept
(304) 843-1600
newvrindaban.com

West Virginia Derby
Chester; early August
(800) 80-40-HOT
moreatmountaineer.com

Upper Ohio Valley Italian Heritage Festival
Wheeling; late July
(304) 233-1090
italyfest.org

Heritage Blues Fest
Wheeling; mid August
(304) 238-6064
heritagemusicfest.com

Oglebayfest
Wheeling; early October
(304) 243-4000 or (800) 624-6988
oglebay.com

Winter Festival of Lights
Wheeling; late November through January 2
(304) 243-4000
oglebay.com

mound during the first excavation in 1838. A gift shop is located in the museum complex. The museum and park are open year-round, except for major holidays, from 10 a.m. to 4:30 p.m. Mon through Sat and 1 to 5 p.m. Sun. Admission is free. Call (304) 843-4131 for more information.

Just across the street from Delf Norona is one of the 500 best places to visit in the US, according to *US News & World Report*. The **West Virginia State Penitentiary** is a defunct maximum-security prison, closed in 1995 after the inmates sued the state over deplorable living conditions. You understand their perspective within minutes after passing through the entrance to the high-walled Gothic prison. The Pen still casts a sinister presence over Moundsville and has been called one of the most haunted places in America. All of the cells have original graffiti, and you get the chance to be locked behind bars briefly, if that's what you like. The tour's highlight is Old Sparky, the state's original electric chair. Sparky was responsible for nine executions before West Virginia outlawed capital punishment.

In addition to the regular tours, adventuresome visitors can now participate in monthly overnight "ghost hunts" with flashlight tours, spooky movies, and pizza. There's also an "Escape the Pen" adventure game here where so many inmates attempted escapes with dire consequences. Call or visit the website to register. Regular tours are conducted Tues through Sun Apr 1 through Oct 31 on the hour 10 a.m. to 4 p.m. and cost $14 for adults, $11 for seniors, and $8 for children ages 6 to 16. Ghost hunts, twilight tours, overnights, and Thriller

A Penitentiary Experience

In West Virginia you can have the experience of going to prison without ever breaking the law. No, state troopers aren't unduly severe with speeders—the old **West Virginia State Penitentiary** in Moundsville is now a tourist attraction. Its doors were shut to felons in 1995 after the West Virginia Supreme Court ruled its standard 5-foot-by-7-foot cells were cruel and unusual punishment. (In the 1950s, inmates had been triple-bunked in these tiny cells.)

Nowadays, the 1866 Gothic fieldstone prison makes for an eerie tour, with its execution area and Old Sparky, the electric chair constructed by an inmate. Those who visit the facility (Tues through Sun between Apr 1 and Nov 15) will see the guns used by guards, the isolation cells on North Hall where the worst inmates were confined, and the area where 16 correctional officers were taken hostage during a 1986 riot.

Depending upon your tour guide, often a former guard, you'll learn about the personalities of individual prisoners, famous escapes, the workings of the prison coal mine, and other stories.

Thursday night tours are also available. Check the website at wvpentours.com or call (304) 845-6200 for specific information.

Another good stop in Moundsville is the ***Fostoria Glass Museum*** on 511 Tomlinson Ave., where you can see 37,000 pieces of crystal from the famed company's 100-year existence. Some of these one-of-a-kind pieces were made by employees experimenting during their lunch break. The site of the old factory, abandoned in 1986, is just blocks away. At one time Fostoria was the largest producer of handmade glass in the nation, employing more than 1,000 people. Its American pattern, introduced in 1915, is still being made by Lancaster Colony. The museum is open Wed through Sat from 1 to 4 p.m., Mar through Nov, and admission is $4. Call (304) 845-9188 or see fostoriaglass.org for other information about Fostoria.

If you like the glitter of Fostoria crystal, just wait until you see the next stop on the tour, the ***Palace of Gold*** in New Vrindaban, a 10-mile trip northeast of Moundsville, in the steep green hills of Marshall County.

During the late 1960s, when religious and alternative lifestyle communes were cropping up throughout isolated and "live and let live" Appalachia, the Hare Krishnas came to this rural stretch of the Northern Panhandle and forever changed the complexion of the place. Today some 100 residents maintain the sprawling palace—nicknamed America's Taj Mahal—and the surrounding 5,000-acre estate. A tour of the 3,000-square-foot palace includes stops in the west gallery, a room bedecked with marble flooring and giant stained-glass windows, as well as a peek into the temple room with its awesome mural containing 4,000 crystals depicting Lord Krishna's life, radiating from the dome ceiling.

If you'd like to shake your bones a bit, stop off at the county's beautifully maintained ***Grand-Vue Park*** on your way back into town. Bolstered by gas-drilling money, the 650-acre park sprawls over the mountainside, giving unequaled views of Moundsville, especially from the 7,540 feet of ziplines. Grand-Vue also offers eight large modern cabins, 4 luxury treetop cabins, 21 miles of mountain biking trails, disc golf, bungee trampoline, rock climbing tower, aquatic center, 9-hole golf course, and an outdoor amphitheater. For the outdoorsy set, the park just finished a tent campground, RV park, and two bathhouses. The park hosts footraces and mountain biking competitions several times a year. For more information, see grandvuepark.com.

There's a tendency among folks who've never been to West Virginia to dismiss ***Wheeling*** as an industrial has-been, a Rust Belt relic with little or no tourism appeal. Nothing could be further from the truth. Not only is Wheeling loaded with interesting historical and cultural diversions, but it's also a beautiful city with one of the highest concentrations of Victorian homes in the country,

West Virginia Taj Mahal

As you approach the New Vrindaban community from Moundsville, the golden spires of the **Palace of Gold** spike above the trees. This is not what you would expect in West Virginia, but here the palace sits, a memorial to Swami Prabhupada, the founder of the International Society for Krishna Consciousness, also known as Hare Krishna.

The Palace of Gold, sometimes called Appalachia's Taj Mahal, has been listed as one of the nation's eight religious wonders by CNN. Originally designed in 1972 as a home for the community's founder, Prabhupada, the structure became a shrine when he died in 1977.

These days, the dazzling palace and its gardens are open to visitors. The exterior walls alone are covered with more than 8,000 square feet of 22-karat gold leaf, and the interior is decorated with semiprecious gems, marble, and crystal chandeliers. The whole project, from architecture through inlay, was a challenge for the unskilled devotees armed with how-to books and nerve. The palace is a tribute to the power of devotion.

Swan boats float in the intentional community's lotus pond, and peacocks strut along the shore. The sign by the lodge spells out the desired ambience: "You are entering a sacred place. No smoking or intoxicants. No non-vegetarian foods." Gardens of vegetables and roses are spread across the compound, which visitors are allowed to roam.

Krishnas don't pester guests about their religious beliefs. This is a laidback experience where visitors are often invited to the midday meditation and curry meal, but efforts to proselytize are restrained. For seekers, New Vrindaban functions as a pilgrimage site with periodic opportunities to study with recognized spiritual leaders. Participants practice yoga, meditation, and silence. The public is invited to join in celebrating festivals with kirtan (spiritual swaying and dancing). It's a bit surreal, but there's certainly nothing else like Palace of Gold in West Virginia.

The palace, with its adjacent temple and 3,000 rosebushes, is 3 miles off US 250 near the village of Limestone. Tours of the palace are available Apr through Aug, 10 a.m. to 7 p.m. and from Sept through Mar from 10 a.m. to 5 p.m.. Adult admission to the palace is $12; children 6–16 pay $6, and those 5 and under are admitted free.

Lodging and vegetarian Indian and American meals are available in the late spring through early fall. Govinda's is the top vegetarian restaurant in the Ohio Valley, serving classic Indian dinner dishes topped off with creamy lassi drinks. The fragrant Rose Garden Brunches serve a mixture of continental and Indian cuisines, along with kid-pleasing favorites including personal pizzas, fruits, and yogurt made from the milk of resident cows. The Govinda Express lunch menu includes vegetarian burgers, grilled sandwiches, soft tacos, ramen bowls, savories, and macaroni and cheese.

With 10 guest cabins and more than 70 lodge rooms, this is a fine place stay a while. Private rooms range from $77 to $150 and 2-bedroom suites from $196 to $219. Lodging is available at budget rates in the winter

Don't trust your GPS as you approach New Vrindaban; the average navigation system is likely to send you over rough roads and through a creek. Look for directions on the website at www.palaceofgold.com or call (304) 843-1600.

lovely parks (including 1,500-acre Oglebay Park, one of the largest and more heavily used municipal parks in the country), a scenic riverfront, and graceful tree-lined neighborhoods.

This northern city is the birthplace of West Virginia statehood, and you can retrace those tense pre–Civil War times at **Independence Hall,** 16th and Market Streets downtown. This stately 1859 Italian Renaissance building was easily the most state-of-the-art structure in Wheeling at the time of the secession debates, claiming both flush toilets and an air-circulating system, a predecessor to modern air-conditioning. The cooling effect was needed for the heated debates that sprung up here in 1861, when it was decided that the western region of Virginia would break free from the rest of the Old Dominion and form its own Union-aligned state, the Reformed State of Virginia. From 1861 to 1863 the Customs House (as it was called then) served as the state capitol. In 1863 President Lincoln declared West Virginia the 35th state in the union. Following official statehood the capital moved to Charleston, and the three-story building fell into a number of other uses, including a post office and federal court.

In 1912 Independence Hall was restored, and today it houses exhibits relating to the state's history along with period rooms, an interpretive film, and, from time to time, special historical reenactments. Admission is free. The newest exhibit, on the first floor, is *West Virginia: Born of the Civil War.* Independence Hall is open daily year-round from 10 a.m. to 4 p.m. except Sun. Call (304) 238-1300 or visitindependencehallfoundation.org.

BEST ATTRACTIONS IN THE NORTHERN PANHANDLE REGION

Independence Hall
Wheeling
(304) 238-1300
independencehallfoundation.org

Oglebay's Stifel Fine Arts Center
Wheeling
(304) 242-7700
oionline.com

Palace of Gold
Moundsville
(304) 843-1600, ext 0
palaceofgold.com

West Virginia State Penitentiary
Moundsville
(304) 845-6200
wvpentours.com

Wheeling Jamboree
944 Main St
(304) 907-0306
wheelingjamboree.org

The Mountain State has always been a hotbed for country music, producing both large audiences and more than its share of performers who've moved on to Nashville, such as Wheeling natives Brad Paisley and Tim O'Brien. Wheeling is the state's undisputed music capital, thanks to the success of *Jamboree USA* (now called *Wheeling Jamboree*), once the second-oldest live-radio show in the nation. Every Saturday night since 1933, the country music show was been broadcast over radio station WWVA to fans along the eastern seaboard and six Canadian provinces. The first show was broadcast April 1 at midnight at Wheeling's Capitol Theatre; the cost of attending was a whopping 25 cents.

In 1969 the wildly popular show, featuring the rising and established stars of Nashville, moved to the luxurious *Capitol Music Hall* in the middle of downtown. Performers who've graced the stage over the past few years include the likes of Willie Nelson, Styx, Trace Adkins, the Oak Ridge Boys, Frankie Avalon, Tanya Tucker, and the Charlie Daniels Band. The music hall deteriorated over the years, and in 2015 the jamboree moved to the former Eagles Building a block away. The live Jamboree show, now called *Wheeling Jamboree,* is still held Saturday nights. Tickets are usually $25 and can be purchased on the website, wheelingjamboree.org.

The restored Capitol Music Hall, now called the *Capitol Theatre,* still hosts musical shows as well as a Broadway play series, among other events (capitoltheatrewheeling.com). Another former Jamboree venue and West Virginia's oldest theater, the *Victoria,* hosts the Victoria Jamboree on Market Street. This is a variety show with an Elvis impersonator, country, bluegrass and gospel.

You really mustn't leave the Wheeling area without a stop at the *Wheeling Island Hotel-Casino-Racetrack* (wheelingisland.com), if only to listen to the music of the gaming machines and sample the 70-item Islander Buffet. This will give you a chance to drive or walk over the *Wheeling Suspension Bridge,* the first bridge over the Ohio River and, at the time of its construction (1849), the longest single-span suspension bridge in the world. With its striking arched stone entrances, the bridge is considered the nation's most important pre–Civil War engineering structure.

If you like to take in the view at an ambulatory pace, Wheeling's your place. *Wheeling Heritage Rail Trail,* 13 miles of paved historic trails through the city, offers walkers, runners, and cyclists a riverside view. At Pike Island Dam, it connects with the *Brooke Pioneer Trail* for 7 more miles of trail, reaching all the way to Wellsburg. Further endearing the Northern Panhandle to walkers, another rail trail, beginning 10 miles north in Weirton, extends 29 miles to Pittsburgh, Pennsylvania.

There's no doubt folks in the Northern Panhandle take play seriously. A toy museum specializing in Marx items, **Kruger Street Toy and Train Museum,** engenders a special fondness from train lovers. If the lemon-yellow 1926 Baltimore & Ohio caboose C-2019 in the yard doesn't signal the founders' passion for trains, the O-gauge train layout filling an entire room should. In the middle 1970s Allan Robert Miller and his son, Allan Raymond, began actively collecting Lionel toy trains. By the early 1980s, the collection had expanded to include Louis Marx trains, then all toys by Marx and others—classic 1950s play sets, dolls, dollhouses, and other items. They virtually grew out of the house. A museum seemed the natural mode of displaying the extensive collection, and the Victorian schoolhouse at 144 Kruger St. in the Elm Grove section of Wheeling was the perfect fit. The museum has hosted the Marx Toy and Train Collectors National Convention and visiting collections of Mego and NASCAR toys, as well as Santa Claus and the Easter Bunny. Toys, trains, and other mementos are on sale in the gift shop. The museum is open from 9 a.m. to 4 p.m. daily June through Dec and 9 a.m. to 4 p.m., weekends only, the rest of the year. Admission is $12 for adults, $9 for seniors, and $6 for students. Children under 6 are free. For specific information call (304) 242-8133 or visit toyandtrain.com.

Toys still captivate the adult heart, all right, but some grown-up boys (and girls) prefer the bigger, louder toys at **Cabela's** massive outdoor store. The 175,000-square-foot mecca for outdoor enthusiasts features giant aquariums of freshwater fish that you seem to walk through, as well as an indoor mountain, an archery range, and herds of wildlife specimens in a naturalistic setting. Oh yeah, and there's stuff for sale, too. The retail departments include camping, hunting, fishing, marine equipment, all-terrain vehicles, boots, clothing, a bargain cave, a general store, and a 180-seat restaurant. Cabela's sits on a 110-acre site near the Dallas Pike exit of I-70.

northern panhandle trivia

The Ohio River, which first flows into the Mountain State near the town of Chester, begins in Pittsburgh, Pennsylvania, at the confluence of the Allegheny and Monongahela Rivers.

Wheeling's most popular destination, **Oglebay Resort,** can keep a family busy for days. In a setting of 1,650 pastoral acres, Oglebay offers a zoo, 2 museums, 7 restaurants, 271 lodge rooms, 54 deluxe cottages, trails, gardens, 7 specialty shops, an art gallery, Segway tours, pedal boats, stables, tennis, and fishing. Oglebay Resort is a golfer's paradise with four golf courses including two championship courses. The Arnold Palmer Course is the newest course at Oglebay. This Arnold Palmer–designed course opened in 2000. It's also a municipal park—one of the largest in the nation. Oglebay is known for its stunning Winter Festival of Lights, Easter egg hunt, flower show, and golf tournaments.

The park's **Henry Stifel Schrader Environmental Center** has been especially popular of late. Families enjoy the butterfly gardens, where they can watch butterflies flitting among the flowers, as well as a woodland walkway 40 feet off the ground that gives them a bird's-eye vantage into the trees. The native snake exhibit allows them to become more familiar with reptiles in a safe setting. At night the **Spiedel Observatory** draws in stargazers and those interested in specific events in the heavens. The attractive center building is constructed from 97 percent recycled materials including the Wheeling newspaper, plastic bottles, bus tires, and recycled aluminum cans. For more information about Oglebay's environmental center activities, call (304) 242-6855. Oglebay is located on Route 88 North. For more information about the park and resort, call (800) 624-6988 or (304) 243-4000 or go to oglebay-resort.com.

Pickin' and Fiddlin'

Nashville may claim the title of Music City, USA, but the seeds of American country music were planted in the fertile mountain hollows of southern Appalachia, far from the neon glow of Music Row. Music scholars will give credit to such places as Galax, Virginia; Bristol, Tennessee; and the coal camps and logging towns of central and southern West Virginia.

The roots of country music date from 17th-century Ireland and came to the Appalachians with the Scots-Irish settlers a century later. Those Irish ballads, jigs, and reels were transformed into distinctly American mountain music, which evolved into old-time string music and bluegrass, country, and honky-tonk sounds. Although today's prevailing Nashville sound has strayed far from its roots, you can still hear real mountain music throughout the southern Appalachians, especially at the festivals, music parks, and picking parlors of the Mountain State.

For examples of this, check out the Allegheny Echoes workshops in Pocahontas County (304-799-7121; alleghenyechoes.com), the Appalachian String Band Festival at Clifftop (304-438-3005; wvculture.org/stringband), and the Augusta Heritage Center in Elkins (800-624-3157; augustaheritagecenterat Facebook.com). You may also want to take in Charleston's Vandalia Festival, the Mountain State Arts and Crafts Fair in Ripley, Spencer's Black Walnut Festival, and the Wednesday-night jams at Davis and Elkins College's Hermanson Center, and Wheeling's Saturday night Jamboree, a radio show that began in 1933 and soon became a very prominent regional show. More informal gatherings are tucked away in country stores, campgrounds, and coffeehouses. They're not hard to find. Just inquire at any local music store, or if the area is very rural, any store. You're bound to find a pickin' parlor or a front porch fiddlin' within a short drive.

It's toys and Halloween all year long in the old Boggs Run School in Benwood, midway between Moundsville and Wheeling. When Pamela Apkarian-Russell's passion for collecting Halloween artwork, costumes, and memorabilia threatened to overflow their home, she and her husband bought the fortress-like elementary school, moved upstairs, and dedicated the bottom floors to *Castle Halloween Museum.* Visitors tour 250 years of Halloween memorabilia—fortune-telling items, folk art, toys, witches, games, and Easter Witches. Everything you've ever associated with Halloween (with some memento mori, Day of the Dead and Harry Potter thrown in for good measure) can be found in her Castle Halloween Museum, including candy containers, costumes (and the materials/equipment used to make them), games, decorations, noisemakers, movie posters, original artwork, food packaging, autographs and much, much more. More than 35,000 items have been amassed by this serious collector, who has written at least five books on her passion. The $9 tours can be arranged by calling (304) 233-1031. See castlehalloween.com for possible discounts and more information.

The urban facade of Wheeling gives way to peaceful countryside as you wend your way up Route 88 to the historic village of West Liberty, home of West Liberty State College. The school was the oldest academy in West Virginia, established in 1837, and became a college a few years later. Its former president's home now serves area visitors as the Liberty Oaks Bed and Breakfast.

Four miles farther north is another old West Virginia college in the village of Bethany. Here you'll find the redbrick, Gothic-influenced *Bethany College,* a prestigious liberal arts institution that conjures up images of the film *Dead Poets Society.* Dominating the ivy-covered and tree-lined campus, the oldest in West Virginia, is "Old Main," a National Historic Landmark with a 122-foot tower and central building of brick and stone stretching more than the length of a football field and punctuated by 5 arched entrances. It was styled after a similar structure at the University of Glasgow in Scotland.

Also on the college grounds is the *Alexander Campbell Mansion,* the home of Bethany College's founder and a leading figure in the 19th-century religious movement that spawned the Disciples of Christ, Churches of Christ, and Christian Church. The impressive 25-room home was built in four periods, beginning in 1793, and entertained such important figures of the day as Henry Clay, Daniel Webster, Jefferson Davis, and James Garfield. Ask at the Mansion Visitor Center for tours of the college, including the Old Bethany Meeting House, built in 1850. Tours also can be arranged on Saturday by calling (304) 829-7611 or through bethanywv.com.

While on campus you may also want to see the 19th-century *Pendleton Heights,* the college president's house, as well as the *Old Bethany Meeting House* and the *Delta Tau Delta Founders' House.*

About a 30-minute drive north of Bethany puts you in the Chester/ Newell area, the top of the Mountain State. This part of the Northern Panhandle is barely 5 miles wide. Although famous for its Mountaineer Race Track and Gaming Resort and its house-size teapot, this region has also garnered a respectful reputation for its *Homer Laughlin Fiestaware* (fiestafactorydirect.com). The world's largest manufacturer of dinnerware—from china for White House banquet tables to the art deco Fiestaware prized by collectors and recently reissued in new colors, the Newell-based Homer Laughlin plant has produced quality china since 1871. You can watch this bold china coming off the assembly line during plant tours Mon through Thurs at 10:30 a.m. and 12:30 p.m. and buy economically priced dinnerware at the outlet store, open 9:30 a.m. to 5 p.m. Mon through Sat and Sun from noon to 5 p.m. For more information, call (304) 387-1300.

There's a range of accommodations up here in the northern tip of West Virginia—from camping in nature at Tomlinson Run State Park to deluxe rooms at Mountaineer Race Track and Gaming Resort, where the lights never go off.

Not everyone who likes an occasional night in the woods invests in a tent, cookstove, and all the other necessary paraphernalia. Realizing this, *Tomlinson Run State Park* recently constructed 4 weathertight canvas yurts to accommodate carefree campers. Each little round hut is equipped with one or two bunk beds, a lantern, propane stove, cookware, cooler, and picnic table,

---

Anyone for a Large Spot of Tea?

In the middle of the intersection of Routes 2 and 30 north of Chester sits the world's largest teapot, its claim to fame emblazoned on its sides. This chunk of kitsch lured bargain hunters into Devon's pottery outlet during the golden years of highway travel before interstates.

The 14-foot teapot was erected in 1938 by William "Babe" Devon in front of his Chester shop on Route 2. Rumor has it that the teapot is actually a hogshead barrel used in a Hires Root Beer publicity campaign, with a spout and a tin covering added. Nevertheless, for almost 50 years, the teapot coaxed tourists to shop for Fiestaware and other locally produced china. The teapot served as a natural symbol for the region's leading industry, and the home of the world's largest pottery plant and manufacturer of dinnerware, Homer Laughlin. The mile-long plant is located just a few miles down the road.

In 1987 the deteriorating teapot was in danger of demolition. After a grassroots Save the Teapot campaign, the teapot was donated to the city of Chester, and renovation began. In 1990 the world's largest teapot was moved to its present location beside the ramp to Jennings Randolph Bridge.

all for under $65 a night. A convenience store and bathhouse with hot showers are a short stroll away. During the day, you can fish, play miniature golf, hike, or swim. The campground is open April 1 to October 31 and features melodious wake-up calls by songbirds. For reservations, call (800) CALL-WVA or see wvstateparks.com/park/tomlinson-run-state-park.

At the other extreme stands **_Grande Hotel at Mountaineer Casino, Race Track and Gaming Resort_** (moreatmountaineer.com) in Chester. The resort features 1,000 slot machines (open 24 hours a day, 7 days a week) as well as game tables, daily poker tournaments, Thoroughbred racing, golf course, theater, spa, fitness center, indoor pool, and 4 restaurants. Top-name musicians and comedians put on shows in the ballroom. Since 2009 Mountaineer Casino has offered craps, blackjack, roulette, 3-card poker, Let It Ride, and Spanish 21. And when it's time to fold, each of the expansive guest rooms is equipped with fluffy bathrobes, oatmeal soap, and all the amenities. If you don't feel like sleeping, you can usually party till dawn at the Roaring Twenties theme casino. For hotel prices and reservations, call (800) 804-0HOT Or see cnty.com/mountaineer.

Places to Stay in the Northern Panhandle

CHESTER

Mountaineer Casino, Racetrack & Gaming Resort
(800) 80-40-HOT
cnty.com/mountaineer
Expensive

GLEN DALE

Bonnie Dwaine
Bed & Breakfast
505 Wheeling Ave.
(304) 845-7250
bonnie-dwaine.com
Moderate

WELLSBURG

Barn with Inn
4859 Bealls Ridge Rd
(304) 737-0647
Barnwithinn.com
Moderate to expensive

WHEELING

McClure City Center
Hotel
1200 Market St.
(304) 232-0300
mcclurehotelwheeling.com
Moderate

Oglebay Resort
465 Lodge Dr.
(304) 243-4000
oglebay.com
Moderate to expensive

Wheeling Island Hotel
1 S. Stone St.
(304) 232-5050
wheelingisland.com
Moderate

Places to Eat in the Northern Panhandle

WEIRTON

Undo's Italian Family
Restaurant
350 Three Springs Dr.
(304) 723-9700
undos.com
Moderate

FOR MORE INFORMATION

Wheeling Convention and Visitors Center
(304) 233-7709 or (800) 828-3097
wheelingcvb.com

Wetzel County Convention & Visitors Bureau
(304) 398-4910
visitwetzelcounty.com

Top of West Virginia CVB
(304) 797-7001
topofwv.com

WELLSBURG

Drover's Inn 1848 Restaurant
1001 Washington Pike
(304) 737-0188
droversinn1848.com
Moderate

WHEELING

Coleman's Fish Market
22nd and Market Streets
(304) 232-8510.
Budget

Public Market
1401 Main St.
(304) 238-9522
Thepublicmarket.org
Inexpensive

Oglebay Resort, Ihlenfeld Dining Room
465 Lodge Dr.
(304) 243-4080
oglebay.com
Moderate

Wheeling Brewing Co.
2247 Market St.
(304) 905-8757
wheelingbrewing.com
Inexpensive

Mountaineer Country

Mountaineer Country, probably because of its industrial and coal-mining heritage, is also the most ethnically diverse part of the state, with particularly large Italian and Polish populations. Of course, ethnic festivals and eateries are popular here, and the astute traveler won't ever leave hungry.

Traveling north on I-79 into Harrison County, have a look at what early American farm life was like. Between Lost Creek and West Milford lies **_Watters Smith Memorial State Park_** (wvstateparks.com/park/watters-smith-state-park), a 523-acre farm established in 1796 on land originally patented by Patrick Henry and owned by four generations of the Watters Smith family, pioneers in this region. It still contains a hand-hewn 18th-century livestock barn, carpenter and blacksmith shops, a modest 130-year-old home built by a Smith family descendant, and a small museum with frontier farm equipment. Start at the visitor center, then take the self-guided tour. After you've learned a bit of history, cool off in the swimming pool located in the park's recreation area. Docent tours are conducted most days from Memorial Day through Labor Day. Tours at other times of the year are available by reservation only. Small donations are accepted. Call (304) 745-3081.

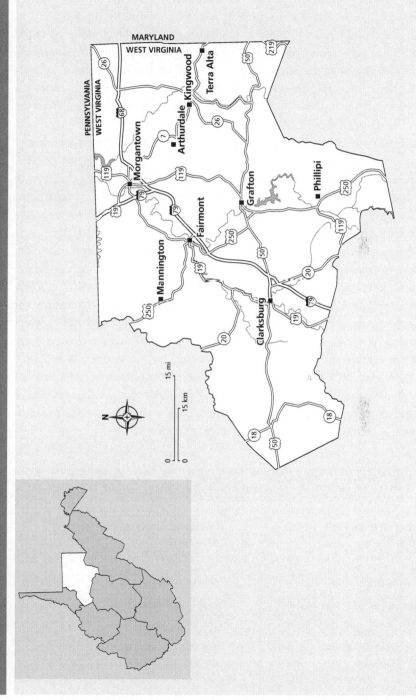

MOUNTAINEER COUNTRY

From here, you're only about 10 miles south of Clarksburg, one of the prettiest and most historic cities in the state. Just off the interstate, it's at the intersection of US 19 and US 50. Clarksburg was established in 1785 and is, among other things, the birthplace of native son Stonewall Jackson. One of the best places to get started on your tour of the city is downtown at **Waldomore,** an 1839 Greek Revival mansion that houses exhibits and information on West Virginia history and culture. It's chock-full of museum-quality pieces from the mid-1800s and holds works by local authors and historical documents from the life and times of Stonewall Jackson.

Also of note at Waldomore is the ***Gray Barker UFO Collection,*** one of the nation's largest unidentified flying object exhibits, featuring 29 file drawers of documents from investigations and sightings as well as a slew of provocative photographs, official records, and correspondence among various international UFO societies. As you might imagine, West Virginia's rural nature—and amazingly dark nighttime skies—make it a treasure trove for all things UFO.

Buckhannon native Gray Barker amassed this large personal collection, and after his death Waldomore assembled it into a museum-quality collection, one that attracts folks from around the world. Barker entered the field of paranormal speculation in 1952, when he went to Braxton County to collect reports from residents who claimed they saw the infamous Flatwoods Monster emerging from a glowing object that landed from the sky. He also investigated the Mothman creature at Point Pleasant, West Virginia, which resulted in his book, *The Silver Bridge*. His final book, *MIB: The Secret Terror Among Us,* became the inspiration for the 1997 summer hit movie *Men in Black.* Clarksburg residents say Barker was not necessarily a believer in UFOs, but was more of a folklorist who would record and publish other people's stories.

BEST ATTRACTIONS IN MOUNTAINEER COUNTRY

Cathedral State Park
Aurora
(304) 735-3771
wvstateparks.com/park/
cathedral-state-park

Cheat River Whitewater Rafting
Albright
(304) 329-2024
Cheatriveroutfitters.com

Prickett's Fort State Park
Fairmont
(304) 363-3030
wwvstateparks.com/park/
pricketts-fort-state-park

Valley Falls State Park
Fairmont
(304) 367-2719
wvstateparks.com/park/
valley-falls-state-park

Don't Worry; You're in West Virginia

When I considered walking the West Fork River Trail's 16 miles between Fairmont and Shinnston, I wasn't as concerned about my physical ability as my safety. Fairmont State College cyclists patrol the rail trail on bicycles daily, I knew; but would a solitary hiker be safe from human harm in the long stretches of lonely forest?

"Oh, honey, you're in West Virginia," said Kathleen Panek, owner of Gillum House B&B in Shinnston. "If you see a man on the trail, he's just going to ask if you're doing all right and if you need anything."

"OK," I said, "if you say so." But I pocketed my mace as I headed out of town along banks quivering with white trilliums. I saw kingfishers and a green heron trolling the West Fork River. (West Fork of what? It should be the Monongahela, but nobody says so.) I spied wild turkeys and a nesting goose, but no humans until I approached Monongah.

There, beside an abandoned coal yard, a young man with big tattoos on his arms was approaching me at a fast clip. Nobody else was in sight.

I clutched my mace in my pocket. He smiled. "How are you, ma'am? Been hiking long?"

"An hour or so."

"Bet you're thirsty. My house is right behind the fire station. Nobody's home. Just go in the front door—it's unlocked—and get you a drink out of the fridge."

I thanked him and unclenched. Honey, you're in West Virginia.

Waldomore and the Gray Barker UFO Collection are open upon request on Tues, Wed, and Fri 9 a.m. to 5 p.m.; Thurs 1 to 8 p.m. David Houchin maintains the collection. Call ahead (304-627-2236) to be sure he is there; the hours fluctuate with his schedule.

Also in the 16-block downtown historic district is the 1807 **Stealey-Goff-Vance House**, 123 W. Main St. (304) 709-4902), with its large collection of American Indian artifacts. This was the home of Cyrus Vance, former secretary of state to Jimmy Carter, during Vance's teen years. Nearby on Main Street on the courthouse grounds is an impressive bronze sculpture, *The Immigrants,* a tribute to the Belgian, Czech, Greek, Hungarian, Irish, Italian, Romanian, and Spanish immigrants who came to the Clarksburg area during the 1880s to work in the glass factories and coalfields. The monument conveys the spirit in which these diverse immigrants pulled together to form a harmonious community that still exists today.

Just north of Clarksburg on US 19 is the historic town of **Shinnston,** settled in 1778 when Levi Shinn built a home in the area. Today the town has

BEST ANNUAL EVENTS IN MOUNTAINEER COUNTRY

Cheat River Festival
Albright; May
(304) 329-3621
Cheatfest.org

PattyFest Music Festival
Fairmont; early June
(304) 641-2376
Pattyfest.org

Preston County Buckwheat Festival
Kingwood; late September
(304) 292-5081

Feast of the Seven Fishes Festival
Fairmont; December
(304) 366-0468
Mainstreetfairmont.org

a population of about 2,200. It supports several pizza places, a museum, and a park with a bocce court as well as the *Chapel of Perpetual Adoration,* where people of all faiths can go for prayer any hour of the day on Sundays, Wednesdays, and Fridays. Shinnston is located at the southern terminus of the *West Fork River Trail,* a 16-mile path running north to Fairmont. On the north side of Fairmont, you can connect with the McTrail to Prickett's Fort State Park, and from there to the Mon River Trail through Morgantown to the Pennsylvania border. Someday soon you'll be able to pedal a network of trails all the way to Pittsburgh, Pennsylvania, or Washington, DC, should you choose such an aerobic holiday. But for many the West Fork River Trail is plenty, thank you, as it wends along its flat course past wildflowers and waterfalls through the company towns of Worthington, Enterprise, and Monongah.

With the active traveler in mind, *Gillum House Bed & Breakfast* can set up bicycle rentals, horse boarding, and shuttle services for those who want to do the scenic trail one-way. Horses get to enjoy the horse B&B (Wade Maley Stables) right on the rail trail, just minutes from the Gillum House. Hosts Kathleen and John Panek also offer motorcycling inn-to-inn packages and will give you an itinerary of covered bridges, craft shops, glass outlets, and other interesting places to visit. If you want to spend a working holiday, the Paneks will even do a three-day seminar on how to run a bed-and-breakfast. The Paneks love the challenge of making breakfasts for special diets, so throw your requirements at them, whether they're sugarless, low-carb, low-fat, or gluten-free. Call (304) 592-0177.

West of Clarksburg on Route 50 is the town of *Salem,* settled in 1792. This is a little city with an unusual history. It was settled by Seventh-Day Baptist families from New Jersey after a two-and-a-half-year journey westward in search of religious freedom. *Fort New Salem* here is a historical park in the process of re-creation. You can head up there through Salem International University's campus for special events such as lantern-lit storytellings, blacksmithing demonstrations, and apple butter festivals. The ***Annual Dulcimer Festival*** draws in players of all levels in early August. The weekend event features hands-on music workshops in mountain dulcimer and hammered dulcimer with additional sessions on penny whistle and bowed psaltery. Public dulcimer

The Mummies of Philippi

They spent much of their short lives hidden away in a mental hospital, but after death these women traveled widely. The mummies of Philippi, two women embalmed by a rural storekeeper and inventor shortly after their deaths, toured with P. T. Barnum's circus and got as far as Paris, France, in the late 19th century.

Now they are the most popular attraction at the Barbour County Historical Society Museum in Philippi. For a paltry $1, visitors can enter the former railroad station restroom to peep at the small, leathery women lying adorned with artificial flowers in their caskets.

They are preserved with Graham Hamrick's Mummifying Fluid; that's also stored in the museum, although a description of his patented formula is not. He claimed his formula was based on the recipe used in the embalming of Jacob in the Bible and that the ingredients were available in any country store.

The label on his embalming fluid reads: "Best in the World, Absolutely Prevents Decomposition, No Such Bleacher is Known, The Fluid that is Always Dependable. Antiseptic, Deodorizer, Disinfectant, Germicide." Hamrick said on his patent application that he wanted to offer a simpler, less-expensive method of embalming. It was also less dangerous to the embalmer, omitting the usual mercury and arsenic. Descriptions of his process compare it to smoking meat.

Hamrick experimented with embalming vegetables and small animals for years before he drove his wagon to the West Virginia Hospital for the Insane in Weston and emerged with the cadavers of two unknown women. Mortuary officials examined the bodies two months later, noting they were perfectly preserved.

Old records suggest that Hamrick also preserved a baby's body, but that disintegrated in the flood of 1985. The mummified women were also damaged, and some say they were laid out on the post office lawn to dry. The mummies belonged to several private citizens before they were reclaimed by Philippi town officials for the museum. "We think of it as a very long wake," said museum curator Olivia Sue Lambert, "which is more than these little ladies were given in life."

The Barbour County Historical Society Museum is located in an old railroad station beside the Philippi covered bridge. Hours are 11 a.m. until 4 p.m. Fri and Sat and 1 to 4 p.m. on Sun, mid-May through mid-Oct. Arrangements for visiting the mummies at other times may be made by calling (304) 457-4846 or (304) 457-3700.

concerts are held on Friday and Saturday nights during the festival. Call (304) 695-2220 or visit fortnewsalemfoundation.org for details.

Just east of Clarksburg on Route 50 is the little town of **Bridgeport.** Founded as a trading post in 1764, it still serves as a good spot to stop for a rest and a bite to eat. There are a number of national chain hotels/motels and restaurants along the highway, but for a real taste of local flavor, go shopping!

Sample the local retail scene by strolling down Main Street, where antiques, unique gifts and specialty West Virginia–made items are popular at local shops. *Almost Heaven Desserts*, Mustard Seed Primitives, Country Peddler, and Art-works have become perennial favorites.

You'll want to save a few coins to give to the folks at **West Virginia Mountain Products**, at I-79, exit 115, near Mount Clare. Housed in the old Quiet Dell School, this is the state's juried largest artisans' cooperative, rich with handmade quilts, stained glass, baskets, pottery, and dolls made by local artists. If your interests go beyond just admiring and purchasing the handiworks, you might want to watch one of the craft demonstrations held here throughout the year. Hours are 10 a.m. to 5 p.m. Mon through Sat. Call (304) 622-3304 for information.

Almost 90 years ago a Civilian Conservation Corps (CCC) camp was operating in the field in back of Quiet Dell School. Now the **West Virginia CCC Camp Museum** shares space with the craft cooperative in the old schoolhouse. On the heels of the stock market crash of 1929, the Great Depression brought hard times. Jobs were hard to find and families became homeless. One of the first things President Franklin Roosevelt did when he took office in 1933 was to set up the CCC to put unemployed young men to work. From that year until the program was phased out in 1942, more than 3 million men worked from 1,600 camps throughout the country. In West Virginia 55,000 young men worked out of 67 camps fighting more than 10,000 forest fires, building hundreds of bridges, planting millions of trees, and developing more than 30 parks.

Camp Harrison was formed so hastily that Quiet Dell was a tent city for 200 men its first season, the summer of 1935. They later built four wooden barracks, work buildings, and a mess hall. Their mission in the county was to improve roads, repair bridges, and grade farmland to slow erosion. The museum contains more than 250 artifacts commemorating the CCC camp experience. A photograph of Pocahontas County's Camp Copperhead (now a privately owned camp) shows a crowd gathered to watch captured copperheads and blacksnakes in snake fight competitions. There are also tools, garments, and soap made by local women to sell to the camp.

The museum and craft shop are open Mon through Sat 10 a.m. to 5 p.m. For more information, call (304) 622-3304 or visit wva-ccc-legacy.org.

Now head into the hinterlands on Route 76 to beautiful Barbour County. There's lots of water here, notably from the lower half of gigantic Tygart Lake. *Audra State Park*, south of the lake off US 119, contains the beautiful Middle Fork River, with its huge rocks for sunbathing and its clear, cool water for diving or kayaking. The beautiful Alum Cave overhang makes for picture-perfect selfies. Meandering back to the north on US 250 places you in *Philippi*, the Barbour County seat. This is where you'll find a treasure of another kind— *Philippi Bridge*, one of the prettiest covered bridges in the country and certainly the most scenic south of New England. In fact, almost half of West Virginia's remaining covered bridges are in the Mountaineer Country region. The Philippi Bridge is located downtown on US 119/250 and spans the width of the Tygart River. It's the only wooden covered bridge that is still a part of a federal highway, and it is also the state's oldest covered bridge, built in 1852. North and South fought the first land battle of the Civil War in Philippi on June 3, 1861, over this bridge. The relatively bloodless battle, irreverently referred to as "the Philippi Races," resulted in a Union rout of Confederate forces threatening the Baltimore & Ohio railroad. The only warning of the Union's predawn surprise attack on camping Confederates came when a local housewife fired a few pistol shots at the Yankees. The Southerners got in only a few shots before breaking lines and running frantically to the south, some still in nightclothes.

This battle—or skirmish—lacked fatalities, but it was not without blood. A cannonball slammed into the leg of a young Confederate soldier named James Hanger, an 18-year-old engineering student. He became the first amputee of the Civil War, but he gained a profession. When he recovered, he whittled a bendable wooden leg with hinges. Hanger was asked to create wooden legs for other Confederate soldiers and eventually started a company that became one of the largest manufacturers of wooden legs in the world. A plaque in Philippi commemorates the fateful cannon blast. For more information about reenactments of the Battle of Philippi, call (304) 457-3700.

The *Barbour County Historical Society Museum* (philippi.org), home of the Philippi mummies, sits on the bank of the Tygart beside the covered bridge. Located in a renovated railroad station, the museum contains Civil War memorabilia, antiques, books, and the mummified remains of two women who lived in a Weston mental hospital. It's open Mon through Sat 11 a.m. to 4 p.m. and Sun 1 to 4 p.m., May 15 to October 15, and by appointment the rest of the year (304-457-4846 or 3700).

Too often folks think of West Virginia house architecture in terms of one-room cabins and company houses. For another glimpse of West Virginia history, go 4 miles north of Philippi to the *Adaland Mansion* (adaland.org), where you can tour the stately 1870 home of Irish settler Augustus Modisett.

Guided tours of the home reveal a carefully restored house with period wallpapers, antique furniture, and gardens straight out of the 19th century. The 1850 barn on the property, a handsome post-and-beam architecture, now serves as a heritage center. Hoop-skirted interpreters occasionally serve afternoon tea at special events. The menu includes scones, fresh fruit, tea sandwiches, dessert, and hot and cold flavored teas. Call (304) 457-1587 for reservations. Adaland is open May 1 to December 31 by appointment. Admission is $10 for adults; free for children under 12.

The Northern Heartland

Rich soil and scenery define this quiet corner of Mountaineer Country, which covers all of Preston, Taylor, and Marion Counties. From the south, the gateway to the region is **Grafton** (graftonwv.org), a tranquil, tree-lined community of 5,000 perched on the upper shores of Tygart Lake. **Tygart Lake State Park** has long been called West Virginia's best kept secret. Now, with splashy new waterpark features, an outfitter for active water adventures, and a new sandy beach, word is getting out about the 10-mile lake. It's no longer just a quiet bass lake. Like most of the towns in the area, Grafton emerged along a wilderness road that opened this part of the Mountain State to civilization in the East. What is now US 50—the brainchild of French engineering genius Claude Crozet—runs through the middle of town. Crozet surveyed and blazed much of the wilderness road (which now extends from Maryland to California) and is credited with being one of the founders of Grafton.

Perhaps the most interesting sidelight here is a shrine that will go straight to the heart of any good mother and child. It's the **International Mother's Day Shrine,** located at Andrews Methodist Church on Main Street, about a mile south of the US 50/119 intersection. Grafton native Anna Jarvis is credited with organizing the first celebration of Mother's Day at the pretty redbrick church in 1908. Miss Jarvis, who was living in Philadelphia at the time, thought it would be a nice gesture to have the church where her mother taught Sunday school for more than 20 years recognize the first Mother's Day on the third anniversary of her mom's death.

The International Mother Day's Shrine, depicting a mother, infant, and small child, was erected adjacent to the 130-year-old church in 1962. A special Mother's Day service is held at the church on that day each year at 2:30 p.m. Guided tours of the historic church and grounds are available year-round by special appointment. The church is also open to the public from April 15 through October 30 every Wed through Fri and Sat, 10 a.m. to 4 p.m. Call (304) 265-1589 or look online at Facebook.com, International Mothers Day Foundation.

The restored farmhouse where Anna Jarvis was born is now a museum containing 5,000 period artifacts, ranging from Anna Jarvis's clothes to Civil War relics. A Mother's Day Founder's Festival is held the second weekend in May. To visit the *Anna Jarvis Birthplace Museum,* go 4 miles south of Grafton on US 119/250. It is open for tours Apr through Dec, Tues through Sat, 9 a.m. to 2 p.m. Admission is $5, children under 6 free. Call (304) 265-5549 or visit annajarvismuseum.com for more details.

There's another important shrine in Grafton, albeit of a different sort. The Grafton National Cemetery is the final resting place for 1,251 Union soldiers, more than 600 of them unknown, who fell victim to the violent clashes that broke out near Grafton The city was a strategic railroad center connecting the interior of West Virginia with Union supply and industrial plants in Parkersburg and Wheeling. A marble obelisk marks the final resting spot of Thornsberry Bailey Brown, the first Union casualty of the Civil War. The beautiful, maple-draped cemetery, dedicated in 1867, is open to the public year-round from dawn to dusk.

If you can grab some fishing line, a bobber, and some fresh night crawlers, head over to the trout pond at Fellowsville's *Cool Springs Park,* also located on US 50, just at the base of rugged Laurel Mountain. Or you might just go in the store and buy a bag of fish food. At the park you'll find a display of antique farm implements, including fascinating old tractors, a water wheel, and threshing machines—reminders of the county's agricultural roots. It's visited by steam train aficionados for its Crab Orchard Coal Company steam engine, complete with cowcatcher. This rusty garden of beautiful old machines policed only by a burro and some ducks is a collector's delight. The park's restaurant serves up a tasty hamburger, and after your meal you can browse through the adjoining gift shop, which is full of local arts and crafts. For information call (304) 454-9511.

Two Belgian immigrants who wanted to pay tribute to World War II veterans helped to create the *Greatest Generation Society Museum* in the old Rowlesburg high school building. The magnificent exhibit, located about 3 miles north of US 50, contains a collection of World War II artifacts and mannequins in authentic German, Belgian, Russian, and US military uniforms, complete with weapons. The scenes, ambience, and lighting are as good as any government military museum. The museum is open Sat and Sun afternoon and is free to veterans and $5 for others. For more information, call Shirley at (304) 329-1240 or Katie at (304) 454-9232 or see rowlesburg.org.

Continue east on US 50 for about another 9 miles to majestic *Cathedral State Park,* a rare Eastern forest of virgin hemlocks up to 12 stories high and 20 feet in circumference—some 400 years old. The 132-acre preserve has been designated a Natural Historical Landmark.

The trees, incidentally, were spared during the timber boom because they were on private property, a mountain resort. Later the land was donated to the state. Although many sentinel trees were felled in the 2012 derecho windstorm, enough survived to preserve the cool, moist atmosphere. Among the park's maze of well-manicured trails, you'll come across imposing stands of yellow

mountaineer countrytrivia

Mountaineer Country is the most ethnically diverse area of the state, with significant populations of residents of Italian, Polish, German, Czech, and Hungarian descent.

birch, red oak, black cherry, maple, chestnut, and beech. As you might imagine, the scene here during the mid-October foliage season is unforgettable. But visit soon. The awe-inspiring trees may not always be here. The hemlocks in this forest are under death threat from the woolly adelgid, a tiny insect that sucks the life from hemlock needles.

Cathedral State Park is about a mile east of the town of Aurora. It's open year-round from 6 a.m. to 10 p.m. Guided park-ranger tours are available by appointment, from spring through fall. Call ahead for hours and special programs at (304) 735-3771.

After a hike through Cathedral, you might come away feeling a bit spiritual. Hold on to that sensation, because just down the road in Silver Lake is *Our Lady of the Pines,* supposedly the smallest church in the 48 states and one of the smallest Roman Catholic churches in the world. The 24-foot-by-12-foot stone structure, with 6 West Virginia–made stained-glass windows, a tiny altar, and 6 pews, can seat at best a dozen worshippers. It was built in 1957 by a local family and today is visited by thousands each year who come to pray, walk the beautiful grounds, and send postcards from the adjacent post office, also one of the smallest anywhere.

Our Lady of the Pines is open daily during daylight hours from spring through fall. The church is tucked away in a pine thicket a block off US 219 across from Silver Lake. There is no admission charge—though donations are welcome—and there is no phone. A tiny post office stands right in back of the chapel, about the size of a single-car garage.

Every great river starts with a trickle from a spring. The Potomac River is no exception. About 6 miles south is the source spring of the mighty Potomac, a river that serves as a border between West Virginia and Maryland for more than 100 miles. Marking the spot of the spring is *Fairfax Stone,* a boundary point established by the wealthy British colonist Thomas Lord Fairfax. The spring marked the northwestern border of Fairfax's land holdings, a vast real estate empire that included what is now almost half of Virginia and most of the West Virginia Eastern Panhandle. You can visit this spot and pay homage to Fairfax and the river that went on to define so much of the history of these states. It's located on a gravel road off US 219 (look for the sign on 219) in a remote stretch of country that must have looked much the same as when Fairfax himself was surveying the area. The Fairfax Stone State Monument is open year-round dawn to dusk. However, do not try to negotiate this road in heavy snowfall. The marker is actually a couple of miles down the gravel road, and if you get stuck there's not a whole lot of traffic coming in or out of this way-off-the-beaten-path site.

More outdoor adventures await farther northwest at Terra Alta. The serpentine drive on CR 53 qualifies as an escapade on its own. At Terra Alta, you can pause at **Alpine Lake Resort** (alpinelake.com), a former hunting preserve now operating as a 2,300-acre community with its own lake, beaches, indoor swimming pool, tubing run, 18-hole golf course, and Nordic ski trails. For reservations at the 35-room motel or restaurant, call (304) 789-2481.

About 10 miles north in **Cranesville Swamp,** you enter a "frost pocket," set aside by The Nature Conservancy as a living artifact from earlier, colder times. Described as Canada in the South, this high, bowl-shaped preserve is the southernmost tamarack (a deciduous pine) forest, a spot where you also see red spruce, insectivorous sundew plants, and cranberries. Birders tramp these boardwalk paths to sight golden-crowned kinglets, saw-whet owls, alder flycatchers, and other rare birds. The swamp has been designated a National Natural Landmark, and its trails are open year-round at no charge.

Isolation and poverty have long been associated with the largely impenetrable hills and hollows of West Virginia. As such, the state has seen its share of social engineering experiments, including the nation's first federal New Deal homestead, **Arthurdale.** This western Preston County community on Route 92 about 25 miles southwest of Cranesville was the pet project of then first lady Eleanor Roosevelt. The federal homesteading plan she helped craft served two purposes: to provide affordable, quality housing and to help boost the Depression-era economy of America's rural areas. Arthurdale became the prototype community, with more than 165 houses built here during 1933.

All but one of the original homes are intact in this tidy community of wide green lots and little white houses. A number of the original homesteading families, many from impoverished mining camps, remain at Arthurdale and help to organize reunions, dinners, and old-time dances. The original Great Hall and some of the stone shops where cooperative craft and manufacturing ventures were housed can be visited. Containers for "Arthur Dale Meat Products," the sausage the homesteaders packaged and sold, sit on the shelves. Arthurdale's

West Virginia: Birthplace of Mother's Day, Father's Day, and Grandparents Day

Call them sentimental if you want, but give West Virginians credit for starting all three family holidays: Mother's Day, Father's Day, and Grandparents Day. Whether it's the importance of family, the precariousness of life in mining towns, or the urge to memorialize loved ones, West Virginians were the first to make a day for it.

It all started with Mother's Day. Although Anna Marie Reeves Jarvis was memorialized by her daughter in the first known Mother's Day service in 1905, the elder Jarvis herself formed Mother's Day Friendship Clubs in Taylor County in the mid-1800s to teach sanitation to mothers. When the Civil War broke out, Jarvis and her clubs refused to take sides, nursing North and South alike. Jarvis let Union general George McClellan use her home in Webster, West Virginia, as he planned the war's first land battle. But she had one stipulation—her house was open to any wounded soldiers, blue or gray.

After the war Jarvis organized a family picnic honoring mothers, called Mother's Friendship Day, to reunite warring sides of the community. While the band played "Auld Lang Syne," teary-eyed neighbors shook hands and hugged.

After Jarvis's death, her daughter Anna Jarvis organized a memorial service for all mothers. Services for the first Mother's Day, May 10, 1908, were held at Andrews Methodist Episcopal Church in Grafton, now the Mother's Day Shrine. But the younger Jarvis's work didn't end there. She persuaded West Virginia governor William Glasscock to proclaim a statewide Mother's Day in 1910 and then started working on US president Woodrow Wilson. The holiday is now celebrated in at least 50 countries.

The historical Mother's Day church, built in downtown Grafton in 1873, is open for tours. An annual Mother's Day service still recognizes all mothers. The Anna Jarvis Birthplace Museum in Webster hosts a two-day festival on Mother's Day weekend.

small museum also shows off some of the homesteaders' lesser known skills. They not only learned to weave their own linens and make pottery, but they also created target kites bearing images of enemy aircraft for the US Army to practice shooting.

Eleanor Roosevelt took a special interest in Arthurdale, regularly visiting to hand out Christmas presents and high school diplomas, and even calling on families. Although the first lady would bring in her wealthy friends to buy quilts and furniture, Arthurdale was not a business success. But many children had healthier, more enriched lives in the experimental agricultural settlement. While the Arthurdale Cemetery is the only cooperative still functioning, Arthurdale

The Birth of Father's Day

Just two months after the first official Mother's Day was celebrated on July 5, 1908, the first Father's Day observance was held 20 miles away at Williams Memorial Methodist Episcopal Church in Fairmont.

The preceding December a mine explosion in nearby Monongah had killed 362 men, leaving 250 widows and more than 1,000 children grieving. Grace Fletcher Clayton, a minister's daughter still missing her own father, persuaded her pastor to perform a special Mass to honor and remember fathers. Although it didn't become an annual event until 1972, the hundreds who attended long remembered the service.

Clayton didn't follow through to get West Virginia to proclaim an annual Father's Day, so credit for the national observance goes to a Washington woman who petitioned her state for the holiday in 1910. But the fact remains that Rev. Robert Webb's service in 1908 was the first Father's Day, and signs at Fairmont's entrances proclaim this.

Although the original Father's Day church building demolished, the congregation, now called Central United Methodist, still celebrates Father's Day with special services on the third Sunday each June. The site on Third Street and Fairmont Avenue is marked with a West Virginia historical marker.

Grandparents Day Started by Mother of 15 Children

A younger holiday, Grandparents Day, came about through the efforts of Marian McQuade, but you'll find no shrine in her hometown of Oak Hill, only a sign on US 19 commemorating her efforts. This mother of 15 lobbied for five years until West Virginia governor Arch Moore proclaimed May 27, 1973, as the first official Grandparents Day.

McQuade, who had started the "Past 80 Party" in Richwood for all West Virginia octogenarians, was saddened by the chronic loneliness of many nursing home residents. She hoped a national holiday would bring attention to their plight. Buoyed by her success, McQuade worked through US Senators Robert Byrd and Jennings Randolph to create a national observance. In 1978 President Jimmy Carter designated the first Sunday after Labor Day as National Grandparents Day when the proposal received unanimous approval in Congress. McQuade died in 2008, shortly after the 30th Grandparents Day.

Heritage is very much alive in its programs, tours, and July New Deal Festival. Now a National Historic District, Arthurdale's homes, Esso station, New Deal Homestead Museum, and craft shop make an interesting tour. On summer weekends interpreters introduce visitors to the farm animals and life in the settlement houses. Arthurdale Heritage is open Mon through Sat year-round from 10 a.m. to 3 p.m. Admission is $11 for adults, $10 for senior citizens, and $7 for children 8 to 17. You can visit their website at arthurdaleheritage.org or contact them at (304) 864-3959.

Lions and tigers and bears, oh my—there's a lot more than history luring folks east of Morgantown. Big cats, bears, and about 30 other species of wild critters live in woodsy **Hovatter's Zoo** near Kingwood. What's more, you can personally feed most of them.

"We're more hands on than most zoos," said Bryan Hovatter, a former animal trainer who runs the zoo with his children.

Many of the animals will eat out of your hand or wait patiently at the end of a chute for the popcorn, granola bar chunks, or other morsels sent down from visitors. All the food is provided by the zoo and appropriate for the animals' diets, in compliance with federal and state regulations.

"The zoo started as a hobby," Hovatter said. "We were breeding and raising animals for movie production companies, and we ended up with so many that we decided to open up to the public."

Some animals have been rescued or retired from show business. A giraffe at the zoo was once a star in *Evan Almighty*, a 2007 retelling of the Noah's ark story. Other critters at Hovatter's include baboons, grizzly and Himalayan bears, chimpanzees, lemurs, wild boars, leopards, camels, monkeys, Bengal tigers, snakes, bobcats, and much more.

The zoo is open from mid-April to October, when cold weather drives the animals into heated barns. Tickets are $13 for people over 13, $11 for 3- to 12-year-olds, and free admission for children under 3. For more information, call (304) 329-3122 or visit westvirginiazoo.com.

Virtually splitting Preston County into two equal halves is the **Cheat River**, which comes out of the mountains of the Potomac Highlands and flows north through the state before emptying into Cheat Lake and ultimately the Monongahela River north of Morgantown.

The Cheat, with its boulder-strewn shoreline and glaciated gorges, is easily the premier whitewater river in northern West Virginia and perhaps third in the state, behind only the Gauley and New Rivers. Consequently the area has attracted several professional river outfitters. For rafting trips on the Cheat, as well as the Potomac, Shenandoah, and other fabled rivers of this region, hook up with either **Wilderness Voyageurs** (800-272-4141; wilderness-voyageurs .com) or **Cheat River Outfitters** (cheatriveroutfitters.com; 304-329-2024) in Albright. Both outfitters offer a range of trips, including overnight, weekend, and extended camping trips. Late-spring trips tend to be the most exciting (because of the high water levels) and are often the most crowded.

If you're content to look at the Cheat, the consensus is that the best view to be had is from the **Cheat Mountain Overlook** at **Coopers Rock State Forest.** Morgantonians, who do get around, claim the 1,200-foot overlook is the most beautiful overlook in the entire state. During the Depression the Civilian Conservation Corps built numerous structures in the forest of the durable old American chestnuts. Eleven of these rustic structures, including the picnic shelters near the overlook, have been included on the National Register of Historic Places. Coopers Rock is 13 miles east of Morgantown on I-68. It gets its name from a professional cooper who hid from the law near the overlook and continued to sell barrels to townspeople. Coopers Rock's 12,000 acres is a good place to hide out, and that may have been the plan when the Jenkins family decided to build the secluded **Mountain Creek Cabins**, where folks escape into the wild, but with hot tubs, air-conditioning, gas-log fireplaces, and pizza delivery. To get info about the deluxe cabins, call (304) 379-7548 or look online at mountaincreekcabins.com.

When the hunger pangs hit, head west to Fairmont, the seat of Marion County, and get ready for an epicurean masterpiece. **Muriale's**, 1742 Fairmont Ave., on the south side of town, could be the best Italian restaurant in the state. The local landmark is famous for its huge portions of wonderful lasagna, ravioli, rigatoni, spaghetti, and cavatelli. Included in the *Who's Who in America's Restaurants,* Muriale's is testament to northern West Virginia's rich Italian heritage. With 6 separate dining rooms, it's a family-friendly kind of place that attracts regular diners from as far away as Pennsylvania and Maryland. Although the star attraction is the pasta, made fresh on the premises, Muriale's also serves hearty steaks, hoagies, pizza, and a wide variety of seafood. It's open daily year-round (except Christmas) from 11 a.m. to 9 p.m. Call (304) 363-3190 or visit murialesrestaurant.com.

One of northern West Virginia's unique treats is the pepperoni roll, invented by Giuseppe Agiro in 1927 as a one-hand lunch for coal miners. His **Country Club Bakery** on Country Club Road in Fairmont still makes those 6-inch buns baked around two sticks of pepperoni. They're best hot out of the oven. The Country Club is open daily, except Wednesday and Sunday. Of course, you can now find pepperoni rolls at Morgantown, Clarksburg, Weston, and out-of-the-way delis in between.

If you've already paid homage to mothers by visiting the International Mother's Day Shrine in Grafton, now you've got your chance to salute fathers. Following Grafton's lead, Fairmont's Central United Methodist Church, 301 Fairmont Ave., was the site of the first observance of Father's Day on July 5, 1908. The so-called **Father's Day Church** is available for tours by calling (304) 366-3351.

While you're in Fairmont, drop over to the **Marion County Museum** on Adams Street beside the courthouse. The former sheriff's home contains three stories of rooms, each room furnished with the artifacts representing a different era in US history. History seen through West Virginia eyes, that is. The emphasis here is on West Virginia's history and its contribution to our nation. The young at heart will love the collection of antique toys and kiddie-scale furniture in the Children's Room. It's open Mon through Sat, 10 a.m. to 2 p.m. in the summer and weekdays only (the same hours) Sept through May. For special arrangements call (304) 367-5398.

Not too far away, at 214 Monroe St., you can show the younger generation that long ago telephones had cords. The *Telephone Museum* contains a variety of switchboards, pay phones, phone booths (when have you seen one of those?), and displays of the various cables, test boards, and wires that linked telephone communication in the good old days. The museum is open Thursday morning and by appointment by calling (304) 363-2393.

Coal Country Miniature Golf is another great place for children—or adults who enjoy the quirky. While putting around mining drills, ventilation fans, and ceiling supports, you learn about the coal industry. But watch out for Big John the miner with the pick. The 30-foot metal statue is constantly rotating, and on the seventh hole you'll need to putt between his feet as they go around. The course is located a mile off I-79, Fairmont exit 137, just off Hopewell Road. It can be reached at (304) 366-9300 or through coalcountrywv .com.

Just north of Fairmont, a rustic log fort perches on a slope above the confluence of Prickett's Creek and the Monongahela River. A re-creation of the original 1774 Prickett's Fort, this building serves up living history of the late 18th century in *Prickett's Fort State Park.* Costumed interpreters demonstrate colonial crafts such as spinning, blacksmithing, weaving, and gunsmithing. The fort sheltered colonists in 16 tiny cabins within its stockade walls. When American Indian attack threatened, up to 80 families would rush into the fort and stay for days or weeks. During its summer season the park also offers concerts, bird walks, craft demonstrations, historical impersonators, and a three-day camp, which allows older children to learn spinning, dyeing, blacksmithing, and natural history. The park is open daily late Apr through the end of Oct, 10 a.m. to 5 p.m. After Labor Day, the park is closed Mondays and Tuesdays. Admission is charged for the historical attractions, but the trails and picnic area are free. Call (800) CALL-WVA or (304) 363-3030 or see www .prickettsfort.org for more information.

Immediately west of Fairmont is the small community of Monongah, a coal-mining town that was the scene of a devastating mine explosion that killed 362 men on December 6, 1907. Congress reacted by toughening mining laws, but in 1968 another explosion less than a mile from Monongah killed 78 men. The victims of these tragedies—and others like them that too often plagued the Mountain State—are remembered at the *West Virginia Miner's Memorial,* a moving, bronze sculpture located in Mary Lou Retton Park, named in honor of the famous Olympic gold medal winner and Marion County native. The park,

Touchdown Mountaineers!

In the Empire State, it's the Big Apple. In California, it's the City of Angels. Illinois boasts the Windy City. Go down the list and you'll see that every state has its version of the Big City. Yes, some West Virginians will even say they have one in Charleston, or perhaps Huntington. But in reality, the biggest city in West Virginia isn't a city at all. It's a football stadium filled to capacity on a gorgeous autumn afternoon. Of course, we're talking about the 61,000-seat Mountaineer Field on the campus of West Virginia University in Morgantown, a sporting shrine of sorts that holds at least 10,000 more people than the entire population of Charleston, the state's largest city. While the Mountaineers may not win every time they take the field, it's always a celebration in Morgantown on a football Saturday. If you plan to go, be wise and take a pair of earplugs . . . or two pairs. Decibel levels after a Mountaineer touchdown have been known to eclipse the noise level of a jet takeoff.

just off US 19, is open daily from dawn to dusk. In Monongah, there's another monument to the miners as well as a stone mother and child, the **Monongah Heroine Statue,** honoring the wives and mothers of the victims of the Monongah Coal Mine Disaster.

The gently rolling countryside west of Fairmont is dotted with beautiful dairy farms and pastureland. Agriculture is still an important part of the economy, and here you can trace its colorful roots by visiting the **Hamilton Round Barn** in Mannington, 10 miles west of Fairmont on US 250. The striking round, wooden barn, commonly known as the Mannington Round Barn, was built as a dairy barn in 1912 by Amos Hamilton. Its unusual architecture was commonplace on dairy farms in Pennsylvania, West Virginia, and Virginia during the late 1800s and early 1900s. This particular barn is the only such restored structure in the state and one of the few remaining south of the Mason-Dixon Line.

Most round barns, including this one, were built into the side of a small hill, enabling the farmer to drive a hay wagon directly into the loft from the rear. Farmer Hamilton's round barn not only sheltered cows and feed, but also was the main residence for the family. Your tour will undoubtedly start in the kitchen and wend around the three stories of living space, which is now full of family heirlooms and farm artifacts—milk coolers, lard presses, butter churns, a children's sleigh, a carriage, and a horse-drawn potato picker. There are even some early West Virginia coal-mining tools on display, as well as musical instruments from an earlier time.

The round barn is open on Fri morning and Sun afternoon, May through Sept. Special tours also can be arranged any time of the year for small groups. In addition, the barn hosts a quilting exhibition every Thursday from 9 a.m. to

1 p.m., and visitors are encouraged to join the circle. A small admission price of $3 per person is charged. Nearby, the **West Augusta Historical Society Museum** contains three floors of Civil War era Americana, from brass ox-horn covers to music boxes. The town's first gas station also has been moved to the grounds. For more information contact the historical society at (304) 986-7053 or westaugustahistorical@gmail.com.

Morgantown

From Mannington, head east back into Fairmont and pick up US 19 north to Morgantown. One of the most stimulating communities in the Mountain State, Morgantown is a harmonic blend of blue bloods, blue collars, bohemians, and college students. It stands as its own subregion in this book because it's really unlike any other community in West Virginia. It is to the Mountain State what Austin is to Texas, Boulder is to Colorado, Madison is to Wisconsin. It's an industrial town with long ties to the nearby northern coalfields and famed glass factories, but it's also a high-tech town anchored by research laboratories maintained by the federal government. **West Virginia University** (WVU; wvu .edu), with some 30,000 students spread across three separate campuses, keeps what would probably be a sleepy town lively year-round.

The university also provides a cultural backdrop that is probably unrivaled among West Virginia cities. The WVU **Creative Arts Center** schedules more than 500 music, theater, and performance art shows a year as well as a host of visual art exhibits. Tours and performance schedules can be had by calling (304) 293-4841 or visiting wvu.edu/creative_arts_center. The center is located about a mile north of downtown off Beechurst Avenue on the Evansdale campus of the university.

Another interesting campus site is the **Core Arboretum** (arboretum .wvu .edu), run by the WVU biology department, featuring 3 miles of trails that wend through a forest of virtually every type of hardwood and pine tree native to West Virginia. Along the way you'll also see an amazing variety of wildflowers, shrubs, and decorative plants common to the state. It's located opposite the arts center on Beechurst. For special tours and bloom and foliage information, you can call the biology department at (304) 293-5201.

Probably the best place to begin your familiarization with the WVU campus is, strangely enough, in downtown Morgantown. Now at One Waterfront Plaza in the Wharf District, the **WVU Visitors Resource Center** (visit.wvu .edu) operates out of the first floor of a multistory building next to the Waterfront Place Hotel. In a few minutes of maneuvering through the high-tech, interactive displays, you'll hear the marching band, learn the layout, and find out more about West Virginia's largest university than if you read five bro-chures. The exhibit follows the course of the university's PRT (Personal Rapid Transit), so the next thing you may want to do is hop into one of the little blue and yellow cars waiting a few blocks away. Or you may opt for a guided bus tour. You may also access the campus map at beta.campusmap.wvu.edu for your electronic guided tour. If you start here you'll learn about WVU's public offerings: the library, Mountainlair student center, Cook-Hayman Pharmacy Museum, WVU Creative Arts Center, and the WVU Student Recreation Center with its climbing wall.

While you're still down by the Monongahela River, you may want to stroll through a few shops, perhaps check out what's happening at the *Hazel Ruby McQuain Park Amphitheatre,* where the summer movies are screened and symphonies are regularly performed. You can also stop by the *Two Water-front Place Hotel* for a single malt scotch. Or you can rent a bicycle at Wams-ley Cycles and shoot out of town for miles on the Caperton, Decker Creek, or Mon River trails.

Despite its skyscraping buildings and energetic downtown, Morgantown has an outdoorsy feel. Hiking boots and parkas appear on the streets more often as suits. The 330-mile *Allegheny Trail* begins at nearby Bruceton Mills and wends its way south to meet the Appalachian Trail at Peters Mountain on the Virginia–West Virginia border. Kayaking, canoeing, and rafting are popular activities on the Cheat, and it's possible to go caving in local wild caves. If you're in town in mid-April, you can catch the annual *Banff Mountain Film Festival,* screened in only a few Southern cities during its world tour.

Scratch around in Morgantown's past and you'll find glassmaking at its core. Although most local glassmaking operations have ceased, you can stroll through the Seneca Center complex of retail shops created in a renovated glass factory on Beechurst Avenue. Constructed in 1898, the center boasts authentic glass manufacturing tools and murals of the glassmaking process. Look for the tower-ing 100-foot glass furnace chimney and red water tower; they're Morgantown landmarks. You may even find some Seneca glass for sale in the antiques shops.

If it's music, indie films, and nightlife you're looking for, the club *123 Pleasant Street* has everything from rock to jazz to rockabilly. Check out their schedule on the website 123pleasantstreet.com. The *Blue Moose Cafe,* at 248 Walnut St., draws connoisseurs of good and sustainably grown coffee and excellent acoustic music. It serves up live music several times a week, hosting local, regional, and national musicians of all genres. You may also walk in on fiction readings, poetry slams, or art receptions at this culturally conscious cybercafe. To check Blue Moose's schedule, call (304) 292-8999 or log on to thebluemoosecafe.com. Black Bear Burritos is also a rocking local hangout, with music several nights a week. It's as known for entertainment as it is for their bigger-than-your-head burrito, quesadilla, and wrap creations. You can mix and match sauces and fillings to create your own Mexican monstrosity with unexpected ingredients like kiwi salsa, garlic potatoes, bleu cheese, Thai peanut curry, and dill sauce.

When you're downtown during the day, hop into a local gallery, pub, or shop. The **Appalachian Gallery** (270 Walnut St.; 304-291-5299; wvcraft.com) is known for its rotating exhibits of works by regional artists, including fine-art glass and books.

At the Old Post Office, 107 High St., you can browse through the **Monongalia Arts Center.** Inside the neoclassical-style building, with its pronounced Doric engaged columns, is Benedum Gallery, housing touring exhibits from around the country. The adjoining Tanner Theater regularly stages plays and community events. The complex is open weekdays 9 a.m. to 4 p.m. and on weekends for special engagements. For more information, call (304) 292-3325.

Lightly populated West Virginia probably isn't the first place to come to mind when thinking of rapid-transit systems, but one of the best in the world can be found in Morgantown. It's the **Personal Rapid Transit,** or PRT, an electrically powered system that transports WVU students to classes across nearly 9 miles in the three-campus university. (If you've ever ridden the People Mover at Disneyland, this is much the same concept.) The computer-automated cars, resembling small subway vehicles, whisk as many as 20 standing students per car at a time at a comfortable 30 miles per hour. Much of the track runs on elevated bridges above town. Nearly 16,000 students ride the 70-plus cars every day; the longest trips last just over 12 minutes. The PRT stops on Walnut Street, on Beechurst Avenue, and near the university's student housing complex, engineering department, and medical center. Studied by city planners, environmentalists, and transit officials worldwide, the WVU system has transported more than 83 million passengers since 1975 without a single injury or a single hydrocarbon released into the air. Students ride the system for free, but visitors are also encouraged to hop aboard. Adults pay a $1 round-trip fee, a minimal charge considering this is one of the most interesting and relaxing ways to tour Morgantown and the university. The PRT is open Mon through Fri 6:30 a.m. to 10 p.m. and Sat 9:30 a.m. to 5 p.m. It's closed Sunday and during university breaks. For more information call (304) 293-5011.

October, as mentioned throughout this book, is a wonderful time to tour West Virginia. In Morgantown it's especially enticing given that this is when the annual **Mountaineer Balloon Festival** lifts off. The color in the sky nearly matches the blazing foliage as dozens of hot-air balloons ascend and exceed the height of the surrounding mountains. Hart Field, aka Morgantown

Municipal Airport, is the site of this festival, which also features an array of balloon races, carnival rides, music attractions, food booths, crafts, and games for the kids. The fete is usually held in the middle of the month, a time when the leaves in the surrounding countryside have reached their peak. In a state that's brimming with festivals, this may be one of the best. For exact dates see Balloons Over Morgantown at Facebook.com.

Spectacular as it is, you don't have to settle on just watching the hot-air balloons from the ground. After a busy day in Morgantown, you need a place to rest those weary bones. The regal ***Hotel Morgan*** is located in the heart of downtown in an eight-story brick building. It is the place for those who like to ditch the car and walk around town, sample the Wharf District, or use the Personal Rapid Transit system. The hotel will happily store bikes overnight. The lobby is still a grand entryway of oak panels, oak pillars, crystal chandeliers, and 24-foot ceilings, but the 80 rooms have been redesigned for today's traveler. Each mini-suite has an oversize desk where real work can be accomplished; rooms include Wi-Fi, flat-screen television, refrigerators, microwaves, room service, and king-size beds. In the morning, you can grab a fresh pastry or make your own waffle in the breakfast lounge before heading out to explore M-town.

Places to Stay in Mountaineer Country

BRUCETON MILLS

Mountain Creek Cabins
(866) 379-7548
mountaincreekcabins.com
Expensive

GRAFTON

Tygart Lake State Park
1240 Paul Malone Rd.
(304) 265-6144
wvstateparks.com/park/
tygart-lake-state-park
Moderate to expensive

KINGWOOD

Preston County Inn
112 W. Main St.
(800) 252-3271 or
(304) 329-2220
prestoncountyinn.com
Inexpensive

MANNINGTON

Curtisville Lake Campground
Curtisville Pike
(304) 363-7037
Mcpark.com/curtisville-lake
Inexpensive

Rhododendron House B&B
306 Mead Ave.
(304) 216-2622
Moderate

MORGANTOWN

The Cranberry
2700 Cranberry Sq.
(304) 403-6300
Cranberrywv.com
Moderate to expensive

Lakeview Golf Resort & Spa
1 Lakeview Dr.
(304) 594-1111
lakeviewresort.com
Inexpensive

Wyndham Hotel Morgan
127 High St.
(304) 292-8200
hotelmorgan.com
Moderate

TERRA ALTA

Alpine Lake Resort
700 W. Alpine Lake Dr.
(304) 789-2481
alpinelake.com
Moderate

Places to Eat in Mountaineer Country

CLARKSBURG

Hart Kitchen Eatery
123 South 4th St
(304) 969-0049
hartkitchen.com
Moderate to expensive

Minard's Spaghetti Inn
813 E. Pike St.
(304) 623-1711
Moderate

FAIRMONT

Poky Dot
1111 Fairmont Ave.
(304) 366-3271
The-poky-dot @Facebook
.com
Moderate

Say-Boys Restaurant
1228 Country Club Rd.
(304) 366-7252
https://sayboys
restaurant.com
Moderate

MORGANTOWN

**Mountain State
Brewing Co**
54 Clay St.
(304) 241-1976
Moderate

**The Restaurants of
Historic Downtown
Morgantown**
(30 restaurants within
1-mile radius), I-68, exit 1
University Ave.
(304) 292-0168
downtownmorgantown
.com/dining

TERRA ALTA

Alpine Lake Resort
Route 7
(304) 789-2481 or
alpinelake.com
Moderate to expensive

Index

A

ACE Adventure
Resort, 111
Actors' Equity theater, 13
Adaland Mansion, 193
Adventures on the
Gorge, 111
African Zion Baptist
Church, 139
Alderson, 102
Alderson's Store, 102
Alexander Campbell
Mansion, 182
Allegheny Trail, 35, 205
Almost Heaven
Desserts, 192
Alpine Lake Resort,
197, 208
American Conservation
Film Festival, 13
American Heritage Music
Hall, 94
Angler's Inn, 25
Anna Jarvis Birthplace
Museum, 195
Annual Dulcimer
Festival, 191
Ansted, 114
Antique Cabins and
Barns, 93
Anvil Restaurant, The, 26
Appalachian Gallery, 206
Appalachian Glass &
Gifts, 73
Appalachian Makers
Market, 90
Appalachian String
Band, 90
Appalachian Trail
Conservancy (ATC), 4
Apple Butter Festival, 3
Arnoldsburg, 170
Arnott House B&B, 170

Arthurdale, 197
Artworks, 192
Audra State Park, 65, 193
Augusta Festival, 29, 45
Augusta Heritage
Center, 45
Autumn Harvest and
Roadkill Cook-off, 29
Avalon Fest, 24
Avalon nudist camp, 24
Avampato Discovery
Museum, 134, 138

B

Bahnhof WVrsthaus, 153
Bailey, "Mad Anne"
Trotter, 142
Baker's Island Recreation
Area, 84
Banff Mountain Film
Festival, 205
Barbour County
Historical Society
Museum, 193
Barboursville, 145
Barn with Inn, 184
Barracks Escape
Room, 94
Battle of Bulltown, 70
Bavarian Inn, 12
Bavarian Inn and Lodge,
25, 26
Bear Wood
Company, 143
Beckley, 116
Beckley Exhibition Coal
Mine, 97, 116
Beech Fork State
Park, 145
Beekeeper Inn, The, 46
Bell Boyd House, 5
Belle Boyd House, 16

Berkeley Springs
Convention & Visitors
Bureau, 25
Berkeley Springs State
Park, 5, 19
Berndine's Five and
Dime, 167
berry picking, 39
Best of Crete, 138
Bethany College, 182
Beury, 112
Beverly Heritage Center,
32, 46
Bhavana Society, 34
Bicentennial Inn, 86
Big Belly Deli, 58
Big Bend
Campground, 38
Big Four Drug Store &
Gift Shop, 106
Big John's Family
Fixin's, 58
Billy Motel, The, 58
Bituminous Coal
Heritage Museum, 133
BlackCat Music Shop &
Studio, 22
Blackwater Falls State
Park, 58
Blaker Mill, 82
Blenko Glass, 134, 140
Blenko Glass
Factory, 144
Blennerhassett Hotel,
160, 170
Blennerhassett Island
State Park, 158
Blennerhassett
Museum, 159
Blueberry Hill, 118
Bluefield, 120
Bluefield Arts
Center, 120

Bluefield Inn, 126
Blue Moon Cafe, 11
Blue Moose Cafe, 205
Bluestone Lake State
    Park, 107
Bonnie Dwaine Bed &
    Breakfast, 184
Booker T. Washington's
    cabin, 138
Bramwell, 122
Brass Pineapple Bed and
    Breakfast, 152
Braxton County
    Convention & Visitors
    Bureau, 68
Brazen Head Inn, 58
Brick House Antiques, 92
Bridge Day, 109
Bridgeport, 192
Bridgeport Clarksburg
    Convention and
    Visitors Bureau, 208
Bridge Road Bistro, 153
Bright Morning Inn, 45
Brooke Pioneer
    Trail, 179
Buckhannon, 77
Buckhannon/Upshur
    County Convention
    and Visitors
    Bureau, 86
Buffalo Trail Cabins, 122
Bulltown
    Campgrounds, 70
Bulltown Historic
    Area, 70
Bunker Hill Antiques
    Associates, 17
Burning Springs, 168
Burnsville Lake, 69
Burnsville Wildlife
    Management Area, 70
Burr, Aaron, 158

C
Cabela's, 180

Cabell-Huntington
    Convention and
    Visitors Bureau, 153
Cabwaylingo State Forest
    Cabins, 152
Cacapon Resort State
    Park, 25
Cacapon State Park, 22
California Park, 167
Camden, 150
Campbell-Flannagan-
    Murrell House
    Museum, 105
Camp Caesar, 83
Canaan Mountain Bike
    Festival, 29
Canaan Valley, 42
Canaan Valley Resort
    State Park, 32, 42
Canaan Valley Resort
    State Park and
    Conference Center, 58
Canal House Cafe, 26
Candlewyck Inn, 32
Cantrell Ultimate
    Rafting, 106
Canyon Rim Visitor
    Center, 109, 110
Capitol Complex, 133
Capitol Music Hall, 179
Capitol Theatre, 179
Capon Springs and
    Farm, 30
Carnegie Hall
    building, 93
Carnifex Ferry Battlefield
    State Park, 64
Carriage Inn Bed and
    Breakfast, 25
Cass Scenic Railroad, 54
Cass Scenic Railroad
    State Park, 51
Castaway Caboose, 49
Castle Halloween
    Museum, 182
Cathedral Café, 127

Cathedral State Park,
    188, 195
Cedar Lakes Craft Center,
    157, 158
Celtic Celebration, 174
Chamber Music
    Society, 138
Chapel of Perpetual
    Adoration, 190
Charleston, 133
Charleston Ballet, 138
Charleston Convention
    and Visitors
    Bureau, 153
Charleston Light Opera
    Guild, 137
Charleston Marriott Town
    Center, 152
Charleston Symphony
    Orchestra, 138
Charles Town, 7
Charles Town Post
    Office, 7
Charles Town Race
    Track, 5
Cheat Mountain Club, 48
Cheat Mountain
    Overlook, 200
Cheat River, 200
Cheat River Festival, 190
Cheat River
    Outfitters, 200
Cheat River Whitewater
    Rafting, 188
Cheese 'N More
    Store, 100
Chief Logan Lodge, 153
Chinn's Family
    Restaurant, 153
Chloe, 170
Christ Church, 17
Christmas in
    Shepherdstown, 3
Christmas Town, 71
Chuck Mathena Center
    for the Performing
    Arts, 118

CJ Maggie's American
Grill, 87
Claremont, 112
Clarion Hotel
Morgan, 207
Clarion Hotel
Morgantown, 208
Clay Center for the Arts
& Sciences, 138
Claymont Court, 10
Coal, 78
Coal Country Miniature
Golf, 202
Coleman's Fish
Market, 185
Comfort Suites,
Parkersburg, 170
Confederate
Cemetery, 94
Conference Center, 82
Contemporary American
Theater Festival, 3, 13
Contentment House
Museum, 114
Cook's Mill, 104
Cool Springs Park, 195
Cooper Gallery, 93
Cooper House, 122
Coopers Rock State
Forest, 200
Core Arboretum, 204
Country Club
Bakery, 201
Country Inn & Spa, 21
Country Peddler, 192
Country Road Cabins,
109, 126
Cowger Guest House, 58
Cranberry Glades Nature
Center, 56
Cranberry Mountain
Lodge, 56
Cranberry, The, 207
Cranesville Swamp, 197
Criel Mound, 139
Cunningham
Farmhouse, 70

Curtisville Lake
Campground, 207
Custard Stand, 85

D
David Harris Riverfront
Park, 149
Da Vinci's
Restaurant, 171
Days Inn by
Wyndham, 86
Deer Creek Valley, 50
DeFluri's Fine
Chocolates, 16
Delf Norona
Museum, 174
Delta Tau Delta
Founders' House, 182
Devil's Backbone, 54
Dirt Bean, 58
Doc's Guest House, 45
Dogwood Arts and Crafts
Festival, 130
Doherty Auditorium, 146
Dolly Sods, 38
Droop Mountain
Battlefield State
Park, 57
Drover's Inn 1848
Restaurant, 185
Durbin & Greenbrier
Valley Railroad, 49

E
Eagle's Nest
Outfitters, 36
East End Bridge, 150
East End Historic
District, 137
Eastern Regional Coal
Archives, 120
Edray Trout Hatchery, 55
Elkhorn Inn, 124
Elk River Touring Center,
32, 53
Elk River Wildlife
Management Area, 69

Ellen's Homemade Ice
Cream, 138, 153
Empty Glass, 138

F
Fairfax Coffee House,
21, 26
Fairfax Stone, 196
Falls of Hills Creek, 55
Farmers' Market, 74
Farm Up Table, 59
Fasnacht, 29
Father's Day Church, 201
Feast of the Ramson,
62, 63
Feast of the Seven Fishes
Festiva, 190
ferry boat, City of
Sistersville, 167
FestivALL, 130
Finn Thai Restaurant, 26
Flatwoods, 69
Flatwoods Monster
Museum, 68
foliage, fall, 44
Fort Ashby, 31
Fort Mill Ridge Wildlife
Management Area, 30
Fort New Salem, 190
Fort Randolph, 151
Fostoria Glass
Museum, 176
Free Spirit
Adventures, 97
French Creek, 78
French Quarter
Restaurant, 141
Friends of Greyhounds
Adoption
Services, 141
Front Porch Restaurant,
41, 59

G
Gad Dam Brewery, 67
Gad Dam Brewing, 87

Gary Bowling's House of
    Art, 120, 121
Gauley River, 64
Gauley River Fest and
    Races, 66
General Adam Stephen
    House, 14
General (horse), 152
General Lewis Inn,
    94, 126
General Lewis Inn and
    Restaurant, The, 127
George Washington
    Heritage Trail, 24
Gerrardstown, 17
Gillum House Bed &
    Breakfast, 190
Glade's Grill at Glade
    Springs Resort, 126
Glade Springs
    Resort, 117
glass country, 141
Glen Ferris Inn, 115
Glenville, 71
Golden Delicious
    Festival, 84
Graceland Inn and
    Conference Center, 58
Grafton, 194
Grafton National
    Cemetery, 195
Graham House, 103
Grande Hotel at
    Mountaineer Casino,
    Race Track and
    Gaming Resort, 184
Grandma's House
    Antiques &
    Collectibles, 106
Grand-Vue Park, 176
Grant County
    Convention & Visitors
    Bureau, 59
Grape Stomping
    Festival, 67
Grape Stomping Wine
    Festival, 62

Grave Creek Mound, 172
Gray Barker UFO
    Collection, 188
Greater Morgantown
    Convention and
    Visitors Bureau, 208
Greatest Generation
    Society Museum, 195
Green Bank
    Telescope, 50
Greenbrier Academy for
    Girls, 102
Greenbrier Bunker, 90
Greenbrier County
    Convention and
    Visitors Bureau, 125
Greenbrier Resort, 90
Greenbrier Resort,
    The, 127
Greenbrier River Trail,
    53, 96, 97
Greenbrier Valley
    Theatre, 94
Greenland Gap Nature
    Preserve, 33
Guest House at Lost
    River, 58
Guest House & Cottage
    of Richwood, 86
Guest House Inn
    on Courthouse
    Square, 126

H
Hampshire County
    Convention & Visitors
    Bureau, 59
Hanging Rock
    Observatory, 100
Harding's Family
    Restaurant, 153
Hardy County
    Convention & Visitors
    Bureau, 59
Harewood, 10
Harmony Ridge
    Gallery, 92

Harpers Ferry, 4
Harpers Ferry
    Campground &
    Cabins, 25
Harpers Ferry Ghost
    Tour, 7
Harpers Ferry National
    Historical Park, 5
Harpers Ferry Toy Train
    Museum, 6
Harper's Old Country
    Store, 40
Hart Kitchen Eatery, 208
Hatfield & McCoy
    Festival, 130
Hatfield & McCoy
    Trails, 132
Haunted
    Parkersburg, 160
Hawks Nest State
    Park, 114
Hawks Nest State Park
    Lodge, 126
Hawk's Nest State Park
    Marina, 110
Hazel Ruby
    McQuain Park
    Amphitheatre, 205
Helvetia, 46
Henderson Hall, 158, 164
Henry Stifel Schrader
    Environmental
    Center, 181
Heritage Blues Fest, 174
Heritage Farm Museum
    and Village, 147
Heritage Farm Museum
    & Village, 134
Heritage Farm
    Village, 153
Herman Dean Firearms
    Collection, 146
Hewitt House B&B, 122
High Country Gallery, 93
Highland Scenic
    Highway, 54
Highlawn Inn, 25

Hillbilly Grill, 87
Hillbrook Inn, 8
Hilton Garden Inn, 25
Hinton, 105
Hinton Railroad Days, 90
Hinton Railroad
    Museum, 105
Historic Bramwell's Tour
    of Homes, 90
Holl's Chocolates, 162
Holly River
    Restaurant, 80
Holly River State
    Park, 80
Hovatter's Zoo, 200
Huntersville Arch, 54
Huntington, 145
Huntington Museum of
    Art, 134, 145
Huntington Railroad
    Museum, 150
Hurricane, 141
Hütte Restaurant, The, 46
Hygeia Bath House, 31

I
Ice House Gallery, 21
Ice Mountain, 29
88 Restaurant &
    Lounge, 87
Independence Hall, 178
Inn at Charles Town,
    The, 25
International Mother's
    Day Shrine, 194
International Water
    Tasting Festival, 3
Ireland, 79
Irish Spring Festival,
    62, 79
Isaiah Morgan
    Distillery, 67

J
Jackson County Chamber
    of Commerce, 171

Jackson's Mill Historic
    Area, 81
Jackson's Mill Jubilee, 82
Jamboree U.S.A., 179
James Rumsey
    Monument, 12
Jefferson County
    Convention and
    Visitors Bureau, 25
Jefferson County
    Museum, 7
Jefferson Rock, 6
Jennings Randolph
    Lake, 32
Jericho Cabins and
    B&B, 58
Jerry Run Summer
    Theater, 81
John Brown Museum, 5
John Brown Wax
    Museum, 5
John Henry Park, 104
Johnson House, 70
Jonathan-Louis Bennett
    House, 72

K
Kac-Ka-Pon
    Restaurant, 59
Kaifu, 138
Kanawha Trace, 145
Keyser, 32
Kirkwood Winery, 67
Kitchen Creek
    Bakery, 100
Krodel Park, 151
Kruger Street Toy and
    Train Museum, 180

L
Lakeview Golf Resort &
    Spa, 207
Landmark Studio for the
    Arts, 67
Lascaux Micro-
    Theater, 77
La Trattoria, 26

Laury's, 138
Lazy-A Campground, 18
leaves, autumn, 44
Lewisburg, 92
Lewis County
    Convention and
    Visitors Bureau, 86
Lewis Theatre, 93
Liberty Station Lodge &
    Tavern, 123
lighthouse, 66
Little Indian, 138
Little Sister oil well, 166
L. Norman Dillon Farm
    Museum, 18
Loafer's Glory B&B and
    Camping, 58
Locust Creek Covered
    Bridge, 57
Log House Homestead
    B&B, 170
Los Agaves, 138
Lost River State Park, 32
Lost River Trading
    Post, 36
Lost World Caverns, 95
Lost World Natural
    History Museum, 96
Lot 12 Public House, 26
Lover's Lane, 84

M
Malden, 138
Maple Syrup Festival, 47
Mardi Gras Casino &
    Resort, 141, 152
Maria's Garden and
    Inn, 22
Marion County
    Convention and
    Visitors Bureau, 208
Marion County
    Museum, 201
Market on Courthouse
    Square, 106
Marshall University, 145

Martinsburg/Berkeley
County Convention
and Visitors
Bureau, 25
Matewan, 128
Matewan Depot
Museum, 131
McClure City Center
Hotel, 184
McWhorter Cabin, 82
Mercer County
Convention and
Visitors Bureau, 125
Mid-Ohio Valley Multi-
Cultural Festival, 156
Milo's Café, 58
Milton, 144
Minard's Spaghetti
Inn, 208
Mineral Springs Motel, 86
Mine Wars Museum, 131
Moncove Lake State
Park, 100
Monongahela National
Forest, 38
Monongah Heroine
Statue, 203
Monongalia Arts
Center, 206
Monroe Co. Carriage
Museum, 101
Monroe County
Historical Society
Museum, 101
Morgan Cabin, 17
Morgan's Grove Park, 11
Morris Harvey House
B&B, 126
Mothman Festival, 130
Mothman Museum, 152
Mountain Creek Cabins,
201, 207
Mountaineer Balloon
Festival, 206
Mountaineer Casino,
Racetrack & Gaming
Resort, 184

Mountaineer Hotel, 153
Mountaineer Opry
House, 145
Mountaineer Wall, 41
Mountain Heritage Arts
and Crafts Festival, 3
Mountain Laurel Country
Store, 69
Mountain Stage, 137
Mountain State Apple
Harvest Festival, 3, 14
Mountain State Arts and
Crafts Fair, 156, 157
Mountain State Brewing
Co, 208
Mountain State Forest
Festival, 29
Mountwood Park, 163
Mountwood Park
Cabins, 170
Mullins 1847
Restaurant, 58
Muriale's, 201
Museum of Radio and
Technology, 147
Museum of the Berkeley
Springs, 19
Mustard Seed
Primitives, 192
Mystery Hole, 114

N
Naked Olive Lounge,
The, 26
Nancy Hanks
Memorial, 33
National Radio
Astronomy
Observatory, 32, 49
Nature Wonder
Weekend, 156
New River, 108
New River Gateway
Convention and
Visitors Bureau, 125
New River Gorge
Bridge, 109

New River Gorge Bridge
Day, 90
New River Gorge
National River, 97
New River Jetboats, 110
New Vrindahan Festival
of Colors, 174
North Bend Rail
Trail, 166
North Bend State Park,
158, 166, 170
North Fork Mountain
Inn, 58
North House
Museum, 93
Norton House, 139
Nutting Bird Café, 181

O
Oakhurst Links, 91
Oglebayfest, 174
Oglebay Resort, 180, 184
Oglebay Resort, Ihlenfeld
Dining Room, 185
Oglebay's Stifel Fine Arts
Center, 178
Ohio River Islands
National Wildlife
Refuge, 165
O'Hurley's General
Store, 5
O'Hurley's General
Store, 12
Oil and Gas
Museum, 161
Old Bethany Meeting
House, 182
Old Fields Church, 34
Old Green Hill
Cemetery, 15
Old Matewan National
Bank Building, 131
Old Mill Bakery, 143
Old Stone Presbyterian
Church, 93
Old World Libations, 104

One Thin Dime
Museum, 120
123 Pleasant Street, 205
Organ Cave, 96, 97
Original Flavor Bistro,
67, 87
Otter and Oak, 106
Our Lady of the
Pines, 196
Outdoor Theatre
West Virginia at
Grandview, 97

P
PageVawter House, 114
Palace of Gold, 176,
177, 178
Parkersburg, 157
Parkersburg Convention
and Visitors
Bureau, 157
PattyFest Music
Festival, 190
Paw Paw, 23
Paw Paw Tunnel, 24
Pearl S. Buck
Homestead, 56
Pence Springs Flea
Market, 102
Pence Springs Hotel, 102
Pendleton Heights, 182
Perry House, 122
Personal Rapid
Transit, 206
Phantom of Silver Run
ghost story walk, 167
P&H Family
Restaurant, 171
Philippi, 191, 193
Philippi Bridge, 193
Philippi Convention &
Visitors Bureau, 208
Pickens, 47
Pinnacle Rock State
Park, 123
Pipestem Gorge, 107

Pipestem Resort State
Park, 97, 107,
126, 127
Playa Bowls, 138
Pocahontas County
Convention and
Visitors Bureau, 59
Pocahontas Trail, 123
Point Pleasant, 150
Point Pleasant Battle
Monument State
Park, 150
Point Pleasant River
Museum, 151
Poky Dot, 208
Potato Festival, 62, 64
Potomac Eagle Scenic
Railroad, 29
Preston County
Buckwheat
Festival, 190
Preston County Inn, 207
Prickett's Fort State
Park, 188
Prickett's Fort State
Park, 202
Pringle Tree, 78
Prospect Peak, 22
Public Market,
Wheeling, 185
Pullman Square, 147
Putnam County
Convention and
Visitors Bureau, 153
PW's Home Bistro, 126

R
rafting, 110, 111
ramps, 63
Ramps & Rails
Festival, 29
Randolph County
Convention and
Visitors Bureau, 59
Ravenswood, 156
Rehoboth Church, 100

Resort at Glade
Springs, 126
Restaurants of Historic
Downtown
Morgantown, 208
Rhododendron House
B&B, 207
Richwood, 62
Richwood Convention &
Visitors Bureau, 86
RiffRaff Arts
Collective, 119
Ritter Park, 149
River Riders, 6
Riverwise Labyrinth, 97
Roane County Chamber
of Commerce, 171
Robert's Antiques, 92
Robey Theatre, 169
Rock Hall Tract, 8
Roman Bath House, 19
Romney, 30
Ron Hinkle Glass, 78
Roundhouse, 15
Rumsey Steamboat
Museum, 11

S
Sago Miners'
Memorial, 78
Sahara, 138
Salem, 190
Salt Sulphur Springs, 101
Sandstone Falls, 106
Sarge's Dive Shop, 66
Saunders One Room
School House
Museum, 103
Savannah's, 153
Say-Boys Restaurant, 208
Segway, 53
Seneca Center, 205
Seneca Rocks, 39
Seneca Rocks Mountain
Guides, 41
Shanghai, 18
Shepherdstown, 10

Shepherd University, 13
Shinnston, 189
Silo Rapids, 112
Sirianni's, 58
Sisters Coffee House, 118
Sistersville, 165
Sistersville Ferry, 166
Sites Homestead, 40
Sleep Inn, 86, 152
Smoke Camp Crafts, 74
Smoke Hole Gorge, 37
Smoot Theatre, 162
Snowshoe Mountain
    Resort, 32, 52
Snowshoe Mountain
    Resort, the Embers, 59
South Charleston
    Convention and
    Visitors Bureau, 153
South Charleston
    Interpretive
    Center, 140
Southern Interpretive
    Center of the Coal
    Heritage Trail, 123
Southern West Virginia
    Convention and
    Visitors Bureau, 125
Spat's at the
    Blennerhassett, 171
Spencer, 168
Spiedel Observatory, 181
Spruce Knob, 41
Stardust Cafe, 127
Star Theatre, 21
State Fair of West
    Virginia, 90
Stealey-Goff-Vance
    House, 189
Stephens Outdoor
    Railways, 163
stern-wheelers, 159
Stillwaters, 76
St. John's Chapel, 100
St. Marys, 164
St. Michael's Church, 70

Stonewall Jackson
    Dam, 74
Stonewall Jackson
    Lake, 74
Stonewall Jackson Lake
    State Park, 74
Stonewall Jackson
    Resort, 76
St. Patrick's Day
    Celebration, 130
St. Peter's Catholic
    Church, 5
Strawberry Festival, 77
Summersville Convention
    and Visitors
    Bureau, 86
Summersville Lake, 66
Summit Bechtel Family
    National Scout
    Reserve, 111
Summit Lake, 92
Summit Lake
    Campground, 55
Summit Point
    Motorsports Park, 9
Summit Theatre, 120
Sumnerite First Free
    School, 162
Sunny Pointe Guest
    House, 86
Sunset Berry Farm &
    Produce, 102
Sunshine Farm and
    Gardens, 98
Sutton, 67
Sutton Lake, 69
Sweet Springs, 99

T
Taggart Hall Civil War
    History Museum, 30
Tamarack, 97, 117
Taste of Our Towns
    (TOOT) Fest, 90
Taste of Parkersburg, 156
Taylor Bookstore, 138
Telephone Museum, 202

Terror of the Tug, 125
Third Street Deli, 171
Thomas House, 122
Thomas Shepherd
    Inn, 25
Thomas Shepherd's
    gristmill, 11
Thorny Mountain Fire
    Tower, 54
Three Rivers Avian
    Center, 107
Thurmond, 113
Tomlinson Run State
    Park, 183
Top of West Virginia
    CVB, 185
Town Run, 11
Town's Inn, 25
Trans-Allegheny Lunatic
    Asylum, 65, 71
Travelers' Repose, 49
TreeTops Canopy
    tour, 112
Triple Brick Building, 14
Tri-Rivers Trail, 63
Troubadour Lounge, 20
Trough, the, 36
Trout Pond Recreation
    Area, 36
Tucker County
    Convention and, 59
Tudor's Biscuit
    World, 127
Tu-Endie-Wei State
    Park, 150
Tuscarora Church, 14
Twin Falls Resort State
    Park, 127
Two Waterfront Place
    Hotel, 205
Tygart Lake State Park,
    194, 207

U
Undo's Italian Family
    Restaurant, 184
Union, 100

Union National Historic
District, 100
Upper Ohio Valley
Italian Heritage
Festival, 174

V
Valley Falls State
Park, 188
Valley Gem
Sternwheeler, 162
Valley Springs
Furniture, 100
Vandalia Gathering,
130, 136
Vault on Main, 67
Vault on Main, The, 87
Veterans Memorial
Museum, 105
Victoria Theater, 179

W
Waffle Rock, 33
Wake Robin Gallery, 104
Waldomore, 188
Wardensville Garden
Market, 36
Warm Hollow, 128
Washington's Lands
Museum, 156
Water Monster's
Daughter, 143
Water Ways, 133
Watoga State Park, 53
Watters Smith Memorial
State Park, 186
Watts Roost Vineyard, 98
Waves of Fun, 143
Webster County
Development
Authority, 86
Webster County Nature
Tour, 83
Webster County
Woodchopping
Festival, 83
Welch, 125

Wells Inn, 165
Wesley Chapel, 77
West Augusta Historical
Society Museum, 204
West Augusta Historical
Society Round
Barn, 203
West Fork River
Trail, 190
Weston, 71
Weston and Gauley
Bridge Turnpike, 70
West Virginia Black
Walnut Festival, 156
West Virginia CCC Camp
Museum, 192
West Virginia Coal
Festival, 130, 133
West Virginia Country
Music Hall of
Fame, 20
West Virginia Cultural
Center, 134
West Virginia Derby, 174
West Virginia Glass
Museum of American
Glass, 73
West Virginia Highlands
Artisans Group, 44
West Virginia Honey
Festival, 156
West Virginia
Jackson's Mill and
Farmstead, 65
West Virginia Jamboree,
178, 179
West Virginia Liars
Contest, 75
West Virginia Miner's
Memorial, 202
West Virginia Molasses
Festival, 170
West Virginia Mountain
Products, 192
West Virginia Museum of
American Glass, 65

West Virginia Radio Hall
of Fame, 147
West Virginia's Largest
Yard Sale, 62
West Virginia State
Capitol Complex, 134
West Virginia State Farm
Museum, 151
West Virginia State Folk
Festival, 62, 71
West Virginia State
Museum and, 134
West Virginia State
Penitentiary, 175, 178
West Virginia State
University's Booker
T. Washington
Institute, 139
West Virginia State
Wildlife Center, 78
West Virginia
University, 204
West Virginia Wesleyan
College, 77
West Virginia Wildlife
Center, 65
Wetzel County
Convention & Visitors
Bureau, 185
Wheeling, 176
Wheeling Brewing
Co., 185
Wheeling Convention
and Visitors Center,
185
Wheeling Heritage Rail
Trail, 179
Wheeling Inn/Knights
Inn, 184
Wheeling Island
Racetrack and
Gaming Center, 179
Wheeling Suspension
Bridge, 179
White Grass, 42
White Oak Blueberry
Farm, 98

White Sulphur Springs National Fish Hatchery, 91

Whitewater rafting, 111

Wild Bean Coffee Shop, 94

Wild Edibles Festival, 29

Wilderness Lake Chalets, 86

Wildwood, 116

Williams River, 55

Williamstown, 164

Williamstown Antique Mall, 164

Willow Island Locks and Dam, 165

Winter Festival of Lights, 174

Winterplace Ski Resort, 117

Wolf Creek Gallery, 93

Women's Park, 138

Wonderment Puppet Theatre, 16

Woodcraft, 163

Woods Resort, 25

Woolen Willow, 164

World War I Memorial Building, 124

WSG Gallery, 16

WV Glass Gathering, 62

WV Renaissance Festival, 90

WVU Creative Arts Center, 204

WVU Visitors Resource Center, 204

Y

Ya'Sou Greek Restaurant, 127

Yoder's Country Kettle, 100

Youth Museum of Southern West Virginia, 116